THE MOST WINNING SMILE

A BRIEF RECORD
OF OUR SPORTS RECORDS

☐ First reinforced athletic balls with composition covers

☐ First reinforced round athletic balls with a controlled nylon winding

☐ First self-sealing all-rubber valve

☐ First series of junior-sized inflated balls

☐ First raised-seam composition-constructed basketball

☐ First last-built leather football

☐ First athletic balls with Icosahedron® construction

☐ First single-hose regulator approved by the U.S. Navy

☐ First basketballs with sure-grip Formula 1™ covers

☐ First pressureless racquetballs

These firsts won't be our last. Our record-setting sports performances stretch back over half a century. And we're keeping the string going with on-going research and development programs to assure that the newest, finest sporting goods products will continue to carry our world-famous brand.

AMF
Voit

Santa Ana, California 92704

GUINNESS SPORTS RECORD BOOK
By Norris McWhirter

1979-1980

Stan Greenberg, associate editor

David A. Boehm, American editor

Steve Morgenstern,
associate American editor

GUINNESS SPORTS RECORD BOOK, 7th EDITION
*A Bantam Book / published by arrangement with
Sterling Publishing Co., Inc.*

PRINTING HISTORY
Original Sterling edition published 1972
Bantam edition / October 1980
2nd printing .... June 1981

PRINTED IN THE UNITED STATES OF AMERICA

11 10 9 8 7 6 5 4 3 2

CONTENTS

EVOLUTION OF SPORTS RECORDS IN THE 20TH CENTURY

	Start of the Century—January 1, 1901	*Middle of the Century—January* 1, 1951	*Present-Day Record—December*, 1978
Greatest Weight Lift	4,133 lbs.—Louis Cyr (Canada), 1896	4,133 lbs.—Louis Cyr (Canada), 1896	6,270 lbs.—Paul Anderson (U.S.), 1957
Fastest 100 meters	10.8 secs.—Luther Cary (U.S.) and 4 others, 1891–1900	10.3 secs.—Percy Williams (Canada) and 6 others, 1930–1935	9.95 secs.—James Ray Hines (U.S.), 1968
Fastest One Mile	4m 12.8s—W. G. George (U.K.), 1886	4m 01.3s—Gunder Hägg (Sweden), 1945	3m 49.4s—John Walker (N.Z.), 1975
One Hour Running	11 miles 932 yds.—W. G. George (U.K.), 1884	12 miles 29 yds.—Viljo Heino (Finland), 1945	13 miles 24⅔ yards—Jos Hermens (Netherlands), 1976
Highest High Jump	6′ 5⅝″—M. Sweeney (U.S.), 1895	6′ 11″—Lester Steers (U.S.), 1941	7′ 8″—Vladimir Yashchenko (U.S.S.R.), 1978
Highest Pole Vault	11′ 10½″—R. Clapp (U.S.), 1898	15′ 7¾″—Cornelius Warmerdam (U.S.), 1942	18′ 8¼″—David Roberts (U.S.), 1976
Long Jump	24′ 7¾″—P. O'Connor (U.K.), 1900	26′ 8¼″—Jesse Owens (U.S.), 1935	29′ 2½″—Robert Beamon (U.S.), 1968
Longest Shot Put	48′ 2″—D. Horgan (U.K.), 1897	58′ 10¾″—Jim Fuchs (U.S.), 1950	72′ 8″—Udo Beyer (E. Germany), 1978
Longest Discus Throw	122′ 3½″—R. Sheldon (U.S.), 1899	186′ 11″—Fortune Gordien (U.S.), 1949	233′ 5″—Wolfgang Schmidt (E. Germany), 1978
Longest Hammer Throw	169′ 4″—J. J. Flanagan (U.S.), 1900	196′ 5″—Imre Németh (Hungary), 1950	263′ 6″—Karl-Heinz Riehm (W. Germany), 1978
Longest Javelin Throw	161′ 9¾″—E. Lemming (Sweden), 1899	258′ 2″—Yrjo Nikkanen (Finland), 1938	310′ 4″—Miklos Nemeth (Hungary), 1976
One Hour Walking	8 miles 270 yds.—W. J. Sturgess (U.K.), (Amateur), 1895	8 miles 1,025 yds.—John Mikaelsson (Sweden), 1945	8 miles 1,700 yds.—Daniel Bautista (Mexico), 1978
Longest Ski Jump	116½′—O. Tanberg (Norway), 1900	442¾′—Dan Netzell (Sweden), 1950	593′ 10″—Bogdan Norcic (Yugoslavia) 1977
Fastest 500 meters Ice Skating	45.2 sec.—P. Ostlund (Norway), 1900	41.8 sec.—Hans Engnestangen (Norway), 1938	37.00 sec.—Evgeni Kulikov (US.S.R.), 1975
Fastest 100 meters Swim (long course)	1m. 14.0s. (no turn)—J. Nutall (U.K.), 1893	55.8 sec.—Alexandre Jany (France), 1947	49.44 sec.—Jonty Skinner (S. Africa), 1976
Cycling Paced (m.p.h.)	62.27—C. M. Murphy (U.S.), 1899	>80—L. Vanderstuyft (Belgium), 1928	140.5—Allan V. Abbott (U.S.), 1973
Fastest 1 mile Racehorse (excluding straightaways)	1m. 35.5s.—*Salvator* in U.S., 1890	1m. 33.4s.—*Citation* in U.S., 1950	1m. 32.2s.—*Dr. Fager* in U.S., 1968
Highest Mountain Climbed (feet)	22,834—Aconcagua, Argentina, 1897	26,492—Annapurna I, Nepal, 1950	29,028—Everest, Nepal-Tibet, 1953

SPORTS, GAMES AND PASTIMES

Earliest. The origins of sport stem from the time when self-preservation ceased to be the all-consuming human preoccupation. Archery was a hunting skill in Mesolithic times (by *c.* 8000 B.C.), but did not become an organized sport until about 300 A.D., among the Genoese. The earliest dated evidence for sport is *c.* 2450 B.C. for fowling with throwing sticks and hunting. Ball games by girls, depicted on Middle Kingdom murals at Beni Hasan, Egypt, have been dated to *c.* 2050 B.C.

Fastest. The highest speed reached in a non-mechanical sport is in sky-diving, in which a speed of 185 m.p.h. is attained in a head-down free-falling position, even in the lower atmosphere. In delayed drops, a speed of 614 m.p.h. has been recorded at high rarefied altitudes. The highest projectile speed in any moving ball game is *c.* 180 m.p.h. in pelota (jai-alai). This compares with 170 m.p.h. (electronically-timed) for a golf ball driven off a tee.

Slowest. In amateur wrestling, before the rules were modified toward "brighter wrestling," contestants could be locked in holds for so long that single bouts could last for 11 hours 40 min. In the extreme case of the 2-hour 41-minute pull in the regimental tug o'war in Jubbulpore, India, on August 12, 1889, the winning team moved a net distance of 12 feet at an average speed of 0.00084 m.p.h.

Longest. The most protracted sporting test was an automobile duration test of 222,618 miles by Appaurchaux and others in a Ford Taunus. This was contested over 142 days in 1963. The distance was equivalent to 8.93 times around the equator.

The most protracted non-mechanical sporting event is the *Tour de France* cycling race. In 1926, this was over 3,569 miles, lasting 29 days. The total damage to the French national economy due to the interest in this annual event, now reduced to 23 days, is immense, and is currently estimated to be in excess of $1,900,000,000.

Largest Field. The largest field for any ball game is that for polo with 12.4 acres, or a maximum length of 300 yards and a width, without side-boards, of 200 yards.

Most Participants. The *Stramilano* 22-kilometer run around Milan, Italy, attracted over 50,000 runners on April 16, 1978.

In May, 1971, the "Ramblin' Raft Race" on the Chattahoochee River at Atlanta, Georgia, attracted 37,683 competitors on 8,304 rafts.

According to a report issued in 1977, 50 million people are actively involved in 220,000 physical culture and sports groups in the U.S.S.R., using 3,175 stadiums and 58,970 indoor gymnasiums. It is estimated that some 29 per cent of the population of East Germany participate in sport regularly.

Worst Disasters. The worst disaster in recent history was when an estimated 604 were killed after some stands at the Hong Kong Jockey Club race course collapsed and caught fire on February 26, 1918. During the reign of Antoninus Pius (138–161 A.D.) the upper wooden tiers in the Circus Maximus, Rome, collapsed during a gladiatorial combat, killing 1,112 spectators.

Youngest and Oldest Sports Record Breakers. The youngest age at which any person has broken a world record is 12 years 298 days in the case of Gertrude Ederle (born October 23, 1906) of the United States, who broke the women's 880-yard freestyle swimming world record with 13 minutes 19.0 seconds at Indianapolis, Indiana on August 17, 1919.

The oldest person to break a world record is Irish-born John J. Flanagan (1868–1938), triple Olympic hammer throw champion for the U.S., 1900–1908, who set his last world record of 184 feet 4 inches at New Haven, Connecticut, on July 24, 1909, aged 41 years 196 days.

Youngest and Oldest Internationals. The youngest age at which any person has won international honors is 8 years in the case of Joy Foster, the Jamaican singles and mixed-doubles table tennis champion in 1958. It would appear that the greatest age at which anyone has actively competed for his country is 72 years 280 days in the case of Oscar G. Swahn (Sweden) (1847–1927), who won a silver medal for shooting in the Olympic Games at Antwerp on July 26, 1920. He qualified for the 1924 Games, but was unable to participate because of illness.

Most Versatile Athletes. Charlotte (Lottie) Dod (1871–1960) won the Wimbledon singles title (1887 to 1893) five times, the British Ladies Golf Championship in 1904, an Olympic silver medal for archery in 1908, and represented England at hockey in 1899. She also excelled at skating and tobogganing.

MOST PARTICIPANTS: 37,683 people on 8,304 rafts entered the "Ramblin' Raft Race" on the Chattahoochee River.

MOST VERSATILE WOMAN ATHLETE: Mildred (Babe) Didrikson Zaharias (U.S.) was an All-American basketball player and an Olympic medalist, with the silver medal in the high jump and gold medals in the javelin throw and the hurdles in the 1932 Games.
Turning professional, she first trained as a boxer and then switched to golf, eventually winning 19 championships.

Mildred (Babe) Didrikson Zaharias (U.S.) was an All-American basketball player, took the silver medal in the high jump and gold medals in the javelin throw and hurdles in the 1932 Olympics. Turning professional, she first trained as a boxer, and then, switching to golf, eventually won 19 championships, including the U.S. Women's Open and All-American Open. She holds the women's world record also for longest throw of a baseball—296 feet.

Youngest and Oldest Champions. The youngest person to have successfully participated in a world title event was a French boy, whose name is not recorded, who coxed the winning Netherlands pair at Paris on Aug. 26, 1900. He was not more than 10 and may have been as young as 7. The youngest individual Olympic winner was Marjorie Gestring (U.S.), who took the springboard diving title at the age of 13 years 9 months at the Olympic Games in Berlin in 1936. Oscar G. Swahn (see above) was aged 65 years 258 days when he won the gold medal in the 1912 Olympic Running Deer team shooting competition.

Longest Reign. The longest reign as a world champion is 27 years (1928–55) by the Basque tennis player, Pierre Etchebaster (born in France, 1893), who retired undefeated at age 62 in 1955 as world amateur real (royal) tennis champion.

Greatest Earnings. The greatest fortune amassed by an individual in sport is an estimated $59,250,000 by the boxer Muhammad Ali Haj to October, 1978. The most for a single event is a purse of $6,500,000 won by Ali in his title fight against Ken Norton, fought in New York City on September 28, 1976.

The highest-paid woman athlete in the world is ice skater Janet Lynn (*née* Nowicki) (U.S.) (born April 6, 1953) who in 1974 signed a $1,500,000 three-year contract. In 1974 she earned more than $750,000.

Largest Trophy. The world's largest trophy for a particular sport is the Bangalore Limited Handicap Polo Tournament Trophy. This massive cup is 6 feet tall and was presented in 1936 by the Raja of Kolanka.

Heaviest Sportsmen. The heaviest sportsman of all time was the wrestler William J. Cobb of Macon, Georgia, who in 1962 was billed as the 802-lb. "Happy Humphrey." The heaviest player of a ball game was Bob Pointer, the 487-lb. tackle, formerly on the 1967 Santa Barbara High School football team.

Most Expensive. The most expensive of all sports is the racing of large yachts—"J" type boats and International 12-meter boats. The owning and racing of these is beyond the means of individual millionaires and is confined to multi-millionaires or syndicates.

Largest Crowd. The greatest number of live spectators for any sporting spectacle is the estimated 1,500,000 who lined the route of the 81st annual Boston Marathon on April 18, 1977. The race was won by Jerome Drayton of Canada. However, spread over 23 days, it is estimated that more than 10,000,000 see the annual *Tour de France* along the route.

The largest crowd traveling to any sporting event is "more than 400,000" for the annual *Grand Prix d'Endurance* motor race on the Sarthe circuit near Le Mans, France. The record stadium crowd was one of 199,854 for the Brazil *vs.* Uruguay match in the Maracanã Municipal Stadium, Rio de Janeiro, Brazil, on July 16, 1950.

The largest television audience for a single sporting event (excluding Olympic events) was the 400,000,000 who watched the final of the 1976 World Cup soccer competition.

Best Attended Sports Funeral

A crowd estimated between 60,000 and 70,000 people attended the funeral of the 1960 and 1964 Olympic marathon champion Abebe Bikila (Ethiopia), at Addis Ababa, in October, 1973.

Aerobatics

Earliest. The first aerobatic maneuver is generally considered the sustained inverted flight in a Bleriot of Célestin-Adolphe Pégoud, at Buc, France on September 21, 1913, but Lieut. Peter Nikolayevich Nesterov, of the Imperial Russian Air Service, performed a loop in a Nieuport Type IV monoplane at Kiev, U.S.S.R. on August 27, 1913.

World Championships. Held biennially since 1960 (excepting 1974), scoring is based on the system devised by Col. José Aresti of Spain. The competitions consist of two compulsory and two free programs.

Most Titles. The world championships team competition has been won on four occasions by the U.S.S.R. No individual has won more than one title, the most successful competitor being Igor Egorov (U.S.S.R.) who won in 1970, was second in 1976, fifth in

1972 and eleventh in 1968. The most successful in the women's competition has been Lidia Leonova (U.S.S.R.) with first place in 1976, third in 1972 and fifth in 1970.

Loops. John "Hal" McClain performed 1,501½ inside loops in a Pitts S–2A over Long Beach, California, on December 16, 1973.

Archery

Earliest References. The discovery of stone arrowheads at Border Cave, Northern Natal, South Africa, in deposits exceeding the Carbon 14 dating limit, indicates that the bow was invented *ante* 46,000 B.C. Archery developed as an organized sport at least as early as the 3rd century A.D. The world governing body is the *Fédération Internationale de Tir à l'Arc* (FITA), founded in 1931.

Flight Shooting. The longest flight shooting records are achieved in the footbow class. In the unlimited footbow division, the professional Harry Drake of Lakeside, California, holds the record at 1 mile 268 yards, shot at Ivanpah Dry Lake, California, on October 24, 1971. The crossbow record is 1,359 yds. 29 inches, held by Drake and set at same venue on October 14–15, 1967. The unlimited handbow class (*i.e.* standing stance with bow of any weight) record is 1,164 yards 2 feet 9 inches by Don Brown (b. 1946) at Wendover, Utah, on September 18, 1977.

HOLDER OF THREE FLIGHT-SHOOTING RECORDS: Harry Drake is the master with the footbow (1 mile 268 yards), handbow and crossbow. Here he is trying to break his own unlimited footbow record.

Sultan Selim III shot an arrow 1,400 Turkish *pikes* or *gez* near Istanbul, Turkey, in 1798. The equivalent English distance is somewhere between 953 and 972 yards.

Highest Scores. The world records for a single FITA round are: men, 1,318 points (of a possible 1,440) by Giancarlo Ferrari (Italy) at Viareggio, Italy, October 15–16, 1977; and women, 1,304 points (possible 1,440) by Zebiniso Rustamova (U.S.S.R.) at Milan, Italy, on October 3, 1977.

There are no world records for Double FITA rounds, but the highest scores achieved in either a world or Olympic championship are: men, 2,571 points (possible 2,880) by Darrell Pace (U.S.) posted at the 1976 Olympics at Montreal, Canada, July 27–30, 1976; women, 2,515 by Luann Ryon (U.S.) at Canberra, Australia, February 11–12, 1977.

Most Titles. The greatest number of world titles (instituted 1931) ever won by a man is four by Hans Deutgen (Sweden) in 1947–48–49–50. The greatest number won by a woman is seven by Mrs. Janina Spychajowa-Kurkowska (Poland) in 1931–32–33–34, 1936, 1939 and 1947.

Oscar Kessels (Belgium) has participated in 21 world championships since 1931.

Olympic Medals. Hubert van Innis (Belgium) (1866–1961) won 6 gold and 3 silver medals in archery events at the 1900 and 1920 Olympic Games.

Greatest Pull. Gary Sentman of Roseburg, Oregon, drew a longbow weighing a record 176 lbs. to the maximum draw on the arrow (28¼ inches) at Forksville, Pennsylvania, on September 20, 1975.

Highest 24-Hour Score. The highest recorded score over 24 hours by a pair of archers is 62,967 during 55 Portsmouth Rounds (60 arrows at 20 yards with a 2-inch diameter 10 ring) shot by John Cox and Harry Loughran at Starlight Archery West, Royal Oak, Michigan, August 11–12, 1978.

Auto Racing

Earliest Races. There are various conflicting claims, but the first automobile race was the 201-mile Green Bay-to-Madison, Wisconsin, run in 1878, won by an Oshkosh steamer.

In 1887, Count Jules Felix Philippe Albert de Dion de Malfiance (1856–1946) won the *La Velocipede* 19.3-mile race in Paris in a De Dion steam quadricycle in which he is reputed to have exceeded 37 m.p.h.

The first "real" race was from Paris to Bordeaux and back (732 miles) June 11–13, 1895. The winner was Emile Levassor (1844–97) (France) driving a Panhard-Levassor two-seater with a 1.2-liter Daimler engine developing 3½ h.p. His time was 48 hours 47 min. (average speed 15.01 m.p.h.). The first closed circuit race was held over 5 laps of a mile dirt track at Narragansett Park, Cranston,

Rhode Island, on September 7, 1896. It was won by A. H. Whiting, who drove a Riker electric.

The oldest auto race in the world, still being regularly run, is the R.A.C. Tourist Trophy (40th race held in 1976), first staged on the Isle of Man on September 14, 1905. The oldest continental race is the French Grand Prix (55th in 1977) first held on June 26–27, 1906. The Coppo Florio, in Sicily, has been irregularly held since 1900.

Fastest Circuits. The highest average lap speed attained on any closed circuit is 221.160 m.p.h. by Mark Donohue, Jr. (1937–75) (U.S.) who lapped the 2.66-mile 33-degree banked tri-oval at Alabama International Motor Speedway, Talladega, Alabama, in 43.299 seconds, driving a 5,374-c.c. turbocharged Porsche 917/30 Can-Am car on August 9, 1975.

The highest average race lap speed for a closed circuit is more than 195 m.p.h. by Richard Brickhouse (U.S.) driving a 1969 Dodge Daytona Charger powered by a 6,981-c.c. 600-b.h.p. V8 engine, during a 500-mile race on the tri-oval at Alabama International Motor Speedway, Talladega, Alabama, on September 14, 1969

The fastest road circuit was the Francorchamps circuit near Spa, Belgium, then 14.10 kilometers (8 miles 1,340 yards) in length. It was lapped in 3 minutes 13.4 seconds (average speed of 163.086 m.p.h.) on lap seven of the Francorchamps 1,000-kilometer sports car race on May 6, 1973, by Henri Pescarolo (b. Paris, France, September 25, 1942) driving a 2,933-c.c. V12 Matra-Simca MS 670 Group 5 sports car. The race lap average speed record at Berlin's AVUS track was 171.75 m.p.h. by Bernd Rosemeyer in a 6-liter V16 Auto Union in 1937.

The fastest world championship Grand Prix circuit in current use is the 2,932-mile course at Silverstone, Northamptonshire, England (opened 1948). The race lap record is 1 minute 18.45 seconds (average speed 134.558 m.p.h.) by Danny Ongais (U.S.) driving a Parnelli-Cosworth VPJ 6B on October 1, 1978. The practice lap record is 1 minute 16.07 seconds (138.7 m.p.h.) by Bengt Ronnie Peterson (1944–1978) in a 2,993-c.c. Lotus 78 Cosworth V8 on March 18, 1978.

Fastest Races. The fastest race in the world is the NASCAR Grand National 125-mile event on the 2½-mile 31-degree banked tri-oval at Daytona International Speedway, Daytona Beach, Florida. The record time is 40 minutes 55 seconds (average speed 183.295 m.p.h.) by William Caleb "Cale" Yarborough (born March 27, 1939) of Timmonsville, South Carolina, driving a 1969 Mercury V8, on February 19, 1970.

The fastest road race was the 1,000-kilometer (621-mile) sports car race held on the Francorchamps circuit (8 miles 1,340 yards) near Spa, Belgium. The record time for this 71-lap (622.055-mile) race was 4 hours 1 minute 9.7 seconds (average speed 154.765 m.p.h.) by Pedro Rodriguez (1940–71) of Mexico and Keith Jack "Jackie" Oliver (b. Chadwell Heath, Essex, England, Aug. 14, 1942), driving a 4,998-c.c. flat-12 Porsche 917K Group 5 sports car on May 9, 1971.

Toughest Circuits. The Targa Florio (first run 1906) was widely acknowledged to be the most arduous race. Held on the Piccolo Madonie Circuit in Sicily, it covered eleven laps (492.126 miles) and involved the negotiation of 9,350 corners over severe mountain gradients and narrow rough roads.

The record time was 6 hours 27 minutes 48.0 seconds (average speed 76.141 m.p.h.) by Arturo Francesco Merzario (b. Civenna, Italy, March 11, 1943) and Sandro Munari (Italy) driving a 2,998.5-c.c. flat-12 Ferrari 312 P Group 5 sports car in the 56th race on May 21, 1972. The lap record was 33 minutes 36.0 seconds (average speed 79.890 m.p.h.) by Leo Juhani Kinnunen (born Tampere, Finland, Aug. 5, 1943) on lap 11 of the 54th race in a 2,997-c.c. flat-8 Porsche 908/3 Spyder Group 6 prototype sports car on May 3, 1970.

The most gruelling and slowest Grand Prix circuit is that for the Monaco Grand Prix (first run on April 14, 1929), run through the streets and around the harbor of Monte Carlo. It is 3.312 km. (2.058 miles) in length and has 11 pronounced corners and several sharp changes of gradient. The race is run over 75 laps (154.348 miles) and involves on average about 1,600 gear changes.

The record for the race is 1 hour 55 minutes 14.66 seconds (average speed 80.358 m.p.h.) by Patrick Depailler (b. France, August 9, 1944) driving an Elf-Tyrrell 008 Ford on May 7, 1978. The race lap record is 1 minute 28.65 seconds (average speed 83.67 m.p.h.) by Andreas-Nikolaus "Niki" Lauda (b. Austria, February 22, 1949) driving a Brabham-Alfa Romeo BT46 on May 7, 1978. The practice lap record is 1 minute 28.34 seconds (average speed 83.865 m.p.h.) by Carlos Alberto Reutemann (b. Argentina, April 12, 1942) in a Ferrari 312T3 on May 4, 1978.

MOST LE MANS WINS (left): Jacky Ickx shares the record of 4 wins with another Belgian, Oliver Gendebien. **GRAND PRIX CHAMPION** (right): Jackie Stewart (#5) has won 27 Grand Prix races.

FASTEST AT INDY: Mark Donohue (# 66) raced the Indianapolis 500 in a record 3 hours 4 minutes 5.54 seconds in 1977.

Le Mans

The greatest distance ever covered in the 24-hour *Grand Prix d'Endurance* (first held on May 26–27, 1923) on the old Sarthe circuit (8 miles 650 yards) at Le Mans, France, is 3,314.221 miles by Dr. Helmut Marko (b. Graz, Austria, April 27, 1943) and Jonkheer Gijs van Lennep (b. Bloemendaal, Netherlands, March 16, 1942) driving a 4,907-c.c. flat-12 Porsche 917K Group 5 sports car on June 12–13, 1971. The record for the current circuit is 3,134.52 miles by Didier Pironi (b. March 26, 1952) and Jean-Pierre Jaussaud (b. June 3, 1937) (average speed 130.60 m.p.h.) in an Alpine Renault, June 10–11, 1978. The race lap record (8.475 mile lap) is 3 minutes 34.2 seconds (average speed 142.24 m.p.h.) by Jean Pierre Jabouille (b. France, October 1, 1942) driving an Alpine Renault on June 11, 1978. The practice lap record is 3 minutes 27.6 seconds by Jacques-Bernard "Jacky" Ickx (b. Belgium, January 1, 1945) in a turbocharged 2.1-liter Porsche 936/78 on June 7, 1978.

Most Wins. The race has been won by Ferrari cars nine times, in 1949, 1954, 1958 and 1960–61–62–63–64–65. The most wins by one man is four by Oliver Gendebien (Belgium), who won in 1958, 1960–61–62, and by Jacky Ickx (Belgium), who won in 1969, 1975–76–77.

Indianapolis 500

The Indianapolis 500-mile race (200 laps) was inaugurated on May 30, 1911. The most successful driver has been Anthony Joseph "A.J." Foyt, Jr., who won in 1961, 1964, 1967 and 1977.

The record time is 3 hours 4 minutes 5.54 seconds (average speed 162.962 m.p.h.) by Mark Donohue (b. New Jersey, March 18, 1937, d. 1975) driving a 2,595-c.c. 900-b.h.p. turbocharged Sunoco McLaren M16B-Offenhauser on May 27, 1972. The record prize fund was $1,116,807 for the 61st race on May 29, 1977. The individual prize record is $271,697.72 by Al Unser (b. Albuquerque, New Mexico, May 29, 1939) on May 30, 1970.

DRIVING CHAMPION: Juan-Manuel Fangio has won the World Drivers' Championships five times.

The race lap record is 46.71 seconds (average speed 192.678 m.p.h.) by Danny Ongais of Costa Mesa, California, driving a 2.6-liter turbocharged Parnelli-Cosworth DFX on lap 42 of the race held on May 29, 1977. The 4-lap qualifying record is 2 minutes 58.08 seconds (average speed 202.156 m.p.h.) by Tom Sneva (b. U.S., June 1, 1948) driving a Penske-Cosworth DFX turbocharged PC6 on May 20, 1978.

Fastest Pit Stop. Bobby Unser (U.S.) took 4 seconds to take on fuel on lap 10 of the Indianapolis 500 on May 30, 1976.

Duration Record

The greatest distance ever covered in one year is 400,000 kilometers (248,548.5 miles) by François Lecot (1879–1949), an innkeeper from Rochetaillée, France, in a 1,900-c.c. 66-b.h.p. Citroën 11 sedan mainly between Paris and Monte Carlo, from July 22, 1935 to July 26, 1936. He drove on 363 of the 370 days allowed.

The world's duration record is 185,353 miles 1,741 yards in 133 days 17 hours 37 minutes 38.64 seconds (average speed 58.07 m.p.h.) by Marchand, Presalé and six others in a Citroën on the Montlhéry track near Paris, during March–July, 1933.

Most Successful Drivers

Based on the World Drivers' Championships, inaugurated in 1950, the most successful driver is Juan-Manuel Fangio (born Balcarce, Argentina, June 24, 1911), who won five times in 1951–54–55–56–57. He retired in 1958, after having won 24 Grand Prix races (2 shared).

The most successful driver in terms of race wins is Richard Lee Petty (born Randleman, North Carolina, July 2, 1937) with 185 NASCAR Grand National wins from 1960 to November, 1977. His best year was 1967 with 27 victories.

The most Grand Prix victories is 27 by Jackie Stewart of Scotland between September 12, 1965 and August 5, 1973. Jim Clark, O.B.E. (1936–1968) of Scotland holds the record of Grand Prix victories in one year with 7 in 1963. He won 61 Formula One and Formula Libre races between 1959 and 1968. The most Grand Prix starts is 176 (out of a possible 184) between May 18, 1958, and Jan. 26, 1975, by Norman Graham Hill, O.B.E. (1929–1975). He took part in 90 *consecutive* Grands Prix between November 20, 1960 and October 5, 1969.

Oldest and Youngest World Champions. The oldest was Juan-Manuel Fangio, who won his last World Championship on August 18, 1957, aged 46 years 55 days. The youngest was Emerson Fittipaldi (Brazil) who won his first World Championship on September 10, 1972, aged 25 years 273 days.

Oldest and Youngest Grand Prix Winners and Drivers. The youngest Grand Prix winner was Bruce Leslie McLaren (1937–70) of New Zealand, who won the U.S. Grand Prix at Sebring, Florida, on December 12, 1959, aged 22 years 104 days. The oldest Grand Prix winner was Tazio Giorgio Nuvolari (1892–1953) of Italy, who won the Albi Grand Prix at Albi, France, on July 14, 1946, aged 53 years 240 days. The oldest Grand Prix driver was Louis Alexandre Ghiron (born Monaco, August 3, 1899), who finished 6th in the Monaco Grand Prix on May 22, 1955, aged 55 years 292 days.

The youngest Grand Prix driver was Christopher Arthur Amon (b. Bulls, New Zealand, July 20, 1943) who took part in the Belgian Grand Prix on June 9, 1963, aged 19 years 324 days.

Land Speed Records

The highest speed ever recorded by a wheeled vehicle was achieved by Gary Gabelich (b. San Pedro, California, August 29, 1950), at Bonneville Salt Flats, Utah, on October 23, 1970. He drove

FASTEST CAR: A top speed of 631.367 m.p.h. was set in this car with Gary Gabelich at the wheel.

the Reaction Dynamics *The Blue Flame*, weighing 4,950 lbs. and measuring 37 feet long, powered by a liquid natural gas-hydrogen peroxide rocket engine developing a maximum static thrust of 22,000 lbs. On his first run, at 11:23 a.m. (local time), he covered the measured kilometer in 3.543 seconds (average speed 631.367 m.p.h.) and the mile in 5.829 seconds (617.602 m.p.h.). On the return run, at 12:11 p.m. his times were 3.554 seconds for the kilometer (629.413 m.p.h.) and 5.739 seconds for the mile (627.287 m.p.h.). The average times for the two runs were 3.5485 seconds for the kilometer (630.388 m.p.h.) and 5.784 seconds for the mile (622.407 m.p.h.). During the attempt only 13,000 lbs. s.t. was used and a peak speed of 650 m.p.h. was momentarily attained.

The most successful land speed record breaker was Major Sir Malcolm Campbell (1885–1948) (U.K.). He broke the official record nine times between September 25, 1924, with 146.157 m.p.h. in a Sunbeam, and September 3, 1935, when he achieved 301.129 m.p.h. in the Rolls-Royce-engined *Bluebird*.

The world speed record for compression-ignition-engined cars is 190.344 m.p.h. (average of two runs over measured mile) by Robert Havemann of Eureka, California, driving his *Corsair* streamliner, powered by a turbocharged 6,981-c.c. 6-cylinder GMC 6-71 diesel engine developing 746 b.h.p., at Bonneville Salt Flats, Utah, in August, 1971. The faster run was made at 210 m.p.h.

Dragging

Piston-Engined. The lowest elapsed time recorded by a piston-engined dragster is 5.637 seconds by Donald Glenn "Big Daddy" Garlits (born 1932) of Seffner, Florida, driving his rear-engined AA-F dragster, powered by a 7,948-c.c. supercharged Dodge V8 engine during the National Hot Rod Association's Supernationals at Ontario Motor Speedway, California, on October 11, 1975.

The highest terminal velocity recorded is 252.10 m.p.h. by Shirley Muldowney (U.S.) in January, 1977.

The world record for two runs in opposite directions over 440 yards from a standing start is 6.70 seconds by Dennis Victor Priddle (b. 1945) of Yeovil, Somerset, England, driving his 6,424-c.c. supercharged Chrysler dragster, developing 1,700 b.h.p. using nitromethane and methanol, at Elvington Airfield, England, on October 7, 1972. The faster run took 6.65 seconds.

Rocket or Jet-Engined. The highest terminal velocity recorded by any dragster is 377.754 m.p.h. (elapsed time 4.65 seconds) by Norman Craig Breedlove (b. March 23, 1938) of Los Angeles, California, driving his *English Leather Special* rocket dragster at Bonneville Salt Flats, Utah, in Sept. 1973. The lowest elapsed time recorded by any dragster is 4.55 seconds by Sam Miller of Wayne, New Jersey, in the hydrogen-peroxide rocket-powered *Pollution Packer* at Seattle International Raceway, Kent, Washington, on May 31, 1975.

Terminal velocity is the speed attained at the end of a 440-yard run made from a standing start and elapsed time is the time taken for the run.

LONGEST RALLY: Joginder Singh of Kenya (left) has won the annual East African Safari 3 times, most recently in 1976.

Stock Car Racing

Richard Petty of Randleman, North Carolina, was the first stock car driver to attain $1,000,000 lifetime earnings on August 1, 1971. His earnings through the 1976 season were over $2,500,000. Petty also holds the NASCAR records for most races won (180) and most victories in a single season (27 in 1967).

Rallies

Earliest. The earliest long rally was promoted by the Parisian daily *Le Matin* in 1907 from Peking, China to Paris, over a route of about 7,500 miles. Five cars left Peking on June 10. The winner, Prince Scipione Borghese, arrived in Paris on August 10, 1907 in his 40 h.p. Itala accompanied by his chauffeur, Ettore, and Luigi Barzini.

Longest. The world's longest ever rally event was the *Singapore Airlines* London—Sydney Rally run over 19,329 miles starting from Covent Garden, Greater London, on August 14, 1977, ending at the Sydney Opera House, passing through 17 countries. It was won on September 28, 1977, by Andrew Cowan, Colin Malkin and Michael Broad in a Mercedes 280E.

The longest rally held annually is the East African Safari (first run 1953), run through Kenya, Tanzania and Uganda, which is up to 3,874 miles long, as in the 17th Safari held on April 8–12, 1971. It has been won a record three times by Joginder Singh (Kenya) in 1965, 1974 and 1976.

Go-Kart Circumnavigation

The only recorded instance of a go-kart being driven around the world was a circumnavigation by Stan Mott, of New York, who drove a Lambretta-engined 175-c.c. Italkart with a ground clearance of two inches, 23,300 land miles through 28 countries from February 15, 1961, to June 5, 1964, starting and finishing in New York.

Pikes Peak Race

The Pikes Peak Auto Hill Climb, Colorado (instituted 1916) has been won by Bobby Unser 13 times between 1956 and 1974 (10 championship, 2 stock and 1 sports car title). On June 30, 1968, in the 46th race, he set an absolute record of 11 minutes 54.9 seconds in his 5,506-c.c. Chevrolet championship car over the 12.42-mile course, rising from 9,402 to 14,110 feet through 157 curves. Unser also holds the course records for stock cars (13 minutes 13.6 seconds in a Dodge Dart) and sports cars (13 minutes 19.1 seconds in a Lotus).

Badminton

Origins. The game was devised c. 1863 at Badminton Hall in Avon, England, the seat of the Dukes of Beaufort. The oldest club is the Newcastle Badminton Club, England, formed as the Armstrong College Club, on January 24, 1900.

International Championships. The International Championship or Thomas Cup (instituted 1948) has been won six times by Indonesia in 1957–58, 1960–61, 1963–64, 1969–70, 1972–73 and 1975–76.

The Ladies International Championship or Uber Cup (instituted 1956) has been won four times by Japan (1966, 1969, 1972 and 1978).

Most Titles Won. The record number of All-England Championship (instituted 1899) titles won is 21 by Sir George Thomas (1881–1972) between 1903 and 1928. The record for men's singles is 8 by Rudy Hartono of Indonesia (1968–74, 76). The most, including doubles, by women is 17, a record shared by Miss M. Lucas (1899–1910) and Mrs. G. C. K. Hashman (née Judy Devlin) (U.S.) from 1954 to 1967, who won a record 10 singles titles.

Shortest Game. In the 1969 Uber Cup in Djakarta, Indonesia, Miss N. Takagi (Japan) beat Miss P. Tumengkol in 9 minutes.

Marathons. The longest singles match between two players is 60 hours 15 minutes by Julian Marcus and Philip Holding of Warwick School, Warwick, England, July 17–19, 1978. Karen Haubrich of La Jolla, California, played continuous singles against a number of different opponents for 72 hours 17 minutes on August 17–20, 1977.

Longest Hit. Frank Rugani drove a shuttlecock 79 feet 8½ inches in indoor tests at San Jose, California, on February 29, 1964.

HOME RUN CHAMP
Japanese baseball star
Sadaharu Oh beat
Hank Aaron's record
with number 756 on
September 3, 1977.

Baseball

Origins. An English woodcut of "Base-Ball" dated 1744 is the earliest known reference.

Earliest Games. The earliest game on record under the Cartwright rules was on June 19, 1846, in Hoboken, N.J., where the "New York Nine" defeated the Knickerbockers 23 to 1 in 4 innings. The earliest all-professional team was the Cincinnati Red Stockings in 1869.

Home Runs

Henry L. (Hank) Aaron broke the record set by George H. (Babe) Ruth (New York AL) of 714 home runs in a lifetime when he hit No. 715 on April 8, 1974. Between 1954 and 1974 he hit 733 home runs in the National League. In 1975, he switched over to the American League and in that year and 1976, when he finally retired, he hit 22 more, bringing his lifetime total to 755, the major league record.

The Japanese slugger, Sadaharu Oh (b. May 20, 1940), of the Yomiuri Giants, beat Aaron's record by hitting his 756th home run on September 3, 1977.

An all-league record of 800 in a lifetime has been claimed for Josh Gibson (1911–47) of the Homestead Grays of the Negro League, who was elected in 1972 to the Baseball Hall of Fame in Cooperstown, New York. Gibson hit 84 round-trippers in one season.

The longest home run ever measured was one of 618 feet by Roy Edward Carlyle in a minor league game at Emeryville Ball Park, California, on July 4, 1929. Babe Ruth hit a 587-foot homer at Tampa, Florida, in 1919.

800 HOME RUNS: Josh Gibson hit 800 lifetime home runs for the Homestead Grays of the Negro League, and 84 in one season. He was never able to play in the major leagues, but was posthumously elected to the Baseball Hall of Fame in 1972.

Fastest Pitcher

The fastest pitcher in the world is L. Nolan Ryan of the California Angels who, on August 20, 1974, in Anaheim Stadium, was electronically clocked at a speed of 100.9 m.p.h.

Longest Throw

The longest throw of a 5–5¼-oz. baseball is 445 feet 10 inches by Glen Gorbous (b. Canada) on August 1, 1957. Mildred "Babe"

FASTEST PITCHER: L. Nolan Ryan (California AL), who can throw a pitch 100.9 m.p.h., set a new modern record with 383 strikeouts in the 1973 season. He has also tied Sandy Koufax with 4 no-hit games.

Didrikson (later Mrs. George Zaharias) (1914–56) threw a ball 296 feet at Jersey City, New Jersey, on July 25, 1931.

Do-Nothing Record

Toby Harrah of the Texas Rangers (AL) played an entire double-header at shortstop on June 26, 1976, without having a chance to make any fielding plays, assists or putouts.

Hit by Pitch

Ron Hunt, an infielder who played with various National League teams from 1963 to 1974, led the league in getting hit by pitched balls for a record seven consecutive years. His career total is 243, also a major league record.

Fastest Base Runner

Ernest Evar Swanson (1902–73) took only 13.3 seconds to circle the bases at Columbus, Ohio, in 1932, averaging 18.45 m.p.h.

Youngest Player

The youngest major league player of all time was the Cincinnati pitcher, Joe Nuxhall, who started his career in June, 1944, aged 15 years 10 months 11 days.

Largest Stadium

The Cleveland Municipal Stadium in Cleveland, Ohio, has a seating capacity of 76,977.

MAJOR LEAGUE ALL-TIME RECORDS
(including 1978 season)

Individual Batting

Highest percentage, lifetime (5,000 at-bats)
.367 Tyrus R. Cobb, Det. AL, 1905–26; Phil. AL, 1927–28

Highest percentage, season (500 at-bats) (Leader in each league)
.438 Hugh Duffy, Bos. NL, 1894
.422 Napoleon Lajoie, Phil. AL, 1901

Most games played
3,298 Henry L. Aaron, Mil. NL, 1954–65, Atl. NL, 1966–74; Mil. AL, 1975–76

Most consecutive games played
2,130 Henry Louis Gehrig, N.Y. AL, June 1, 1925 through Apr. 30, 1939

Most runs, lifetime
2,244 Tyrus R. Cobb, Det. AL, 1905–1926; Phil. AL, 1927–28; 24 years

Most runs batted in, season
190 Lewis R. (Hack) Wilson, Chi. NL, 155 games, 1930

HIGHEST BATTING AVERAGE for a season in the American League was .422 by Nap Lajoie of Philadelphia in 1901.

HOME RUN KING: Henry L. (Hank) Aaron played in the National League for 21 seasons before switching to the American League for his last two seasons (1975–76). He hit a record 755 home runs in his career and also holds records for lifetime runs batted in (2,297) and most total bases (6,856).

Individual Batting Records (continued)

Most runs batted in, game
  12 James L. Bottomley, St. L. NL, Sept. 16, 1924

Most runs batted in, inning
  7 Edward Cartwright, St. L. AA, Sept. 23, 1890

Most base hits
  4,191 Tyrus R. Cobb, Det. AL, 1905–26; Phil. AL, 1927–28; 24 years

Most runs, season
  196 William R. Hamilton, Phil. NL, 131 games, 1894

Most runs batted in, lifetime
  2,297 Henry L. Aaron, Mil. NL, 1954–65, Atl. NL, 1966–74; Mil. AL, 1975–76

Most base hits, season
  257 George H. Sisler, St. L. AL, 154 games, 1920

Most hits in succession
  12 M. Frank (Pinky) Higgins, Bos. AL, June 19–21 (4 games), 1938; Walter Dropo, Det. AL, July 14, July 15, 2 games, 1952

Most base hits, consecutive, game
  7 Wilbert Robinson, Balt. NL, June 10, 1892, 1st game (7-ab), 6-1b, 1-2b

  Renaldo Stennett, Pitt. NL, Sept. 16, 1975 (7-ab), 4-1b, 2-2b, 1-3b

  Cesar Gutierrez, Det. AL, June 21, 1970, 2nd game (7-ab) 6-1b, 1-2b (extra-inning game)

Most consecutive games batted safely, season
  56 Joseph P. DiMaggio, N.Y. AL (91 hits—16-2b, 4-3b, 15 hr), May 15 to July 16, 1941

Most long hits, season
  119 George H. (Babe) Ruth, N.Y. AL (44-2b, 16-3b, 59 hr), 152 games, 1921

Most total bases, lifetime
  6,856 Henry L. Aaron, Mil. NL, 1954–65, Atl. NL, 1966–74; Mil. AL, 1975–76

Most total bases, season
  457 George H. (Babe) Ruth, N.Y. AL, 152 g. (85 on 1b, 88 on 2b, 48 on 3b, 236 on hr), 1921

Most total bases, game
  18 Joseph W. Adcock, Mil. NL (1-2b, 4-hr), July 31, 1954

Sluggers' percentage
(The percentage is obtained by dividing the "times at bat" into total bases.)
Highest slugging percentage, lifetime
  .690 George H. (Babe) Ruth, Bos.-N.Y. AL, 1914–34; Bos. NL, 1935

Triple-Crown winners
(Most times leading league in batting, runs batted in and home runs.)
  2 Rogers Hornsby, St. L. NL, 1922, 1925
  Theodore S. Williams, Bos. AL, 1942, 1947

Most one-base hits (singles), season
202 William H. Keeler, Balt. NL, 128 games, 1898

Most two-base hits, season
67 Earl W. Webb, Bos. AL, 151 games, 1931

Most three-base hits, season
36 J. Owen Wilson, Pitts. NL, 152 games, 1912

Most home runs, lifetime
755 Henry L. Aaron, Mil. NL, 1954 (13), 1955 (27), 1956 (26), 1957 (44), 1958 (30), 1959 (39), 1960 (40), 1961 (34), 1962 (45), 1963 (44), 1964 (24), 1965 (32); Atl. NL, 1966 (44), 1967 (39), 1968 (29), 1969 (44), 1970 (38), 1971 (47), 1972 (34), 1973 (40), 1974 (20); Mil. AL, 1975 (12), 1976 (10)

Most home runs, season (154-game schedule)
60 George H. (Babe) Ruth, N.Y. AL (28 home, 32 away), 151 gs. 1927

Most home runs, season (162-game schedule)
61 Roger E. Maris, N.Y. AL (30 home, 31 away), 161 gs. 1961

RECORD SLUGGER: Babe Ruth (New York AL) still holds the record for 60 home runs in a 154-game season, most long hits (119), most total bases (457), and most bases on balls (170) in a season and had a lifetime slugging percentage of .690.

Most home runs, bases filled, lifetime
23 Henry Louis Gehrig, N.Y. AL, 1927–1938

Most home runs with bases filled, season
5 Ernest Banks, Chi. NL, May 11, 19, July 17 (1st game), Aug. 2, Sept. 19, 1955
James E. Gentile, Balt. AL, May 9 (2), July 2, 7, Sept. 22, 1961

Most home runs, with bases filled, same game
2 Anthony M. Lazzeri, N.Y. AL, May 24, 1936
James R. Tabor, Bos. AL (2nd game), July 4, 1939
Rudolph York, Bos. AL, July 27, 1946
James E. Gentile, Balt. AL, May 9, 1961 (consecutive at-bats)
Tony L. Cloninger, Atl. NL, July 3, 1966
James T. Northrup, Det. AL, June 24, 1968 (consecutive at-bats)
Frank Robinson, Balt. AL, June 26, 1970 (consecutive at-bats)

Most bases on balls, game
6 James E. Foxx, Bos. AL, June 16, 1938

Most bases on balls, season
170 George H. (Babe) Ruth, N.Y. AL, 152 games, 1923

Most home runs, one month
18 Rudolph York, Det. AL, Aug. 1937

Most consecutive games hitting home runs
8 R. Dale Long, Pitt. NL, May 19–28, 1956

Most home runs, one doubleheader
5 Stanley F. Musial, St. L. NL, 1st game (3), 2nd game (2), May 2, 1954
Nathan Colbert, S.D. NL, 1st game (2), 2nd game (3), Aug. 1, 1972

Most consecutive pinch hits, lifetime
9 David E. Philley, Phil. NL, Sept. 9, 11, 12, 13, 19, 20, 27, 28, 1958; Apr. 16, 1959

Most Valuable Player, as voted by Baseball Writers Association
3 times James E. Foxx, Phil. AL, 1932, 33, 38
Joseph P. DiMaggio, N.Y. AL, 1939, 41, 47
Stanley F. Musial, St. L. NL, 1943, 46, 48
Lawrence P. (Yogi) Berra, N.Y. AL, 1951, 54, 55
Roy Campanella, Bklyn. NL, 1951, 53, 55
Mickey C. Mantle, N.Y. AL, 1956, 57, 62

BASE STEALER: Lou Brock (St. Louis NL) stole 118 bases in 153 games in 1974. His lifetime total of 917 stolen bases is the record for any player in the 20th century.

Base Running

Most stolen bases, lifetime
937   William R. Hamilton, K.C. AA, 1888–89; Phil. NL 1890–95; Bos. NL 1896–1901

Most stolen bases, lifetime since 1900
917   Louis C. Brock, Chi.-St. L. NL, 1961–78

Most stolen bases, season since 1900
118   Louis C. Brock, St. L. NL, 153 games, 1974

Most stolen bases, game
7   George F. (Piano Legs) Gore, Chi. NL, June 25, 1881
    William R. (Sliding Billy) Hamilton, Phil. NL, 2nd game, 8 inn., Aug. 31, 1894

Most times stealing home, game
2   by 9 players

Most times stealing home, lifetime
35   Tyrus R. Cobb, Det.-Phil. AL, 1905–28

Fewest times caught stealing, season (50+ attempts)
2   Max Carey, Pitt. NL, 1922 (53 atts.)

Pitching

Most games, lifetime
1,070   J. Hoyt Wilhelm, N.Y.-St. L.-Atl.-Chi.-L.A. (448) NL, 1952–57, 69–72; Clev.-Balt.-Chi.-Cal. (622) AL, 1957–69

Most complete games, lifetime
751   Denton T. (Cy) Young, Clev.-St. L.-Bos. NL (428); Bos.-Clev. AL (323), 1890–1911

Most complete games, season
74   William H. White, Cin. NL, 1879

Most innings pitched, game
26   Leon J. Cadore, Bklyn. NL, May 1, 1920
    Joseph Oeschger, Bos. NL, May 1, 1920

Lowest earned run average, season
0.90   Ferdinand M. Schupp, N.Y. NL, 1916 (140 inn)
1.01   Hubert B. (Dutch) Leonard, Bos. AL, 1914 (222 inn)
1.12   Robert Gibson, St. L. NL, 1968 (305 inn)

Most games won, lifetime
511   Denton T. (Cy) Young, Clev. NL (239) 1890–98; St. L. NL 1899–1900; Bos. AL (193) 1901–08; Clev. AL (29) 1909–11; Bos. NL (4) 1911

Most games won, season
60   Charles Radbourne, Providence NL, 1884

Most consecutive games won, lifetime
24   Carl O. Hubbell, N.Y. NL, 1936 (16); 1937 (8)

Most consecutive games won, season
19   Timothy J. Keefe, N.Y. NL, 1888
    Richard W. Marquard, N.Y. NL, 1912

Most shutout games, season
16   George W. Bradley, St. L. NL, 1876
    Grover C. Alexander, Phil. NL, 1916

Most shutout games, lifetime
113   Walter P. Johnson, Wash. AL, 21 years, 1907–27

Most consecutive shutout games, season
6   Donald S. Drysdale, L.A. NL, May 14, 18, 22, 26, 31, June 4, 1968

Most consecutive shutout innings
58   Donald S. Drysdale, L.A. NL, May 14–June 8, 1968

Most strikeouts, lifetime
3,508 Walter P. Johnson, Wash. AL,
1907–27

Most strikeouts, season
505 Matthew Kilroy, Balt. AA, 1886
(Distance 50 ft)
383 L. Nolan Ryan, Cal. AL, 1973
(Distance 60 ft 6 in.)

Most strikeouts, game (9 inn) since 1900:
19 Steven N. Carlton, St. L. NL vs
N.Y., Sept. 15, 1969 (lost)
G. Thomas Seaver, N.Y. NL vs
S.D., Apr. 22, 1970
L. Nolan Ryan, Cal. AL, vs Bos.,
Aug. 12, 1974

Most strikeouts, extra-inning game
21 Thomas E. Cheney, Wash. AL vs
Balt. (16 inns), Sept. 12, 1962
(night)

Most no-hit games, lifetime
4 Sanford Koufax, L.A. NL, 1962–
63–64–65
L. Nolan Ryan, Cal. AL, 1973(2)–
74-75

Most consecutive no-hit games
2 John S. Vandermeer, Cin. NL,
June 11–15, 1938

Perfect game—9 innings

1880 John Lee Richmond, Wor-
cester vs Clev. NL, June 12 1–0
John M. Ward, Prov. vs
Buff. NL, June 17 AM...... 5–0

1904 Denton T. (Cy) Young,
Bos. vs Phil. AL, May 5 ... 3–0

1908 Adrian C. Joss, Clev. vs Chi.
AL, Oct. 2...................... 1–0

†1917 Ernest G. Shore, Bos. vs
Wash. AL, June 23 (1st g.) 4–0

1922 C. C. Robertson, Chi. vs
Det. AL, April 30............ 2–0

**1956 Donald J. Larsen, N.Y. AL
vs Bklyn. NL, Oct. 8...... 2–0

1964 James P. Bunning, Phil.
NL vs N.Y., June 21 (1st
g.) 6–0

1965 Sanford Koufax, L.A. NL
vs Chi., Sept. 9............... 1–0

1968 James A. Hunter, Oak. AL
vs Minn., May 8............... 4–0

Special mention

1959 Harvey Haddix, Jr., Pitt. vs Mil.
NL, May 26, pitched 12 "perfect" innings, allowed hit in 13th
and lost

---

†Starting pitcher, "Babe" Ruth, was
banished from game by Umpire Owens
after giving first batter, Morgan, a base
on balls. Shore relieved and while he
pitched to second batter, Morgan was
caught stealing. Shore then retired next
26 batters to complete "perfect" game.

**World Series game.

LONGEST-LASTING PITCHER:
Hoyt Wilhelm, knuckleball pitcher for 9
teams in both leagues, played in 1,070
major league games between 1952 and
1972, and had a lifetime ERA of 2.52.

Club Batting

Highest percentage, season
.343 Phil. NL, 132 games, 1894

Highest percentage, season since 1900
.319 N.Y. NL, 154 games, 1930

Most runs, one club, game
36 Chi. NL (36) vs Louisville (7),
June 29, 1897

Most runs, one club, inning
18 Chi. NL, 7th inning, Sept. 6, 1883

Most runs, both clubs, inning
19 Wash. AA (14), Balt. (5), 1st inn.,
June 17, 1891
Clev. AL (13), Bos. (6), 8th inn.,
April 10, 1977

Most hits, one club, 9 inning game
36 Phil. NL, Aug. 17, 1894

Most hits, one club, inning
18 Chi. NL, 7th inning, Sept. 6, 1883

Fewest hits, both clubs, game
1 Chi. NL (0) vs L.A. (1), Sept. 9,
1965

Most home runs, one club, season (154-
game schedule)
221 N.Y. NL, 155 games, 1947
Cin. NL, 155 games, 1956

Most home runs, one club, season (162-
game schedule)
240 N.Y. AL, 163 games, 1961

Club Batting Records (continued)

Fewest home runs (135 or more games), one club, season
  3 Chi. AL, 156 games, 1908

Most stolen bases (1900 to date), one club, season
  347 N.Y. NL, 154 games, 1911

Most stolen bases, one club, inning
  8 Wash. AL, 1st inning, July 19, 1915
     Phil. NL, 9th inning, 1st g., July 7, 1919

Club Fielding

Highest percentage, one club, season
  .985 Balt. AL, 1964

Fewest errors, season
  95 Balt. AL, 163 games, 1964
      Cin. NL, 162 games, 1977

Most double plays, club, season
  217 Phil. AL, 154 games, 1949

Most double plays, club, game
  7 N.Y. AL, Aug. 14, 1942
     Houst. NL, May 4, 1969

General Club Records

Shortest and longest game by time
  51 minutes N.Y. NL (6), Phil. (1), 1st g., Sept. 28, 1919
  7:23 S.F. NL (8) at N.Y. (6) 23 inn., 2nd g., May 31, 1964

Longest 9-inning game
  4:18 S.F. NL (7) at L.A. (8), Oct. 2, 1962

Fewest times shutout, season
  0 Bos. NL, 1894 (132 g.)
     Phil. NL, 1894 (127 g.)
     N.Y. AL, 1932 (155 g.)

Most consecutive innings shutting out opponents
  56 Pitt. NL, June 1-9, 1903

Highest percentage games won, season
  .798 Chi. NL (won 67, lost 17), 1880
  .763 Chi. NL (won 116, lost 36), 1906
  .721 Clev. AL (won 111, lost 43), 1954

Most games won, season (154-game schedule)
  116 Chi. NL, 1906

Most consecutive games won, season
  26 N.Y. NL, Sept. 7 (1st g.) to Sept. 30 (1 tie), 1916

Most pitchers used in a game, 9 innings, one club
  9 St. L. AL vs Chi., Oct. 2, 1949

Managers' consecutive championship records
5 years Charles D. (Casey) Stengel, N.Y. AL, 1949–50–51–52–53

World Series Records

Most series played
  14 Lawrence P. (Yogi) Berra, N.Y., AL, 1947, 49–53, 55–58, 60–63

Highest batting percentage (20 g. min.), total series
  .391 Louis C. Brock, St. L. NL, 1964, 67–68 (g-21, ab-87, h-34)

Highest batting percentage, 4 or more games, one series
  .625 4-game series, George H. (Babe) Ruth, N.Y. AL, 1928

Most runs, total series
  42 Mickey C. Mantle, N.Y. AL, 1951–53, 55–58, 60–64

Most runs, one series
  10 Reginald M. Jackson, N.Y. AL, 1977

Most runs batted in, total series
  40 Mickey C. Mantle, N.Y., AL, 1951–53, 55–58, 60–64

Most runs batted in, game
  6 Robert C. Richardson, N.Y. AL, (4) 1st inn., (2) 4th inn., Oct. 8, 1960

Most runs batted in, consecutive times at bat
  7 James L. (Dusty) Rhodes, N.Y. NL, first 4 times at bat, 1954

Most base hits, total series
  71 Lawrence P. (Yogi) Berra, N.Y. AL, 1947, 49–53, 55–58, 60–61

Most home runs, total series
  18 Mickey C. Mantle, N.Y. AL, 1952 (2), 53 (2), 55, 56 (3), 57, 58 (2), 60 (3), 63, 64 (3)

Most home runs, one series
  5 Reginald M. Jackson, N.Y. AL, 1977

Most home runs, game
  3 George H. (Babe) Ruth, N.Y. AL, Oct. 6, 1926; Oct. 9, 1928
     Reginald M. Jackson, N.Y. AL, 1977

Pitchers' Records

Pitching in most series
  11 Edward C. (Whitey) Ford, N.Y. AL, 1950, 53, 55–58, 60–64

WORLD SERIES RUNS: Reggie Jackson belted 3 homers in a game and 5 in the 6-game series in 1977.

Most victories, total series
  10 Edward C. (Whitey) Ford, N.Y. AL, 1950 (1), 55 (2), 56 (1), 57 (1), 60 (2), 61 (2), 62 (1)

All victories, no defeats
  6 Vernon L. (Lefty) Gomez, N.Y. AL, 1932 (1), 36 (2), 37 (2), 38 (1)

Most games won, one series
  3 games in 5-game series
    Christy Mathewson, N.Y. NL, 1905
    J. W. Coombs, Phil. AL, 1910
Many others won 3 games in series of more games.

Most shutout games, total series
  4 Christy Mathewson, N.Y. NL. 1905 (3), 1913

Most shutout games, one series
  3 Christy Mathewson, N.Y. NL. 1905

Most strikeouts, one pitcher, total series
  94 Edward C. (Whitey) Ford, N.Y. AL, 1950, 53, 55–58, 60–64

Most strikeouts, one series

23 in 4 games Sanford Koufax, L.A. NL, 1963

18 in 5 games Christy Mathewson, N.Y. NL, 1905

20 in 6 games C. A. (Chief) Bender, Phil. AL, 1911

35 in 7 games Robert Gibson, St. L. NL, 1968

28 in 8 games W. H. Dinneen, Bos. AL, 1903

Most strikeouts, one pitcher, game
  17 Robert Gibson, St. L. NL, Oct. 2, 1968

Highest attendance

420,784 L.A. NL, World Champions vs Chi. AL, 4–2, 1959

Most Series Won
  22 New York AL, 1923, 1927, 1928, 1932, 1936, 1937, 1938, 1939, 1941, 1943, 1947, 1949, 1950, 1951, 1952, 1953, 1956, 1958, 1961, 1962, 1977, 1978

Baseball records by Seymour Siwoff. Elias Sports Bureau.

World Series Attendance

The World Series record attendance is 420,784 (6 games with total receipts of $2,626,973.44) when the Los Angeles Dodgers beat the Chicago White Sox 4 games to 2, October 1–8, 1959.

The single game record is 92,706 for the fifth game (receipts $552,774.77) at the Memorial Coliseum, Los Angeles, on October 6, 1959.

SHOOTING STAR:
Ted St. Martin sank
2,036 consecutive free
throws in June, 1977.

Basketball

Origins. *Ollamalitzli* was a 16th-century Aztec precursor of basketball played in Mexico. If the solid rubber ball was put through a fixed stone ring placed high on one side of the stadium, the player was entitled to the clothing of all the spectators. The captain of the losing team often lost his head (by execution). Another game played much earlier, in the 10th century B.C. by the Olmecs in Mexico, called *Pok-ta-Pok*, also resembled basketball in its concept of a ring through which a round object was passed.

Modern basketball was devised by the Canadian-born Dr. James A. Naismith (1861–1939) at the Training School of the International Y.M.C.A. College at Springfield, Massachusetts, in December, 1891. The first game played under modified rules was on January 20, 1892. The first public contest was on March 11, 1892. The game is now a global activity.

The International Amateur Basketball Federation (F.I.B.A.) was founded in 1932.

Most Accurate Shooting. The greatest goal-shooting demonstration was made by a professional, Ted St. Martin, now of Jacksonville, Florida, who, on June 25, 1977, scored 2,036 consecutive free throws.

In a 24-hour period, May 31–June 1, 1975, Fred L. Newman of San Jose, California, scored 12,874 baskets out of 13,116 attempts (98.15 per cent). Newman has also made 88 consecutive free throws while blindfolded at the Central Y.M.C.A., San Jose, California, on February 5, 1978.

Longest Field Goal. The longest recorded field goal in a game was made from a measured distance of 86 feet by Barry Hutchings, 15, of Sutherlin High School, Sutherlin, Oregon, on March 22, 1976.

In practice in 1953, Larry Slinkard of Arlington Heights High School, Arlington, Illinois, scored with a shot from 88 feet.

Tallest Players

The tallest player of all time is reputed to be Mu Tieh-Chu (China) who competed against a Japanese All-Star team in 1978, when he measured 7 feet 9¾ inches. The tallest woman player is Iuliana Semenova (U.S.S.R.) who is reputed to stand 7 feet 2 inches tall and weigh 281 lbs. The tallest N.B.A. player is Tom Burleson, who is 7 feet 4 inches tall.

Greatest Attendances. The Harlem Globetrotters played an exhibition to 75,000 in the Olympic Stadium, West Berlin, Germany, in 1951. The largest indoor basketball crowd was at the Astrodome, Houston, Texas, where 52,693 watched a game on January 20, 1968, between the University of Houston and U.C.L.A.

The Harlem Globetrotters have traveled over 6,000,000 miles, visited 94 countries on six continents, and have been watched by an estimated 80,000,000 spectators. They have won over 12,000 games,

MILLIONS OF FANS:
Meadowlark Lemon was a star player for the Harlem Globetrotters, who have performed before an estimated 80 million people.

losing less than 350, but many were not truly competitive. The team was founded by Abraham M. Saperstein (1903–66) of Chicago, and their first game was played at Hinckley, Illinois, on January 7, 1927.

Olympic Champions

The U.S. won all seven Olympic titles from the time the sport was introduced to the Games in 1936 until 1968, without losing a single match. In 1972, in Munich, their run of 64 consecutive victories was broken when they lost 51–50 to the U.S.S.R. in a much-disputed final match. They regained the Olympic title in Montreal in 1976, again without losing a game.

World Champions

Brazil, the U.S.S.R. and Yugoslavia are the only countries to win the World Championship (instituted 1950) on more than one occasion. Brazil won in 1959 and 1963; the U.S.S.R. in 1967 and 1974; Yugoslavia in 1970 and 1978.

In 1975, the U.S.S.R. won the women's championship (instituted 1953) for the fifth consecutive time since 1959.

Marathon

The longest reported marathon is 75 hours by two teams of 5 (no substitutes) from Bethany College, West Virginia, October 5–8, 1977.

NATIONAL BASKETBALL ASSOCIATION
Regular Season Records
Including 1977–78 *Season*

The National Basketball Association's Championship series was established in 1947. Prior to 1949, when it joined with the National Basketball League, the professional circuit was known as the Basketball Association of America.

SERVICE

Most Games, Lifetime
1,270 John Havlicek, Bos. 1963–78

Most Games, Consecutive, Lifetime
844 John Kerr, Syr.-Phil.-Balt., Oct. 31, 1954–Nov. 4, 1965

Most Complete Games, Season
79 Wilt Chamberlain, Phil. 1962

Most Complete Games, Consecutive, Season
47 Wilt Chamberlain, Phil. 1962

Most Minutes, Lifetime
47,859 Wilt Chamberlain, Phil.-S.F.-L.A. 1960–73

Most Minutes, Season
3,882 Wilt Chamberlain, Phil. 1962

SCORING

Most Seasons Leading League
7 Wilt Chamberlain, Phil. 1960–62; S.F. 1963–64; S.F.-Phil. 1965; Phil. 1966

Most Points, Lifetime
31,419 Wilt Chamberlain, Phil.-S.F.-L.A. 1960–73

Most Points, Season
4,029 Wilt Chamberlain, Phil. 1962

Most Seasons 1000+ Points
16 John Havlicek, Bos. 1963–78

Most Points, Game
100 Wilt Chamberlain, Phil. vs. N.Y., Mar. 2, 1962

Most Points, Half
59 Wilt Chamberlain, Phil. vs. N.Y., Mar. 2, 1962

Most Points, Quarter
33 George Gervin, S.A. vs. N.O., Apr. 9, 1978

Most Points, Overtime Period
13 Earl Monroe, Balt. vs. Det., Feb. 6, 1970
Joe Caldwell, Atl. vs. Cin., Feb. 18, 1970

Highest Scoring Average, Lifetime (400 + games)
30.1 Wilt Chamberlain, Phil.-S.F.-L.A. 1960–73

Highest Scoring Average, Season
50.4 Wilt Chamberlain, Phil. 1962

Field Goals Made

Most Field Goals, Lifetime
12,681 Wilt Chamberlain, Phil.-S.F.-L.A. 1960–73

Most Field Goals, Season
1,597 Wilt Chamberlain, Phil. 1962

Most Field Goals, Consecutive, Season
35 Wilt Chamberlain, Phil. Feb. 17–28, 1967

Most Field Goals, Game
36 Wilt Chamberlain, Phil. vs. N.Y., Mar. 2, 1962

Most Field Goals, Half
22 Wilt Chamberlain, Phil. vs. N.Y., Mar. 2, 1962

Most Field Goals, Quarter
13 David Thompson, Den. vs. Det., Apr. 9, 1978

Field Goals Attempted

Most Field Goal Attempts, Lifetime
23,930 John Havlicek, Bos. 1963–1978

Most Field Goal Attempts, Season
3,159 Wilt Chamberlain, Phil. 1962

Most Field Goal Attempts, Game
63 Wilt Chamberlain, Phil. vs. N.Y., Mar. 2, 1962

Most Field Goal Attempts, Half
37 Wilt Chamberlain, Phil. vs. N.Y., Mar. 2, 1962

Most Field Goal Attempts, Quarter
21 Wilt Chamberlain, Phil. vs. N.Y., Mar. 2, 1962

Field Goal Percentage

Most Seasons Leading League
9 Wilt Chamberlain, Phil. 1961; S.F. 1963; S.F.-Phil. 1965; Phil. 1966–68; L.A. 1969, 72–73

Highest Percentage, Lifetime
.549 Kareem Abdul-Jabbar, Mil.-L.A. 1970–78

Highest Percentage, Season
.727 Wilt Chamberlain, L.A. 1973

LONGEST SERVICE: John Havlicek played in a record 1,270 games for the Boston Celtics.

Free Throws Made

Most Free Throws Made, Lifetime
7,694 Oscar Robertson, Cin.-Mil. 1961–74

Most Free Throws Made, Season
840 Jerry West, L.A. 1966

Most Free Throws Made, Consecutive, Season
60 Rick Barry, G.S. Oct. 22–Nov. 16, 1976

Most Free Throws Made, Game
28 Wilt Chamberlain, Phil. vs. N.Y., Mar. 2, 1962

Most Free Throws Made (No Misses), Game
19 Bob Pettit, St.L. vs. Bos., Nov. 22, 1961

Most Free Throws Made, Half
19 Oscar Robertson, Cin. vs. Balt., Dec. 27, 1964

Most Free Throws Made, Quarter
14 Rick Barry, S.F. vs. N.Y., Dec. 6, 1966

FREE THROW LEADER: Jerry West sank 840 free throws in his 1966 season for L.A.

Basketball (N.B.A.) continued

Free Throws Attempted

Most Free Throw Attempts, Lifetime
11,862 Wilt Chamberlain, Phil.-S.F.-L.A. 1960–73

Most Free Throw Attempts, Season
1,363 Wilt Chamberlain, Phil. 1962

Most Free Throw Attempts, Game
34 Wilt Chamberlain, S.F. vs. N.Y., Nov. 27, 1963

Most Free Throw Attempts, Half
22 Oscar Robertson, Cin. vs. Balt., Dec. 27, 1964

Most Free Throw Attempts, Quarter
16 Oscar Robertson, Cin. vs. Balt., Dec. 27, 1964
Stan McKenzie, Phoe. vs. Phil., Feb. 15, 1970
Pete Maravich, Atl. vs. Chi., Jan. 2, 1973

Free Throw Percentage

Most Seasons Leading League
7 Bill Sharman, Bos. 1953–57, 59, 61

Highest Percentage, Lifetime
.896 Rick Barry, S.F.-G.S. 1966–67, 73–78

Highest Percentage, Season
.945 Ernie Di Gregorio, Buff. 1977

REBOUNDS

Most Seasons Leading League
11 Wilt Chamberlain, Phil. 1960–62; S.F. 1963; Phil. 1966–68; L.A. 1969, 71–73

Most Rebounds, Lifetime
23,924 Wilt Chamberlain, Phil.-S.F.-L.A. 1960–73

Most Rebounds, Season
2,149 Wilt Chamberlain, Phil. 1961

Most Rebounds, Game
55 Wilt Chamberlain, Phil. vs. Bos., Nov. 24, 1960

Most Rebounds, Half
32 Bill Russell, Bos. vs. Phil., Nov. 16, 1957

Most Rebounds, Quarter
18 Nate Thurmond, S.F. vs. Balt., Feb. 28, 1965

Highest Average (per game), Lifetime
22.9 Wilt Chamberlain, Phil.-S.F.-L.A. 1960–73

Highest Average (per game), Season
27.2 Wilt Chamberlain, Phil. 1961

ASSISTS

Most Seasons Leading League
8 Bob Cousy, Bos. 1953–60

Most Assists, Lifetime
9,887 Oscar Robertson, Cin.-Mil. 1961–74

Most Assists, Season
910 Nate Archibald, K.C.-Omaha 1973

Most Assists, Game
29 Kevin Porter, N.J. vs. Hou. Feb. 24, 1978

Most Assists, Half
19 Bob Cousy, Bos. vs. Minn., Feb. 27, 1959

ASSIST SPECIALIST: Oscar Robertson holds the record for setting up plays with 9,887 assists in his lifetime, highest average (9.5) per game lifetime and highest average (11.5) in one season.

Most Assists, Quarter
12 Bob Cousy, Bos. vs. Minn., Feb.
    27, 1959
   John Lucas, Hou. vs. Mil.,
    Oct. 27, 1977
Highest Average (per game), Lifetime
9.5 Oscar Robertson, Cin.-Mil.
    1961–74
Highest Average (per game), Season
11.5 Oscar Robertson, Cin. 1965

PERSONAL FOULS

Most Personal Fouls, Lifetime
3,855 Hal Greer, Syr.-Phil. 1959–73
Most Personal Fouls, Season
366 Bill Bridges, St. L. 1968
Most Personal Fouls, Game
8 Don Otten, T.C. vs. Sheb., Nov.
   24, 1949
Most Personal Fouls, Half
6 By many. Last:
   Roger Brown, Det. vs. G.S.,
    Mar. 25, 1977
Most Personal Fouls, Quarter
6 Connie Dierking, Syr. vs. Cin.,
    Nov. 17, 1959
   Henry Akin, Seattle vs. Phil.,
    Dec. 20, 1967
   Bud Ogden, Phil. vs Phoe., Feb.
    15, 1970
   Don Smith, Hou. vs. Clev.,
    Feb. 8, 1974
   Roger Brown, Det. vs. G.S.,
    Mar. 25, 1977

DISQUALIFICATIONS
(Fouling Out of Game)

Most Disqualifications, Lifetime
127 Vern Mikkelsen, Minn., 1950–59
Most Disqualifications, Season
26 Don Meineke, Ft. W. 1953
Most Games, No Disqualifications, Lifetime
1,045 Wilt Chamberlain, Phil.-S.F.-
     L.A. 1960–73 (Entire Career)

TEAM RECORDS
(ot = overtime)

Most Seasons, League Champion
13 Boston 1957, 59–66, 68–69, 74,
   76
Most Seasons, Consecutive, League Champion
8 Boston 1959–66
Most Seasons, Division Champion
14 Boston 1957–65, 72–76
Most Seasons, Consecutive, Division Champion
9 Boston 1957–65
Most Games Won, Season
69 Los Angeles, 1972
Most Games Won, Consecutive, Season
33 Los Angeles Nov. 5, 1971–Jan.
   7, 1972
Most Games Won, Consecutive, Start of Season
15 Washington Nov. 3–Dec. 4, 1948

REBOUND RECORD-HOLDER:
Wilton Norman (the Stilt) Chamberlain is probably the greatest basketball player of all time. He made 55 rebounds in one game, 2,149 in a season. He also set records of 100 points in a game, 4,029 points in a season, most free throws made (28) in a game, and other records.

Most Games Won, Consecutive, End of Season
14 Milwaukee Feb. 28–Mar. 27,
   1973
Most Games Lost, Season
73 Philadelphia 1973
Most Games Lost, Consecutive, Season
20 Philadelphia Jan. 9–Feb. 11,
   1973
Most Games Lost, Consecutive, Start of Season
15 Denver Oct. 29–Dec. 25, 1949
   Cleveland Oct. 14–Nov. 10, 1970
   Philadelphia Oct. 10–Nov. 10,
    1973
Highest Percentage, Games Won, Season
.841 Los Angeles 1972
Lowest Percentage, Games Won, Season
.110 Philadelphia 1973

Team Scoring

Most Points, Season
10,143 Philadelphia 1967
Most Games, 100+ Points, Season
81 Los Angeles 1972
Most Games, Consecutive, 100+ Points, Season
77 New York 1967
Most Points, Game
173 Boston vs Minn. Feb. 27, 1959
Most Points, Both Teams, Game
316 Phil. (169) vs N.Y. (147) Mar. 2,
    1962
   Cin.(165) vs San Diego (151)
    Mar. 12, 1970
Most Points, Half
97 Atlanta vs San Diego Feb. 11,
   1970

Basketball (N.B.A.) continued

Most Points, Quarter
58 Buffalo vs Bos. Oct. 20, 1972
Widest Victory Margin, Game
63 Los Angeles (162) vs Golden State (99) Mar. 19, 1972

Field Goals Made

Most Field Goals, Season
3,972 Milwaukee 1971
Most Field Goals, Game
72 Boston vs Minn. Feb. 27, 1959
Most Field Goals, Both Teams, Game
134 Cin. (67) vs San Diego (67) Mar. 12, 1970
Most Field Goals, Half
40 Boston vs Minn. Feb. 27, 1959
     Syracuse vs Det. Jan. 13, 1963
Most Field Goals, Quarter
23 Boston vs Minn. Feb. 27, 1959
     Buffalo vs Bos. Oct. 20, 1972

Field Goals Attempted

Most Field Goal Attempts, Season
9,295 Boston 1961
Most Field Goal Attempts, Game
153 Philadelphia vs. L.A. Dec. 8, 1961 (3 ot)
150 Boston vs Phil. Feb. 3, 1960
Most Field Goal Attempts, Both Teams, Game
291 Phil. (153) vs L.A. (138) Dec. 8, 1961 (3 ot)
274 Bos. (149) vs Det. (125) Jan. 27, 1961
Most Field Goal Attempts, Half
83 Philadelphia vs Syr. Nov. 4, 1959
     Boston vs Phil. Dec. 27, 1960
Most Field Goal Attempts, Quarter
47 Boston vs Minn. Feb. 27, 1959
Highest Field Goal Percentage, Season
.509 Milwaukee 1971

Free Throws Made

Most Free Throws Made, Season
2,434 Phoenix 1970
Most Free Throws Made, Game
59 Anderson vs Syr. Nov. 24, 1949 (5 ot)
Most Free Throws Made, Both Teams, Game
116 And. (59) vs Syr. (57) Nov. 24, 1949 (5 ot)
Most Free Throws Made, Half
36 Chicago vs Phoe. Jan. 8, 1970
Most Free Throws Made, Quarter
24 St. Louis vs Syr. Dec. 21, 1957

Free Throws Attempted

Most Free Throw Attempts, Season
3,411. Philadelphia 1967
Most Free Throw Attempts, Game
86 Syracuse vs And. Nov. 24, 1949 (5 ot)
71 Chicago vs Phoe. Jan. 8, 1970

Most Free Throw Attempts, Both Teams, Game
160 Syr. (86) vs And. (74) Nov. 24, 1949 (5 ot)
127 Ft. W. (67) vs Minn. (60) Dec. 31, 1954
Most Free Throw Attempts, Half
48 Chicago vs. Phoe. Jan. 8, 1970
Most Free Throw Attempts, Quarter
30 Boston vs Chi. Jan. 9, 1963
Highest Free Throw Percentage, Season
.821 K.C.-Omaha 1975

Rebounds

Most Rebounds, Season
6,131 Boston 1961
Most Rebounds, Game
112 Philadelphia vs Cin. Nov. 8, 1959
     Boston vs Det. Dec. 24, 1960
Most Rebounds, Both Teams, Game
215 Phil. (110) vs L.A. (105) Dec. 8, 1961 (3 ot)
196 Bos. (106) vs Det. (90) Jan. 27, 1961
Most Rebounds, Half
62 Boston vs Phil. Nov. 16, 1957
     New York vs Phil. Nov. 19, 1960
     Philadelphia vs Syr. Nov. 9, 1961
Most Rebounds, Quarter
40 Philadelphia vs Syr. Nov. 9, 1961

Assists

Most Assists, Season
2,338 New York 1978
     Phoenix 1978
Most Assists, Game
60 Syracuse vs Balt. Nov. 15, 1952 (1 ot)
52 Chicago vs Atl. Mar. 20, 1971
Most Assists, Both Teams, Game
89 Det. (48) vs Clev. (41) Mar. 28, 1973 (1 ot)
88 Phoe. (47) vs San Diego (41) Mar. 15, 1969
Most Assists, Half
29 Chicago vs Atl. Mar. 20, 1971
Most Assists, Quarter
16 Boston vs Minn. Feb. 27, 1959
     Chicago vs Atl. Mar. 20, 1971

Personal Fouls

Most Personal Fouls, Season
2,470 Atlanta 1978
Most Personal Fouls, Game
66 Anderson vs Syr. Nov. 24, 1949 (5 ot)
Most Personal Fouls, Both Teams, Game
122 And. (66) vs Syr. (56) Nov. 24, 1949 (5 ot)
97 Syr. (50) vs N.Y. (47) Feb. 15, 1953
Most Personal Fouls, Half
30 Rochester vs Syr. Jan. 15, 1953
Most Personal Fouls, Quarter
18 Portland vs. Atl., Jan. 16, 1977

Billiards

Earliest Mention. The earliest recorded mention of billiards was in France in 1429, and it was mentioned in England in 1588 in inventories of the Duke of Norfolk's Howard House and the Earl of Leicester's property in Essex. The first recorded public room for billiards in England was the Piazza, Covent Garden, London, in the early part of the 19th century.

Rubber cushions were introduced in 1835 and slate beds in 1836.

Highest Breaks. Tom Reece (England) made an unfinished break of 499,135, including 249,152 cradle cannons (2 points each), in 85 hours 49 minutes against Joe Chapman at Burroughes' Hall, Soho Square, London, between June 3 and July 6, 1907. This was not recognized because press and public were not continuously present. The highest certified break made by the anchor cannon is 42,746 by W. Cook (England) from May 29 to June 7, 1907. The official world record under the then baulk-line rule is 1,784 by Joe Davis in the United Kingdom Championship on May 29, 1936. Walter Lindrum (Australia) made an official break of 4,137 in 2 hours 55 minutes against Joe Davis at Thurston's, London, on January 19–20, 1932, before the baulk-line rule was in force. The amateur record is 862 by Norman Dagley in the European amateur championships in Middlesbrough, Cleveland, England, on March 16, 1978.

Fastest Century. Walter Lindrum (1898–1960) of Australia made an unofficial 100 break in 27.5 seconds in Australia on October 10, 1952. His official record is 100 in 46.0 seconds, set in Sydney in 1941.

RIGHT ON CUE:
Willie Hoppe
was undisputed master of
3-cushion billiards from
1906 through 1952.

LONGEST POOL RUN: Michael Eufemia pocketed 625 balls in a row in February, 1960.

Most World Titles. The greatest number of world championship titles (instituted 1870) won by one player is eight by John Roberts, Jr. (England) in 1870 (twice), 1871, 1875 (twice), 1877 and 1885 (twice). Willie Hoppe (U.S.) won 51 "world" titles in the U.S. variant of the game between 1906 and 1952.

Most Amateur Titles. The record for world amateur titles is four by Robert Marshall (Australia) in 1936–38–51–62.

Pool

Pool or championship pocket billiards with numbered balls began to become standardized $c.$ 1890. The greatest exponents were Ralph Greenleaf (U.S.) (1899–1950), who won the "world" professional title 19 times (1919–1937), and William Mosconi (U.S.), who dominated the game from 1941 to 1957.

Michael Eufemia holds the record for the greatest continuous run, pocketing 625 balls without a miss on February 2, 1960 before a large crowd at the Logan Billiard Academy, Brooklyn, New York.

Patrick Young pocketed 10,752 balls in 24 hours at the Camden Arms in London on May 2–3, 1978.

The longest recorded game by 2 players is 150 hours by Paul Heffron and Lee Hayden of Hensol Hospital, Pontyclun, Wales, October 20–26, 1978.

3-Cushion Billiards

This pocketless variation dates back to 1878. The most successful exponent, 1906–52, was William F. Hoppe (b. October 11, 1887, Cornwall-on-Hudson, New York; d. February 1, 1959) who won 51 billiards championships in all forms.

Bobsledding and Tobogganing

Origins. The oldest known sled is dated *c.* 6500 B.C. and came from Heinola, southern Finland. Modern world championships were inaugurated in 1924. Four-man bobs were included in the first Winter Olympic Games at Chamonix, France, in 1924 and two-man boblets from the third Games at Lake Placid, New York, in 1932.

Olympic and World Titles. The Olympic four-man bob has been won four times by Switzerland (1924–36–56–72). The U.S. (1932, 1936), Italy (1956, 1968) and West Germany (1952 and 1972) have won the Olympic boblet event twice. The most medals won by an individual is 6 (two gold, two silver, two bronze) by Eugenio Monti (Italy) from 1956 to 1968.

The world four-man bob has been won 12 times by Switzerland (1924–36–39–47–54–55–56–57–71–72–73–75). Italy won the two-man title 14 times (1954–56–57–58–59–60–61–62–63–66–68–69–71–75). Eugenio Monti (Italy) (b. January 23, 1928) has been a member of 11 world championship crews.

Tobogganing

The word toboggan comes from the Micmac American Indian word *tobaakan.* The oldest tobogganing club in the world, founded in 1887, is at St. Moritz, Switzerland, home of the Cresta Run and site of the introduction of the skeleton one-man racing toboggan.

The skeleton one-man toboggan dates, in its present form, from 1892. On the 1,325-yard-long Cresta Run at St. Moritz, Switzerland, dating from 1884, the record from the Junction (2,913 feet) is 42.96 seconds (average 63.08 m.p.h.) by Poldi Berchtold of Switzerland in January, 1975. The record from Top (3,977 feet) is 53.24 seconds, also by Berchtold in January, 1975. Momentary speeds of 90 m.p.h. have been attained.

The greatest number of wins in the Cresta Run Grand National (instituted 1885) is eight by the 1948 Olympic champion Nino Bibbia (Italy) (b. September 9, 1924) in 1960–61–62–63–64–66–68–73. The greatest number of wins in the Cresta Run Curzon Cup (instituted in 1910) is eight by Bibbia in 1950–57–58–60–62–63–64–69 who hence won the Double in 1960–62–63–64. The greatest number of descents made in a season is 7,832 during 1976.

Lugeing

In lugeing the rider adopts a sitting, as opposed to a prone position. Official international competition began at Klosters, Switzerland, in 1881. The first European championships were at Reichenberg (now East) Germany, in 1914 and the first world championships at Oslo, Norway, in 1953. The International Luge Federation was formed in 1957. Lugeing became an Olympic sport in 1964.

Most World Titles. The most successful rider in the world championships is Thomas Köhler (East Germany) (b. June 25, 1940), who won the single-seater title in 1962, 1964 (Olympics),

1966, and 1967, and shared in the two-seater title in 1967 and 1968 (Olympics). Margit Schumann (East Germany) has won 5 times—in 1973, 1974, 1975, 1976 (Olympics) and 1977.

Highest Speed. The fastest luge run is at Krynica, Poland, where speeds of more than 80 m.p.h. have been recorded.

Bowling

Origins. Bowling can be traced to articles found in the tomb of an Egyptian child of 5200 B.C. where there were nine pieces of stone to be set up as pins at which a stone "ball" was rolled. The ball first had to roll through an archway made of three pieces of marble. There is also resemblance to a Polynesian game called *ula maika* which utilized pins and balls of stone. The stones were rolled a distance of 60 feet. In the Italian Alps about 2,000 years ago, the underhand tossing of stones at an object is believed the beginnings of *bocci*, a game still widely played in Italy and similar to bowling. Bowling at pins probably originated in ancient Germany as a religious ceremony. Martin Luther is credited with the statement that nine was the ideal number of pins. In the British Isles, lawn bowls were preferred to bowling at pins. In the 16th century, bowling at pins was the national sport in Scotland. How bowling at pins came to the United States is a matter of controversy. Early British settlers probably brought lawn bowls and set up what is known as Bowling Green at the tip of Manhattan Island in New York but perhaps the Dutch under Henry Hudson were the ones to be credited. Some historians say that in Connecticut the tenth pin was added to evade a legal ban against the nine-pin game in 1845 but others say that ten pins was played in New York City before this and point to Washington Irving's "Rip Van Winkle" written about 1818 as evidence.

Lanes. In the U.S. there were 8,698 bowling establishments with 151,725 lanes in 1977 and about 65,000,000 bowlers.

The world's largest bowling center is the Tokyo World Lanes Center, Japan, with 252 lanes.

Organizations. The American Bowling Congress (ABC) comprises 4,700,000 men who bowl in leagues and tournaments. The Women's International Bowling Congress (WIBC) has a membership of 4,100,000.

World Championships

The Fédération Internationale des Quilleurs world championships were instituted in 1954. The highest pinfall in the individual men's event is 5,963 for 28 games by Ed Luther (U.S.) at Milwaukee, Wisconsin, in 1971.

In the women's event (instituted 1963) the record is 4,615 pins in 24 games by Annedore Haefker (West Germany) at Tolworth, Surrey, England, in 1975.

League Scores

Highest Men's. The highest individual score for three games is 886 by Allie Brandt of Lockport, New York, in 1939. Maximum possible is 900 (three perfect games). Highest team score is 3,858 by Budweisers of St. Louis in 1958.

The highest season average attained in sanctioned competition is 239 by Jim Lewis of Schenectady, New York, in 88 games in a 3-man league in 1975–76.

Highest Women's. The highest individual score for three games is 818 by Bev Ortner (now of Tucson, Arizona) in Galva, Iowa in 1968. Highest team score is 3,379 by Freeway Washer of Cleveland in 1960. (Highest in WIBC tournament play is 737 by D. D. Jacobson in 1972.)

Consecutive Strikes. The record for consecutive strikes in sanctioned match play is 33 by John Pezzin (born 1930) at Toledo, Ohio, on March 4, 1976.

Most Perfect Scores. The highest number of sanctioned 300 games is 27 (through 1978) by Elvin Mesger of Sullivan, Missouri. The maximum 900 for a three-game series has been recorded three times in unsanctioned games—by Leo Bentley at Lorain, Ohio, on March 26, 1931; by Joe Sargent at Rochester, New York, in 1934; and by Jim Murgie in Philadelphia, on February 4, 1937.

ABC Tournament Scores

Highest Individual. Highest three-game series in singles is 801 by Mickey Higham of Kansas City, Missouri, in 1978. Best three-game total in any ABC event is 804 by Lou Veit of Milwaukee, Wisconsin, in team in 1977. Jim Godman of Vero Beach, Florida, holds the record for a nine-game All-Events total with 2,184 (731–749–704) set in Indianapolis, Indiana, in 1974. ABC Hall of Famers Fred Bujack of Detroit, Michigan, and Bill Lillard of Houston, Texas, have won the most championships with 8 each. Bujack shared in 3 team and 4 team All-Events titles between 1949 and 1955, and also won the individual All-Events title in 1955. Lillard bowled on Regular and team All-Events champions in 1955 and 1956, the Classic team champions in 1962 and 1971, and won regular doubles and All-Events titles in 1956.

Highest Doubles. The ABC record of 558 was set in 1976 by Les Zikes of Chicago and Tommy Hudson of Akron, Ohio. The record score in a doubles series is 1,453, set in 1952 by John Klares (755) and Steve Nagy (698) of Cleveland.

Perfect Scores. Les Schissler of Denver scored 300 in the Classic team event in 1967, and Ray Williams of Detroit scored 300 in regular team play in 1974. In all, there have been only thirty-four 300 games in the ABC tournament. There have been 19 perfect games in singles, 12 in doubles, and three in team play.

Best Finishes in One Tournament. Les Schissler of Denver won the singles, All-Events, and was on the winning team in 1966 to tie Ed Lubanski of Detroit and Bill Lillard of Houston as the only men to win three ABC crowns in one year. The best four finishes in one ABC tournament were third in singles, second in doubles, third in team and first in All-Events by Bob Strampe, Detroit, in 1967, and first in singles, third in team and doubles and second in All-Events by Paul Kulbaga, Cleveland, in 1960.

Attendance. Largest attendance on one day for an ABC tournament was 5,257 in Milwaukee in 1952. The total attendance record was set at Reno, Nevada, in 1977 with 174,953 in 89 days.

Youngest and Oldest Winners. The youngest champion was Harold Allen of Detroit who was a 1915 doubles winner at the age of 18. The oldest champion was Eddie Nicholas of Austin, Texas, who, at the age of 70, was a winner in the 1978 Booster team event. The oldest doubles team in ABC competition totaled 165 years in 1955: Jerry Ameling (83) and Joseph Lehnbeutter (82), both from St. Louis.

Professional Bowlers Association Records

Most Titles. Earl Anthony of Tacoma, Washington, has won a lifetime total of 30 PBA titles. The record number of titles won in one PBA season is 8, by Mark Roth of North Arlington, New Jersey, in 1978.

Consecutive Titles. Only three bowlers have ever won three consecutive professional tournaments—Dick Weber in 1961, Johnny Petraglia in 1971, and Mark Roth in 1977.

Highest Earnings. The greatest lifetime earnings on the Professional Bowlers Association circuit have been won by Earl Anthony of Tacoma, Washington, who has taken home $627,701. Mark Roth of North Arlington, New Jersey, won a record $134,500 in the 1978 season.

Perfect Games. A total of 86 perfect (300-point) games were bowled in PBA tournaments in 1978. Dick Weber rolled 3 perfect games in one tournament (Houston, Texas) in 1965, as did Billy Hardwick of Louisville, Kentucky (in the Japan Gold Cup competition) in 1968, and Roy Buckley of Columbus, Ohio (at Chagrin Falls, Ohio) in 1971.

Don Johnson of Las Vegas, Nevada, bowled at least one perfect game in 11 consecutive seasons (1965–1975).

Strikes and Spares in a Row

In the greatest finish to win an ABC title, Ed Shay set a record of 12 strikes in a row in 1958, when he scored a perfect game for a total of 733 in the series.

The most spares in a row is 23, a record set by Lt. Hazen Sweet of Battle Creek, Michigan, in 1950.

Longest Career. William H. Bailey (born January 4, 1891) has been bowling in the Hamilton City Ten Pin League, Ontario, Canada, for 72 consecutive years.

Marathons

Tom Destowet bowled for 150 hours 15 minutes in Dublin, California, April 2–8, 1978. He bowled 709 games.

Richard Dewey, 46, of Omaha, Nebraska, bowled 1,472 consecutive games in 114½ hours, June 5–10, 1975. He bowled with both his right and left hands, averaged 159 through his first 750 games and 126 for all 1,472.

EARLY CODIFIER: Jack Broughton (left) wrote the earliest prize ring rules in the 18th century.

Boxing

Earliest References. Boxing with gloves was depicted on a fresco from the Isle of Thera, Greece, which has been dated 1520 B.C. The earliest prize-ring code of rules was formulated in England on August 16, 1743, by the champion pugilist Jack Broughton (1704–89), who reigned from 1729 to 1750. Boxing, which had in 1867 come under the Queensberry Rules, formulated for John Sholto Douglas, 9th Marquess of Queensberry, was not established as a legal sport in Britain until after a ruling of Mr. Justice Grantham following the death of Billy Smith (Murray Livingstone) as the result of a fight on April 24, 1901, at Covent Garden, London.

Longest Fight. The longest recorded fight with gloves was between Andy Bowen of New Orleans and Jack Burke in New Orleans, on April 6–7, 1893. The fight lasted 110 rounds and 7 hours 19 minutes from 9:15 p.m. to 4:34 a.m., but was declared a no contest (later changed to a draw) when both men were unable to continue. The longest recorded bare knuckle fight was one of 6 hours 15 minutes between James Kelly and Jack Smith at Fiery Creek, Dalesford, Victoria, Australia, on December 3, 1855. The greatest recorded number of rounds is 276 in 4 hours 30 minutes, when Jack Jones beat Patsy Tunney in Cheshire, England, in 1825.

Shortest Fight. There is a distinction between the quickest knockout and the shortest fight. A knockout in 10½ seconds (including a 10-second count) occurred on September 26, 1946, when Al Couture struck Ralph Walton while the latter was adjusting a gum shield in his corner at Lewiston, Maine. If the time was accurately taken it is clear that Couture must have been more than half-way across the ring from his own corner at the opening bell.

The shortest fight on record appears to be one in a Golden Gloves tournament in Minneapolis, Minnesota, on November 4, 1947, when Mike Collins floored Pat Brownson with his first punch and the contest was stopped, without a count, 4 seconds after the bell.

The shortest world heavyweight title fight occurred when Tommy Burns (1881–1955) (*né* Noah Brusso) of Canada knocked out Jem Roche in 1 minute 28 seconds in Dublin, Ireland, on March 17, 1908. The duration of the Clay *vs.* Liston fight at Lewiston, Maine, on May 25, 1965, was 1 minute 52 seconds (including the count) as timed from the video tape recordings despite a ringside announcement giving a time of 1 minute. The shortest world title fight was when Al McCoy knocked out George Chip in 45 seconds for the middleweight crown in New York on April 6, 1914.

Tallest. The tallest boxer to fight professionally was Gogea Mitu (born 1914) of Rumania in 1935. He was 7 feet 4 inches and weighed 327 lbs. John Rankin, who won a fight in New Orleans, in November, 1967, was reputedly also 7 feet 4 inches.

World Heavyweight Champions

Longest and Shortest Reigns. The longest reign of any world heavyweight champion is 11 years 8 months and 7 days by Joe Louis (born Joseph Louis Barrow, at Lafayette, Alabama, May 13, 1914), from June 22, 1937, when he knocked out James J. Braddock in the 8th round at Chicago until announcing his retirement on March 1,

HEAVIEST CHAMPION: Primo Carnera, scaling about 270 lbs., held the heavyweight title for just 350 days.

LONGEST AS CHAMPION: Joe Louis (left) was the heavyweight champion of the world for 11 years 8 months 7 days.

1949. During his reign Louis made a record 25 defenses of his title. The shortest reign was by Leon Spinks (U.S.) (born July 11, 1953) for 212 days from February 15–September 15, 1978.

Heaviest and Lightest. The heaviest world champion was Primo Carnera (Italy) (1906–67), the "Ambling Alp," who won the title from Jack Sharkey in 6 rounds in New York City, on June 29, 1933. He scaled 267 lbs. for this fight but his peak weight was 270 lbs. He had the longest reach at 85½ inches (fingertip to fingertip) and also the largest fists with a 14¾-inch circumference. He had an expanded chest measurement of 53 inches. The lightest champion was Robert James Fitzsimmons (1863–1917), who was born at Helston, Cornwall, England, and, at a weight of 167 lbs., won the title by knocking out James J. Corbett in 14 rounds at Carson City, Nevada, on March 17, 1897.

The greatest differential in a world title fight was 86 lbs. between Carnera (270 lbs.) and Tommy Loughran (184 lbs.) of the U.S., when the former won on points at Miami, Florida, on March 1, 1934.

Tallest and Shortest. The tallest world champion was Primo Carnera, who was measured at 6 feet 5.4 inches by the Physical Education Director at the Hemingway Gymnasium of Harvard, although he was widely reported and believed in 1933 to be 6 feet 8½ inches tall. Jess Willard (1881–1968), who won the title in 1915, often stated as 6 feet 6¼ inches tall, was in fact 6 feet 5¼ inches. The shortest was Tommy Burns (1881–1955) of Canada, world champion from February 23, 1906, to December 26, 1908, who stood 5 feet 7 inches, and weighed 179 lbs.

Oldest and Youngest. The oldest man to win the heavyweight crown was Jersey Joe Walcott (born Arnold Raymond Cream,

OLDEST HEAVYWEIGHT CHAMPION: Jersey Joe Walcott (left) defeated
Ezzard Charles (right) to become heavyweight champion at age 37.

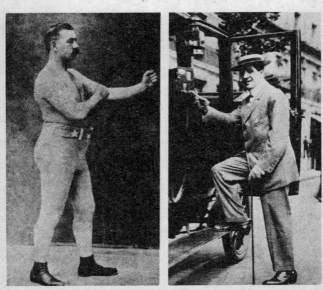

THE EARLIEST TITLE FIGHT pitted John L. Sullivan (left) against "Gentleman
Jim" Corbett (right). It took 21 rounds for Corbett to win the fight.

January 31, 1914, at Merchantville, New Jersey), who knocked out Ezzard Charles on July 18, 1951, in Pittsburgh, when aged 37 years 5 months 18 days. Walcott was the oldest title holder at 38 years 7 months 23 days when he lost to Rocky Marciano on September 23, 1952. The youngest age at which the world title has been won is 21 years 331 days by Floyd Patterson (born Waco, North Carolina, January 4, 1935). After the retirement of Rocky Marciano, Patterson won the vacant title by beating Archie Moore in 5 rounds in Chicago, on November 30, 1956.

Most Recaptures. Muhammad Ali Haj is the only man to regain the heavyweight title twice. He defeated George Foreman on October 30, 1974, having been stripped of his title by the world boxing authorities on April 28, 1967. He lost his title to Leon Spinks on February 15, 1978, but regained it on September 15, 1978 by defeating Spinks in New Orleans.

Undefeated. Rocky Marciano (b. Rocco Francis Marchegiano) (1923–69) is the only heavyweight champion to have been undefeated in his entire professional career (1947–56).

Longest-Lived. Jess Willard was born December 29, 1881, at St. Clere, Kansas, and died in Pacoima, California, on December 15, 1968, aged 86 years 351 days.

Earliest Title Fight. The first world heavyweight title fight, with gloves and 3-minute rounds, was between John L. Sullivan (1858–1918) and "Gentleman" James J. Corbett (1866–1933) in New Orleans, on September 7, 1892. Corbett won in 21 rounds.

World Champions (any weight)

Longest and Shortest Reign. Joe Louis's heavyweight duration record stands for all divisions. The shortest reign has been 54 days by the French featherweight Eugène Criqui from June 2 to July 26, 1923. The disputed flyweight champion Emile Pladner (France) reigned only 47 days from March 2 to April 18, 1929, as did the disputed featherweight champion Dave Sullivan from September 26 to November 11, 1898.

Youngest and Oldest. The youngest at which any world championship has been claimed is 17 years 180 days by Wilfredo Benitez (born September 8, 1958) of Puerto Rico, who won the W.B.A. light-welterweight title in San Juan on March 6, 1976.

The oldest world champion was Archie Moore (b. Archibald Lee Wright, Collinsville, Illinois, December 13, 1913 or 1916), who was recognized as a light-heavyweight champion up to February 10, 1962, when his title was removed. He was then between 45 and 48. Bob Fitzsimmons (1863–1917) had the longest career of any official world titleholder with over 32 years from 1882 to 1914. He won his last world title aged 40 years 183 days in San Francisco on November 25, 1903. He was an amateur from 1880 to 1882.

Greatest "Tonnage." The greatest "tonnage" recorded in any fight is 700 lbs., when Claude "Humphrey" McBride of Oklahoma at 340 lbs. knocked out Jimmy Black of Houston at 360 lbs. in the 3rd round at Oklahoma City on June 1, 1971.

The greatest "tonnage" in a world title fight was 488¾ lbs. when Carnera (259¼ lbs.) fought Paolino Uzcuden (229½ lbs.) of Spain in Rome, Italy, on October 22, 1933.

Smallest Champions. The smallest man to win any world title has been Pascual Perez (1926–1977) who won the flyweight title in Tokyo on November 26, 1954, at 107 lbs. and 4 feet 11½ inches tall. Jimmy Wilde (b. Merthyr Tydfil, 1892, d. 1969, U.K.) who held the flyweight title from 1916 to 1923 was reputed never to have fought above 108 lbs.

Longest Fight. The longest world title fight (under Queensberry Rules) was between the lightweights Joe Gans (1874–1910), of the U.S., and Oscar "Battling" Nelson (1882–1954), the "Durable Dane," at Goldfield, Nevada, on September 3, 1906. It was terminated in the 42nd round when Gans was declared the winner on a foul.

Most Recaptures. The only boxer to win a world title five times at one weight is Sugar Ray Robinson (b. Walker Smith, Jr., in Detroit, May 3, 1920) who beat Carmen Basilio (U.S.) in the Chicago Stadium on March 25, 1958, to regain the world middleweight title for the fourth time. The other title wins were over Jake LaMotta (U.S.) in Chicago on February 14, 1951, Randy Turpin (U.K.) in New York on September 12, 1951, Carl "Bobo" Olson (U.S.) in Chicago on December 9, 1955, and Gene Fullmer (U.S.) in Chicago on May 1, 1957. The record number of title bouts in a career is 33 or 34 (at bantam and featherweight) by George Dixon (1870–1909), *alias* Little Chocolate, of Canada, between 1890 and 1901.

Most Titles Simultaneously. The only man to hold world titles at three weights simultaneously was Henry ("Homicide Hank") Armstrong (born December 12, 1912), now the Rev. Henry Jackson, of the U.S., at featherweight, lightweight and welterweight from August to December, 1938.

Most Knockdowns in Title Fights. Vic Toweel (South Africa) knocked down Danny O'Sullivan of London 14 times in 10 rounds in their world bantamweight fight at Johannesburg, on December 2, 1950, before the latter retired.

All Fights

Largest Purse. Muhammad Ali Haj (born Cassius Marcellus Clay, in Louisville, Kentucky, January 17, 1942) won a reported $6,500,000 in his successful defense of the heavyweight title against Ken Norton (U.S.), held in Yankee Stadium, New York City, on September 28, 1976.

The largest stake ever fought for in the bare-knuckle era was $22,500 in a 27-round fight between Jack Cooper and Wolf Bendoff at Port Elizabeth, South Africa, on July 29, 1889.

Highest Attendances. The greatest paid attendance at any boxing fight has been 120,757 (with a ringside price of $27.50) for the Tunney vs. Dempsey world heavyweight title fight at the Sesquicentennial Stadium, Philadelphia, on September 23, 1926. The indoor record is over 70,000 for the Spinks vs. Ali world heavyweight title fight at the Louisiana Superdome in New Orleans, on September 15, 1978. The gate receipts exceeded $6,000,000, a record total. The highest non-paying attendance is 135,132 at the Tony Zale vs. Billy Pryor fight at Juneau Park, Milwaukee, Wisconsin, on August 18, 1941.

Lowest. The smallest attendance at a world heavyweight title fight was 2,434 at the Clay vs. Liston fight at Lewiston, Maine, on May 25, 1965.

Highest Earnings in Career. The largest known fortune ever made in a fighting career (or any sports career) is an estimated $59,250,000 amassed by Muhammad Ali to October, 1978.

Most Knockouts. The greatest number of knockouts in a career is 141 by Archie Moore (1936 to 1963). The record for consecutive K.O.'s is 44, set by Lamar Clark of Utah at Las Vegas, Nevada, on January 11, 1960. He knocked out 6 in one night (5 in the first round) in Bingham, Utah, on December 1, 1958.

Most Fights. The greatest recorded number of fights in a career is 1,024 by Bobby Dobbs (U.S.), (1858–1930), who is reported to have fought from 1875 to 1914, a period of 39 years. Abraham Hollandersky, *alias* Abe the Newsboy (U.S.), is reputed to have had 1,309 fights in the fourteen years from 1905 to 1918, but many of them were exhibition bouts.

Most Fights Without Loss. Hal Bagwell, a lightweight, of Gloucester, England, was reputedly undefeated in 180 consecutive fights, of which only 5 were draws, between August 15, 1938, and November 29, 1948. His record of fights in the wartime period (1939–46) is very sketchy, however. Of boxers with complete records, Packey McFarland (1888–1936) went undefeated in 97 fights from 1905 to 1915.

Longest Career. The heavyweight Jem Mace, known as "the gypsy" (born at Norwich, England, April 8, 1831), had a career lasting 35 years from 1855 to 1890, but there were several years in which he had only one fight. He died, aged 79, in Jarrow on November 30, 1910. Walter Edgerton, the "Kentucky Rosebud," knocked out John Henry Johnson, aged 45, in 4 rounds at the Broadway A.C., New York City, on February 4, 1916, when aged 63. (See also *Most Fights*, above.)

Most Olympic Gold Medals. The only amateur boxer ever to win three Olympic gold medals is the southpaw László Papp (born 1926 in Hungary), who took the middleweight (1948) and the light-middleweight titles (1952 and 1956). The only man to win two titles in one meeting was Oliver L. Kirk (U.S.), who took both the bantam

GREATEST MATADORS: Multimillionaire El Cordobés (left) is the most financially successful matador in history, and Lagartijo (right) has the most kills to his credit.

and featherweight titles at St. Louis, Missouri, in 1904, when the U.S. won all the titles. Harry W. Mallin (Great Britain) was in 1924 the first boxer ever to defend an Olympic title successfully when he retained the middleweight crown.

The oldest man to win an Olympic gold medal in boxing was Richard K. Gunn (born 1870) of Great Britain who won the featherweight title on October 27, 1908, in London, aged 38.

Bull Fighting

In the latter half of the second millenium B.C., bull leaping was practiced in Crete. Bull fighting in Spain was first reported by the Romans in Baetica (Andalusia) in the third century B.C.

The first renowned professional *espada* (bull fighter) was Francisco Romero of Ronda, in Andalusia, Spain, who introduced the *estoque* and the red *muleta* c. 1700. Spain now has some 190 active matadors. Since 1700, 42 major matadors have died in the ring.

Largest Stadiums and Gate. The world's largest bull-fighting ring, the Plaza, Mexico City, with a capacity of 48,000 was closed in March, 1976. The largest of Spain's 312 bullrings is Las Ventas, Madrid, with a capacity of 24,000.

Most Successful Matadors. The most successful matador measured by bulls killed was Lagartijo (1841–1900), born Rafael Molina, whose lifetime total was 4,867.

The longest career of any full matador was that of Bienvenida (1922–75) (*né* Antonio Mejías) from 1942 to 1974. (Recent Spanish law requires compulsory retirement at age 55.)

Most Kills in a Day. In 1884, Romano set a record by killing 18 bulls in a day in Seville, and in 1949 El Litri (Miguel Báes) set a Spanish record with 114 *novilladas* in a season.

Highest Paid Matadors. The highest paid bull fighter in history is El Cordobés (born Manuel Benitez Pérez, probably on May 4, 1936, in Palma del Rio, Spain), who became a multimillionaire in 1966, during which year he fought 111 *corridas* up to October 4, receiving over $15,000 for each half hour in the ring. In 1970, he received an estimated $1,800,000 for 121 fights.

Paco Camino (b. December 19, 1941) has received $27,200 (2,000,000 *pesetas*) for a *corrida*. He retired in 1977.

Canoeing

Origins. The acknowledged pioneer of canoeing as a sport was John Macgregor, a British barrister, in 1865. The Canoe Club was formed on July 26, 1866.

Most Olympic Gold Medals. Gert Fredriksson (b. November 21, 1919) of Sweden has won the 1,000-meter Kayak singles in 1948, 1952 and 1956, the 10,000-meter Kayak singles in 1948 and 1956, and the 1,000-meter Kayak doubles in 1960. In addition to his 6 Olympic titles he has won 3 other world titles in non-Olympic years: 1,000-meter K.1 in 1950 and 1954, and 500-meter K.1 in 1954.

The most by a woman is 3 by Ludmila Pinayeva (*née* Khvedosyuk, born January 14, 1936) (U.S.S.R.) in the 500-meter K.1 in 1964 and 1968, and the 500-meter K.2 in 1972.

The Olympic 1,000-meter best performance of 3 minutes 06.46 seconds by the 1976 Spanish K.4 represents an average speed of 11.99 m.p.h., and a rate of about 125 strokes per minute.

LONGEST JOURNEY: Randy Bauer (left) and Jerry Mimbach (right) traveled 7,516 miles by paddle and portage in less than 2 years.

ESKIMO ROLLS: Bruce Parry turned in a record 1,000 rolls in 65 minutes 39.3 seconds in 1977.

Longest Journey

The longest canoe journey in history was one of 7,516 miles around the eastern U.S. by paddle and portage, from Lake Itasca, Minnesota, *via* New Orleans, New York and Lake Ontario, by Randy Bauer (born August 15, 1949) and Jerry Mimbach (born May 22, 1952) of Coon Rapids, Minnesota, from September 8, 1974, to August 30, 1976.

The longest journey without portage or aid of any kind is one of 6,102 miles by Richard H. Grant and Ernest Lassey circumnavigating the eastern U.S. from Chicago to New Orleans to Miami to New York, returning back to Chicago *via* the Great Lakes, from September 22, 1930, to August 15, 1931.

Eskimo Rolls. The record for Eskimo rolls is 1,000 in 65 minutes 39.3 seconds by Bruce Parry (b. September 25, 1960) on Lake Lismore, New South Wales, Australia, on December 17, 1977. A "hand-rolling" record of 100 rolls in 3 minutes 58.7 seconds was set in the Bootham School Pool, York, England, on June 14, 1975, by David A. Clapham, 15.

English Channel Crossing. Andrew William Dougall Samuel (Scotland) paddled from Dover, England, to Wissant, France, in 3 hours 33 minutes 47 seconds on September 5, 1976.

The doubles record is 3 hours 20 minutes 30 seconds by Capt. William Stanley Crook and the late Ronald Ernest Rhodes, in their fibreglass K.2 *Accord*, from Dover, England, to Cap Blanc Nez, France, on September 20, 1961.

Longest Open Sea Voyage. Beatrice and John Dowd, Ken Beard and Steve Benson (Richard Gillett replaced him mid-journey) paddled 1,559 miles out of a total journey of 2,010 miles from Venezuela to Miami, Florida, via the West Indies from August 11, 1977, to April 29, 1978, in two Klepper Aerius 20 kayaks.

Highest Altitude. In September, 1976, Dr. Michael Jones and Michael Hopkinson of the British Everest Canoe Expedition canoed down the Dudh Kosi River in Nepal from an altitude of 17,500 feet.

Longest Race. The longest regularly held canoe race in the U.S. is the Texas Water Safari (instituted 1963) which covers the 419 miles from San Marcos to Seadrift, Texas, on the San Marcos and Guadalupe rivers. Robert Chatham and Butch Hodges set the record of 37 hours 18 minutes on June 5–6, 1976.

Downstream Canoeing

River	Miles	Canoer	Location	Duration
Mississippi	2,245	Dr. Gerald Capers, Charles Saunders, Joseph Tagg, Jr.	Lake Itasca, Minnesota, to New Orleans, July 4– Aug. 28, 1937	56 days
Mississippi- Missouri	3,810	Nicholas Francis (Scotland)	Three Forks, Montana, to New Orleans, July 13–Nov. 25, 1977	135 days
Congo	2,600	John and Julie Batchelor (G.B.)	Moasampanga to Banana, May 8– Sept. 12, 1974	128 days
Amazon	3,400	Stephan Z. Bezuk (U.S.) (kayak)	Atalaya to Ponta do Céu, June 21–Nov. 4, 1970	136 days
Nile	4,000	John Goddard (U.S.), Jean Laporte and André Davy (France)	Kagera to the Delta, Nov., 1953–July, 1954	9 months

LONGEST OPEN SEA VOYAGE: The crew for this 2,010-mile kayak adventure was (left to right) John Dowd, Beatrice Dowd, Stephen Benson and Kenneth Beard.

Cave Exploration (Spelunking)

Duration. The endurance record for staying in a cave is 463 days by Milutin Veljkovic (b. 1935) (Yugoslavia) in the Samar Cavern, Svrljig Mountains, northern Yugoslavia from June 24, 1969, to September 30, 1970.

PROGRESSIVE CAVING DEPTH RECORDS

Feet	Cave	Cavers	Date
453	Macocha, Moravia	J. Nagel et al.	May, 1748
741	Grotta di Padriciano, Trieste, Italy	Antonio Lindner et al.	1839
1,076	Grotta di Trebiciano, Trieste	Antonio Lindner et al.	April 6, 1841
1,509	Geldloch, Austria	—	1923
1,574	Antro di Corchia, Tuscany, Italy	E. Fiorentino Club	1934
1,978	Trou du Glaz, Isère, France	P. Chevalier et al.	1947
2,418	Gouffre de la Pierre St. Martin, Bàsses-Pyrénées, France	*Georges Lépineux	Aug. 15, 1953
2,962	Gouffre Berger, Isère, France	*F. Petzl and 6 men	Sept. 25, 1954
3,123	Gouffre Berger, Isère, France	L. Potié, G. Garby et al.	Aug., 1955
3,681	Gouffre Berger, Isère, France	F. Petzl and others	July, 1956
3,715	Gouffre Berger, Isère, France	K. Pearce	Aug., 1963
3,842	Reseau de la Pierre Saint Martin	Ass. de Rech. Spéléo Internationale	Aug., 1966
4,370	Reseau de la Pierre Saint Martin	A.R.S.I.P.	Aug., 1975

N.B.—The Reseau de la Pierre St. Martin has been explored via a number of entrances, and has never been entirely descended at any one time. Consequently, after Aug., 1963, the "sporting" records for greatest descent into a cave should read:

3,743	Gouffre Berger, Isère, France	Spéléo Club de Seine	July, 1968

* Leader

Cricket

Origins. The earliest evidence of the game of cricket is from a drawing depicting two men playing with a bat and ball dated *c.* 1250. The game was played in Guildford, Surrey, at least as early as 1550. The earliest major match of which the score survives was one in which a team representing England (40 and 70) was beaten by Kent (53 and 58 for 9) by one wicket at the Artillery Ground in Finsbury, London, on June 18, 1744. Cricket was played in Australia as early as 1803.

CRICKET (First Class Matches Only)

Batting—Team Scores

Highest Innings
1,107 Victoria vs. N.S.W., Australia, Dec. 27–28, 1926

Highest Innings, Test
903 for 7 dec. England vs. Australia (5th Test), Aug. 20–23, 1938

Batting—Individual Scores

Highest Innings
499 Hanif Mohammad (Pakistan), Jan. 8–11, 1959

Highest Innings, Test
365 no Garfield Sobers (West Indies), Feb. 27–Mar. 1, 1958

Most Runs, Over (6 ball)
36 Garfield Sobers (Nottinghamshire), Aug. 31, 1968

Most Runs, Season
3,816 Denis Compton (Middlesex and England), 1947

Most Runs, Career
61,237 John (Jack) Hobbs (Surrey and England), 1905–34

BOWLING RECORD: Jim Laker of Surrey took 19 wickets for 30 runs in a 1956 match.

Most Runs, Tests
8,032 Garfield Sobers (West Indies), 1953–1974

Test Match Average
99.94 (80 inn.) Donald Bradman (Australia), 1928–1948

Career Average
95.14 (338 inn.) Donald Bradman (Australia), 1927–49

Bowling

Most Wickets, Innings
10 Numerous occasions

Most Wickets, Match
19 Jim Laker (Surrey), July 26–31, 1956

Most Wickets, Season
304 Alfred "Tich" Freeman (Kent), 1928

Most Wickets, Career
4,187 Wilfred Rhodes, 1898–1930

Most Wickets, Tests
309 Lance Gibbs (West Indies), 1958–1976

Wicket Keeping

Most Dismissals, Season
127 Leslie Ames (Kent), 1929

Most Dismissals, Career
1,527 John Murray (Middlesex), 1952–1975

Most Dismissals, Tests
252 Alan Knott (England), 1967–1977

Miscellaneous

Fastest Century
35 min. Percy Fender (Surrey), Aug. 26, 1920

Fastest Bowler
99.7 m.p.h. Jeff Thompson (Australia), Dec. 1975

Most Test Appearances
114 Colin Cowdrey (England), 1954–1975

Longest Cricket Ball Throw (5½ oz. ball)
422 ft. Robert Percival, Apr. 18, 1881

CHAMPION BATSMAN: Sir Garfield Sobers holds records for highest innings (365 not out) and most runs (8,032) in test matches.

Cross-Country Running

International Championships. The earliest international cross-country race was run between England and France on a course 9 miles 18 yards long from Ville d'Avray, outside Paris, on March 20, 1898. The inaugural International Cross-Country Championships took place at the Hamilton Park Racecourse, Glasgow, Scotland, on March 28, 1903. Since 1973 the race has been run under the auspices of the International Amateur Athletic Federation.

The greatest margin of victory in the International Cross-Country Championships has been 56 seconds, or 390 yards, by Jack T. Holden (England) at Ayr Racecourse, Scotland, on March 24, 1934. The narrowest win was that of Jean-Claude Fayolle (France) at Ostend, Belgium, on March 20, 1965, when the timekeepers were unable to separate his time from that of Melvyn Richard Batty (England), who was placed second.

Most Appearances. The runner with the largest number of international championship appearances is Marcel Van de Wattyne of Belgium, who participated in 20 competitions in the years 1946–65.

Most Wins. The greatest number of victories in the International Cross-Country Race is four by Jack Holden (England) in 1933, 1934, 1935 and 1939, by Alain Mimoun-o-Kacha (France) in 1949, 1952, 1954 and 1956, and Gaston Roelants (Belgium) in 1962, 1967, 1969 and 1972. England has won 43 times to 1977.

Largest Field. The largest recorded field was one of 5,321 starters in the Lidingöloppet, near Stockholm, Sweden, on October 3, 1976. There were 4,894 finishers.

Curling

Origins. The earliest illustration of the sport was in one of the winter scenes by the Flemish painter, Pieter Brueghel, *c.* 1560. The club with the earliest records, dating back to 1716, is that at Kilsyth, Scotland. The game was introduced into Canada in 1759. Organized administration began in 1838 with the formation of the Grand (later Royal) Caledonian Curling Club, the international legislative body until 1966. The first indoor ice rink to introduce curling was at Southport, England, in 1879.

The U.S. won the first Gordon International Medal series of matches, between Canada and the U.S., at Montreal in 1884. The first Strathcona Cup match between Canada and Scotland was won by Canada in 1903. Although demonstrated at the Winter Olympics of 1924, 1932 and 1964, curling has never been included in the official Olympic program.

Largest Rink. The world's largest curling rink is the Big Four Curling Rink, Calgary, Alberta, Canada, opened in 1959 at a cost of Can. $2,250,000. Each of the two floors has 24 sheets of ice, the total accommodating 96 teams and 384 players.

Most Titles. The record for the Air Canada Silver Broom (instituted 1959) is 12 wins by Canada, in 1959–60–61–62–63–64–66–

68–69–70–71–72. The most Strathcona Cup wins is seven by Canada (1903–09–12–23–38–57–65) against Scotland.

Perfect Games. A unique achievement is claimed by Mrs. Bernice Fekete of Edmonton, Alberta, Canada, who skipped her rink to two consecutive eight-enders on the same sheet of ice at the Derrick Club, Edmonton, on January 10 and February 6, 1973.

Marathon. The longest recorded curling match is one of 61 hours 20 minutes by eight members of the Playland Curling Club, Victoria, British Columbia, Canada, on March 3–5, 1978. Duration record for 2 curlers is 24 hours 5 minutes by Eric Olesen and Warren Knuth at Racine Curling Club, Racine, Wisconsin on March 30–31, 1978. The weight handled was 27.72 tons each.

Most Durable Player. In 1972, Howard "Pappy" Wood competed in his 65th consecutive annual *bonspiel* since 1908 at the Manitoba Curling Association.

Longest Bonspiel. The longest bonspiel in the world is the Manitoba Bonspiel held in Winnipeg, Canada. There were 728 teams of 4 players in the February, 1977 tournament.

Cycling

Earliest Race. The earliest recorded bicycle race was a velocipede race over two kilometers (1.24 miles) at the Parc de St. Cloud, Paris, on May 31, 1868, won by James Moore (G.B.).

Slow Cycling. David Steel of Tucson, Arizona, stayed stationary without support for 9 hours 15 minutes on November 25, 1977.

Highest Speed. The highest speed ever achieved on a bicycle is 140.5 m.p.h. by Dr. Allan V. Abbott, 29, of San Bernardino, California, behind a windshield mounted on a 1955 Chevrolet over ¾ of a mile at Bonneville Salt Flats, Utah, on August 25, 1973. His speed over a mile was 138.674 m.p.h. Considerable help is provided by the slipstreaming effect of the lead vehicle. Charles Minthorne Murphy (born 1872) achieved the first mile-a-minute behind a pacing locomotive on the Long Island Railroad on June 30, 1899. He took only 57.8 seconds, so averaging 62.28 m.p.h.

Allan Abbott recorded an official unpaced 9.22 sec. for 200 meters (48.52 m.p.h.) at Ontario, California, on April 30, 1977.

The greatest distance ever covered in one hour is 76 miles 604 yards by Leon Vanderstuyft (Belgium) on the Montlhéry Motor Circuit, France, on September 30, 1928. This was achieved from a standing start paced by a motorcycle. The 24-hour record behind pace is 860 miles 367 yards by Hubert Opperman in Australia in 1932.

The greatest distance covered in 60 minutes unpaced is 30 miles 1,258 yards by Eddy Merckx at Mexico City, Mexico, on October 25, 1972. The 24-hour record on the road is 515.8 miles by Teuvo Louhivuori of Finland on September 10, 1974.

Most Olympic Titles. Cycling has been on the Olympic program since the revival of the Games in 1896. The greatest number of gold medals ever won is three by Paul Masson (France) in 1896, Francisco Verri (Italy) in 1906 and Robert Charpentier (France) in 1936. Marcus Hurley (U.S.) won four events in the "unofficial" cycling competition in the 1904 Games.

Tour de France

The greatest number of wins in the Tour de France (inaugurated 1903) is five by Jacques Anquetil (born January 8, 1934) of France, who won in 1957, 1961, 1962, 1963, and 1964, and Eddy Merckx (b. Belgium, 1945) who won five titles (1969–70–71–72–74).

The closest race ever was that of 1968 when after 2,898.7 miles over 25 days (June 27–July 21) Jan Jannssen (Netherlands) (born 1940) beat Herman van Springel (Belgium) in Paris by 38 seconds. The longest course was 3,569 miles on June 20–July 18, 1926. The length of the course is usually about 3,000 miles, but varies from year to year.

The fastest average speed was 23.2 m.p.h. by Anquetil in 1962.

World Titles

The only four cyclists to have won 7 world titles in any single world championship event are Leon Meredith (G.B.) who won the

GREATEST ONE-HOUR RIDE: Leon Vanderstuyft of Belgium rode more than 76 miles in 60 minutes in 1928.

TOUR DE FRANCE CHAMPIONS: Jacques Anquetil of France (left) and Eddy Merckx of Belgium (right) have each achieved 5 Tour de France victories.

Amateur 100-kilometer paced event in 1904–05–07–08–09–11–13; Jeff Scherens (Belgium) who won the Professional sprint title in 1932–33–34–35–36–37 and 1947; Antonio Maspes (Italy) who won the Professional sprint title in 1955–56–59–60–61–62–64; and Daniel Morelon (France) who won the Amateur sprint title in 1966–67–69–70–71–73–75.

Yvonne Reynders (Belgium) won a total of 7 titles in women's events, the pursuits in 1961–64–65 and the road title in 1959–61–63–66. Beryl Burton (G.B.) equalled this total by winning the pursuits title in 1959–60–62–63–66 and the road title in 1960–67.

Endurance

Tommy Godwin (G.B.) in the 365 days of 1939 covered 75,065 miles or an average of 205.65 miles per day. He then completed 100,000 miles in 500 days on May 14, 1940.

The longest cycle tour on record is the more than 402,000 miles amassed by Walter Stolle (b. Sudetenland, 1926), an itinerant lecturer. From January 24, 1959 to December 12, 1976, he covered 159 countries, had 5 bicycles stolen and suffered 231 other robberies, along with over 1,000 flat tires.

Ray Reece, 41, of Alverstoke, England, circumnavigated the world by bicycle (13,325 road miles) between June 14 and November 5 (143 days) in 1971.

John Hathaway of Vancouver, Canada, covered 50,600 miles, visiting every continent from November 10, 1974 to October 6, 1976.

Coast to Coast

The transcontinental record is 13 days 5 hours 20 minutes from Los Angeles to New York (City Hall) by Paul Cornish, 25, March 4–17, 1973. He averaged 225 miles a day.

Stan N. Kuhl (born December 31, 1955) and Steve Jeschien (born August 6, 1956) of Sunnyvale, California, traveled 8,026.7 miles on a tandem bicycle around the U.S. from June 29 to October 3, 1976.

Equestrian Sports

Origin. Evidence of horse riding dates from an Anatolian statuette dated *c.* 1400 B.C. Pignatelli's academy of horsemanship at Naples dates from the sixteenth century. The earliest jumping competition was at the Agricultural Hall, London, in 1869. Equestrian events have been included in the Olympic Games since 1912.

Most Olympic Medals. The greatest number of Olympic gold medals is 5 by Hans-Günter Winkler (West Germany), who won 4 team gold medals as captain in 1956, 1960, 1964 and 1972, and won the individual Grand Prix in 1956. The most team wins in the Prix des Nations is 5 by Germany in 1936, 1956, 1960, 1964, and 1972.

The lowest score obtained by a winner was no faults, by Frantisek Ventura (Czechoslovakia) on *Eliot* in 1928, and by Alwin Schockemöhle (West Germany) on *Warwick Rex* in 1976. Pierre Jonqueres d'Oriola (France) is the only two-time winner of the individual gold medal, in 1952 and 1964.

World Titles. The men's world championship (instituted 1953) has been won twice by Hans-Günter Winkler of West Germany in 1954 and 1955, and Raimondo d'Inzeo of Italy in 1956 and 1960. The women's title (instituted 1965) has been won twice by Jane "Janou" Tissot (*née* Lefebvre) of France on *Rocket* in 1970 and 1974.

Jumping Records. The official *Fédération Equestre Internationale* high jump record is 8 feet 1¼ inches by *Huasó*, ridden by Capt. A. Larraguibel Morales (Chile) at Santiago, Chile, on February 5, 1949, and 27 feet 2¾ inches for long jump over water by *Amado Mio* ridden by Lt.-Col. Lopez del Hierro (Spain), at Barcelona, Spain, on November 12, 1951. *Heatherbloom*, ridden by Dick Donnelly was reputed to have covered 37 feet in clearing an 8-foot-3-inch *puissance* jump at Richmond, Virginia, in 1903. H. Plant on *Solid Gold* cleared 36 feet 3 inches over water at the Wagga Show, N.S.W., Australia, on August 28, 1936. *Jerry M* allegedly cleared 40 feet over water at Aintree, Liverpool, England, in 1912.

At Cairns, Queensland, *Golden Meade* ridden by Jack Martin cleared an unofficially measured 8 feet 6 inches on July 25, 1946. *Ben Bolt* was credited with clearing 9 feet 6 inches at the 1938 Royal Horse Show, Sydney, Australia. The Australian record however is

MOST OLYMPIC GOLD: Hans Winkler of West Germany won 5 gold medals, 1956–72.

8 feet 4 inches by C. Russell on *Flyaway* in 1939 and A. L. Payne on *Golden Meade* in 1946. The world's unofficial best for a woman is 7 feet 5½ inches by Miss B. Perry (Australia) on *Plain Bill* at Cairns, Queensland, Australia, in 1940.

The greatest recorded height reached bareback is 6 feet 7 inches by *Silver Wood* at Heidelberg, Victoria, Australia, on December 10, 1938.

Longest Ride. In 1911, two Texans, Temple and Louis Abernathy, rode 3,619 miles from Coney Island, New York City, to San Francisco, in 62 days. Temple was aged 9 and Louis was 11, and had they taken two days less they would have won a $10,000 prize. One of their horses, *Wylie Haynes*, finished the trip. The other, *Sam Bass* (the oldest member of the party at 16), died in Wyoming and was replaced by another horse.

The Bicentennial "Great American Horse Race," begun on May 31, 1976, from Saratoga Springs, New York, to Sacramento, California (3,500 miles) was won by Virl Norton on *Lord Fauntleroy*—a mule—in 98 days. His actual riding time was 315.47 hours.

Marathon. The duration record in the saddle is 245 hours 15 minutes by Wally Eaglesham in Wagga Wagga, N.S.W., Australia, September 24–October 4, 1976. Marathons of this kind stipulate that mounts must be changed at least every 6 hours.

Michael Grealy (Australia) rode at all paces (including jumping) for 55 hours 26 minutes at Blackwater, Queensland, Australia, on May 5–7, 1978.

Fencing

Origins. Fencing (fighting with single sticks) was practiced as a sport in Egypt as early as *c.* 1360 B.C. The first governing body for fencing in Britain was the Corporation of Masters of Defence founded by Henry VIII before 1540 and fencing was practiced as sport, notably in prize fights, since that time. The foil was the practice weapon for the short court sword from the 17th century. The épée was established in the mid-19th century and the light sabre was introduced by the Italians in the late 19th century.

Most Olympic Titles. The greatest number of individual Olympic gold medals won is three by Ramón Fonst (Cuba) (b. 1883) in 1900 and 1904 (2) and Nedo Nadi (Italy) (1894–1952) in 1912 and 1920 (2). Nadi also won three team gold medals in 1920 making a then unprecedented total of five gold medals at one Olympic meet.

Edoardo Mangiarotti (Italy) (born April 7, 1919) holds the record of 13 Olympic medals (6 gold, 5 silver, 2 bronze), won in the foil and épée competitions from 1936 to 1960.

The women's record is 7 medals (2 gold, 3 silver, 2 bronze) by Ildikó Sagine-Retjöo (formerly Ujlaki-Retjö) (Hungary) (b. May 11, 1937) from 1960 to 1976.

Most World Titles. The greatest number of individual world titles won is four by d'Oriola (see table, page 63), but note that d'Oriola also won 2 individual Olympic titles. Likewise, of the three women foilists with 3 world titles (Helene Mayer, Ellen Müller-Preiss and Ilona Schacherer-Elek) only Elek also won 2 individual Olympic titles.

Ellen Müller-Preiss (Austria) won the women's foil in 1947 and 1949 and shared it in 1950. She also won the Olympic title in 1932.

Italy won the men's foil team 12 times; Hungary the ladies' foil team 11 times; Italy the épée team 10 times and Hungary the sabre team 15 times.

MOST OLYMPIC MEDALS: In a competitive career spanning 24 years, Edoardo Mangiarotti won 13 Olympic medals.

MOST WORLD TITLES: Christian d'Oriola (France) (left) won 4 World Championships and 2 Olympic gold medals.

Most Olympic and Most World Titles

Event	Olympic Gold Medals	World Championships (not held in Olympic years)
Men's Foil, Individual	2 Christian d'Oriola (France) b. Oct. 3, 1928 (1952, 56) 2 Nedo Nadi (Italy) 1894–1952 (1912, 20)	4 Christian d'Oriola (France) (1947, 49, 53, 54)
Men's Foil, Team	5 France (1924, 32, 48, 52, 68)	12 Italy (1929–31, 33–35, 37, 38, 49, 50, 54, 55)
Men's Epée, Individual	2 Ramón Fonst (Cuba) b. 1883 d. 1959 (1900, 04)	3 Georges Buchard (France) b. Dec. 21, 1893 (1927, 31, 33) 3 Aleksey Nikanchikov (U.S.S.R.) b. July 30, 1940 (1966, 67, 70)
Men's Epée, Team	6 Italy (1920, 28, 36, 52, 56, 60)	10 Italy (1931, 33, 37, 49, 50, 53–55, 57, 58)
Men's Sabre, Individual	2 Jean Georgiadis (Greece) b. 1874 (1896, 1906) 2 Dr. Jenő Fuchs (Hungary) b. Oct. 29, 1882 (1908, 12) 2 Rudolf Kárpáti (Hungary) b. July 17, 1920 (1956, 60)	3 Aladar Gerevich (Hungary) (1935, 51, 55) 3 Jerzy Pawlowski (Poland) b. Oct. 25, 1932 (1957, 65, 66) 3 Yacov Rylsky (U.S.S.R.) (1958, 61, 63)
Men's Sabre, Team	9 Hungary (1908, 12, 28, 32, 36, 48, 52, 56, 60)	15 Hungary (1930, 31, 33–35, 37, 51, 53–55, 57, 58, 66, 73, 78)
Women's Foil, Individual	2 Ilona Schacherer-Elek (Hungary) b. 1907 (1936, 48)	3 Helene Mayer (Germany) 1910–53 (1929, 31, 37) 3 Ilona Schacherer-Elek (Hungary) b. 1907 (1934, 35, 51) 3 Ellen Müller-Preiss (Austria) b. May 6, 1912 (1947, 49, 50 (shared))
Women's Foil, Team	4 U.S.S.R. (1960, 68, 72, 76)	11 Hungary (1933–35, 37, 53–55, 59, 62, 67, 73)

Field Hockey

Origin. A representation of two players with curved snagging sticks apparently in an orthodox "bully" position was found in Tomb No. 17 at Beni Hasan, Egypt, and has been dated to *c.* 2050 B.C. There is a reference to the game in Lincolnshire, England, in 1277. The first country to form a national association was England (The Hockey Association) on April 16, 1875.

Earliest International. The first international match was the Wales *vs.* Ireland match on January 26, 1895. Ireland won 3–0.

Highest International Score. The highest score in international field hockey was when India defeated the U.S. 24–1 at Los Angeles, in the 1932 Olympic Games. The Indians were Olympic Champions from the re-inception of Olympic hockey in 1928 until 1960, when Pakistan beat them 1–0 at Rome. They had their seventh win in 1964. Of the 6 Indians who have won 3 Olympic gold medals, two have also won a silver medal—Leslie Claudius in 1948, 1952, 1956 and 1960 (silver), and Udham Singh in 1952, 1956, 1964 and 1960 (silver).

The highest score in a women's international match occurred when England defeated France 23–0 at Merton, Surrey, on February 3, 1923.

The World Cup has been won twice by Pakistan, in 1971 and 1978.

Longest Game. The longest international game on record was one of 145 minutes (into the sixth period of extra time), when Netherlands beat Spain 1–0 in the Olympic tournament at Mexico City on October 25, 1968.

Attendance. The highest attendance at a women's hockey match was 65,165 for the match between England and the U.S. at the Empire Stadium, Wembley, Greater London, on March 11, 1978.

Fishing

Largest Catches. The largest fish ever caught on a rod is an officially ratified man-eating great white shark (*Carcharodon carcharias*) weighing 2,664 lbs., and measuring 16 feet 10 inches long, caught by Alf Dean at Denial Bay, near Ceduna, South Australia, on April 21, 1959. Capt. Frank Mundus (U.S.) harpooned and landed a 17-foot-long 4,500-lb. white shark, after a 5-hour battle, off Montauk Point, Long Island, New York, on June 6, 1964. He was assisted by Peter Brandenberg, Gerald Mallow, Frank Bloom, and Harvey Ferston.

A white pointer shark weighing 3,388 lbs. was caught on a rod by Clive Green off Albany, Western Australia, on April 26, 1976, but this will remain unratified as whale meat was used as bait.

The largest marine animal ever killed by *hand* harpoon was a blue whale 97 feet in length, killed by Archer Davidson in Twofold Bay, New South Wales, Australia, in 1910. Its tail flukes measured 20 feet across and its jaw bone 23 feet 4 inches.

MARTIN'S MARLIN: Larry Martin landing this record Atlantic Blue marlin off St. Thomas in August 1977.

Smallest Catch. The smallest fish ever to win a competition was a smelt weighing $\frac{1}{16}$ of an ounce, caught by Peter Christian at Buckenhain Ferry, Norfolk, England, on January 9, 1977. This beat 107 other competitors.

Spear-fishing. The largest fish ever taken underwater was an 804-lb. giant black grouper by Don Pinder of the Miami Triton Club, Florida, in 1955.

Freshwater Casting. The longest freshwater cast ratified under I.C.F. (International Casting Federation) rules is 574 feet 2 inches by Walter Kummerow (West Germany), for the Bait Distance Double-Handed 30-gram event held at Lenzerheide, Switzerland, in the 1968 Championships.

The longest Fly Distance Double-Handed cast is 257 feet 2 inches by S. Sheen of Norway, also set at Lenzerheide in 1968.

Longest Fight. The longest recorded fight with a fish by an individual is 32 hours 5 minutes by Donal Heatley (b. 1938) (New Zealand) with a broadbill (estimated length 20 feet and weight 1,500 lbs.) off Mayor Island off Tauranga, New Zealand, January 21–22, 1968. It towed the 12-ton launch 50 miles before breaking the line.

Marathon. John Reader fished for 504 hours at Weston-super-Mare, England, on August 20–September 10, 1978.

Fishing

(Sea fish records taken by tackle as ratified by the International Game Fish Association to June 30, 1978. Fresh-water fish records, ratified by *Field & Stream* are marked*.)

Species	Weight in lbs. oz.		Name of Angler	Location	Date
Amberjack	149	0	Peter Simons	Bermuda	June 21, 1964
Barracuda†	83	0	K. J. W. Hackett§§	Lagos, Nigeria	Jan. 13, 1952
Bass (Giant Sea)	563	0	James D. McAdam, Jr.	Anacapa Island, California	Aug. 20, 1968
Black Runner (Cobia)	110	5	Eric Tinworth	Off Mombasa, Kenya	Sep. 8, 1964
*Carp†	55	5	Frank J. Ledwein	Clearwater Lake, Minnesota	July 10, 1952
Cod	98	12	Alphonse J. Bielevich	Isle of Shoals, New Hampshire	June 8, 1969
Marlin (Black)	1,560	0	Alfred C. Glassell, Jr.	Cabo Blanco, Peru	Aug. 4, 1953
Marlin (Atlantic Blue)	1,282	0	Larry Martin	St. Thomas, U.S. Virgin Islands	Aug. 6, 1977
Marlin (Pacific Blue)	1,153	0	Greg D. Perez	Ritidian Point, Guam	Aug. 21, 1969
Marlin (Striped)	417	0	Phillip Bryers	Cavalier Isles, New Zealand	Jan. 14, 1977
Marlin (White)	174	3	Otavia Cunha Reboucas	Vitoria, Brazil	Nov. 1, 1976
*Pike (Northern)	46	2	Peter Dubuc	Sacandaga Reservoir, New York	Sept. 15, 1940
Sailfish (Atlantic)	128	1	Harm Steyn	Luanda, Angola	Mar. 27, 1974
Sailfish (Pacific)	221	0	C. W. Stewart	Santa Cruz I., Galapagos Is.	Feb. 12, 1947
*Salmon (Chinook)§	93	0	Howard C. Rider	Kelp Bay, Alaska	June 24, 1977
Shark (Blue)	437	0	Peter Hyde	Catherine Bay, N.S.W., Australia	Oct. 2, 1976
*Shark (Mako)	1,061	0	James B. Penwarden	Mayor Island, New Zealand	Feb. 17, 1970
Shark (White or Man-Eating)	2,664	0	Alfred Dean	Ceduna, South Australia	Apr. 21, 1959
Shark (Porbeagle)	465	0	Jorge Potier	Cornwall, England	July 23, 1976
Shark (Thresher)‡	739	0	Brian Galvin	Turukaka, New Zealand	Feb. 17, 1975
Shark (Tiger)	1,780	0	Walter Maxwell	Cherry Grove, South Carolina	June 14, 1964
*Sturgeon (White)‡‡	360	0	Willard Cravens	Snake River, Idaho	Apr. 24, 1956
Swordfish	1,182	0	L. E. Marron	Iquique, Chile	May 7, 1953
Tarpon	283	0	M. Salazar	Lago de Maracaibo, Venezuela	Mar. 19, 1965
*Trout (Lake)||	65	0	Larry Daunis	Great Bear Lake, Northwest Terr., Canada	Aug. 8, 1970
Tuna (Allison or Yellowfin)	388	12	Curt Wiesenhutter	San Benedicto Islands, Mexico	Apr. 1, 1977
Tuna (Atlantic Big-eyed)	375	8	Cecil Browne	Ocean City, Maryland	Aug. 26, 1977
Tuna (Pacific Big-eyed)	435	0	Dr. Russel V. A. Lee	Cabo Blanco, Peru	Apr. 17, 1957
Tuna (Bluefin)	1,200	0	Leslie Privano	Chaleur Bay, New Brunswick, Canada	Sept. 22, 1967
Wahoo	149	0	John Pirovano	Cat Cay, Bahamas	June 15, 1962

† A carp weighing 83 lbs. 8 oz. was taken (not by rod) near Pretoria, South Africa. A 60 lb. specimen was taken by bow and arrow by Ben A. Topham in Wythe Co., Virginia, on July 5, 1970. § A salmon weighing 126 lbs. 8 oz. was taken (not by rod) near Petersburg, Alaska. || A 102-lb. trout was taken from Lake Athabasca, northern Saskatchewan, Canada, on August 8, 1961. ** A 1,295-lb. specimen was taken by two anglers off Natal, South Africa, on March 17, 1939, and a 1,500-lb. specimen harpooned inside Durban Harbour, South Africa, in 1933. ‡ W. W. Dowding caught a 922-lb. thresher shark in 1937 on an untested line. †† A barracuda weighing 48 lbs. 6 oz. was caught barehanded by Thomas B. Pace at Panama City Beach, Florida, on April 19 1974. §§ Hackett was only 11 years 137 days old at the time. ‡‡ Glenn Howard caught a sturgeon weighing 394 lbs. on the Snake River, Idaho.

Football

Origins. The origin of modern football stems from the "Boston Game" as played at Harvard. Harvard declined to participate in the inaugural meeting of the Intercollegiate Football Association in New York City in October, 1873, on the grounds that the proposed rules were based on the non-handling "Association" code of English football. Instead, Harvard accepted a proposal from McGill University of Montreal, Canada, who played the more closely akin English Rugby Football. The first football match under the Harvard Rules was thus played against McGill at Cambridge, Mass., in May, 1874. In November, 1876, a New Intercollegiate Football Association, based on modern football, was inaugurated at Springfield, Mass., with a pioneer membership of five colleges.

Professional football dates from the Latrobe, Pa. *vs.* Jeannette, Pa. match at Latrobe, in August, 1895. The National Football League was founded in Canton, Ohio, in 1920, although it did not adopt its present name until 1922. The year 1969 was the final year in which professional football was divided into separate National and American Leagues, for record purposes.

MODERN MAJOR-COLLEGE INDIVIDUAL RECORDS

(Through 1978 Season)

Points
Most in a Game	43	Jim Brown (Syracuse)	1956
Most in a Season	174	Lydell Mitchell (Penn State)	1971
Most in a Career	356	Tony Dorsett (Pittsburgh)	1973–76

Touchdowns
Most in a Game	7	Arnold Boykin (Mississippi)	1951
Most in a Season	29	Lydell Mitchell (Penn State)	1971
Most in a Career	59	Glenn Davis (Army)	1943–46
	59	Tony Dorsett (Pittsburgh)	1973–76

Field Goals
Most in a Game	6	Frank Nester (West Virginia)	1972
	6	Charlie Gogolak (Princeton)	1965
	6	Vince Fusco (Duke)	1976
Most in a Season	22	Matt Bahr (Penn State)	1978
Most in a Career	56	Tony Franklin (Texas A & M)	1975–78

SEASON RECORDS

Total Offense	3,343 yds.	Bill Anderson (Tulsa)	1965
Most Rushing and Passing Plays	580	Bill Anderson (Tulsa)	1965
Most Times Carried	358	Steve Owens (Oklahoma)	1969
Yards Gained Rushing	1,948 yds.	Tony Dorsett (Pittsburgh)	1976
Highest Average Gain per Rush	9.35 yds.	Greg Pruitt (Oklahoma)	1971
Most Passes Completed	296	Bill Anderson (Tulsa)	1965
Most Touchdown Passes	39	Dennis Shaw (San Diego St.)	1969
Highest Completion Percentage	69.3%	Chris Kupec (North Carolina)	1974
Most Yards Gained Passing	3,464 yds.	Bill Anderson (Tulsa)	1965
Most Passes Caught	134	Howard Twilley (Tulsa)	1965
Most Yards Gained on Catches	1,779 yds.	Howard Twilley (Tulsa)	1965
Most Touchdown Passes Caught	18	Tom Reynolds (San Diego St.)	1969
Most Passes Intercepted by	14	Al Worley (Washington)	1968

Longest Service Coach

The longest service head coach was Amos Alonzo Stagg, who served Springfield in 1890–91, Chicago from 1892 to 1932 and College of Pacific from 1933 to 1946, making a total of 57 years.

College Series Records

The oldest collegiate series is that between Princeton and Rutgers dating from 1869, or 7 years before the passing of the Springfield rules. The most regularly contested series is between Lafayette and Lehigh, who have met 114 times between 1884 and the end of 1978.

Longest Streaks

The longest winning streak is 47 straight by Oklahoma. The longest unbeaten streak is 63 games (59 won, 4 tied) by Washington from 1907 to 1917.

Highest Score

The most points ever scored in a college football game was 222 by Georgia Tech, Atlanta, Georgia, against Cumberland University of Lebanon, Tennessee, on October 7, 1916. Tech also set records for the most points scored in one quarter (63) most touchdowns (32) and points after touchdown (30) in a game, and the largest victory margin (Cumberland did not score). There were no first downs.

All-America Selections

The earliest All-America selections were made in 1889 by Caspar Whitney of *The Week's Sport* and later of *Harper's Weekly*.

All-Star Games

The reigning N.F.L. Champions first met an All-Star College selection in the annual August series in Chicago in 1934. The highest scoring match was that of 1940 in which Green Bay beat the All-Stars 45–28. The biggest professional win was in 1949 when Philadelphia won 38–0, and the biggest All-Stars win was in 1943 when Washington was defeated 27–7.

ALL-TIME PROFESSIONAL INDIVIDUAL RECORDS
(Through 1978 Season)

Service

Most Seasons, Active Player
26 George Blanda, Chi. Bears 1949–58; Balt. 1950; AFL: Hou. 1960–66; Oak. 1967–75

Most Games Played, Lifetime
340 George Blanda, Chi. Bears 1949–58; Balt. 1950; AFL: Hou. 1960–66; Oak. 1967–75

Most Consecutive Games Played, Lifetime
266 Jim Marshall, Clev. 1960; Min. 1961–78

Most Seasons, Head Coach
40 George Halas, Chi. Bears 1920–29, 33–42, 46–55, 58–67

Scoring

Most Seasons Leading League
5 Don Hutson, Green Bay 1940–44
Gino Cappelletti, Bos. 1961, 63–66 (AFL)

Most Points, Lifetime
2,002 George Blanda, Chi. Bears 1949–58; Balt. 1950; AFL: Hou. 1960–66; Oak. 1967–75 (9-td, 943-pat, 335-fg)

Most Points, Season
176 Paul Hornung, Green Bay 1960 (15-td, 41-pat, 15-fg)

Most Points, Rookie, Season
132 Gale Sayers, Chi. 1965 (22-td)

GREAT RUNNER:
O. J. Simpson scored the most touchdowns in one season (23) and rushed for most yards gained in one season (2,003 yards in 1973).

Most Points, Game
  40 Ernie Nevers, Chi. Cards vs Chi. Bears, Nov. 28, 1929 (6-td, 4-pat)

Most Points, One Quarter
  29 Don Hutson, Green Bay vs Det., Oct. 7, 1945 (4-td, 5-pat) 2nd Quarter

Touchdowns

Most Seasons Leading League
  8 Don Hutson, Green Bay, 1935–38, 41–44

Most Touchdowns, Lifetime
  126 Jim Brown, Cleve. 1957–65 (106-r, 20-p)

Most Touchdowns, Season
  23 O. J. Simpson, Buff. 1975 (16-r., 7-p.)

Most Touchdowns, Rookie Season
  22 Gale Sayers, Chi. 1965 (14-r, 6-p, 1-prb, 1-krb)

Most Touchdowns, Game
  6 Ernie Nevers, Chi. Cards vs Chi. Bears, Nov. 28, 1929 (6-r)
     William (Dub) Jones, Cleve. vs Chi. Bears, Nov. 25, 1951 (4-r, 2-p)
     Gale Sayers, Chi. vs S. F., Dec. 12, 1965 (4-r, 1-p, 1-prb)

Most Consecutive Games Scoring Touchdowns
  18 Lenny Moore, Balt. 1963–65

Points after Touchdown

Most Seasons Leading League
  8 George Blanda, Chi. Bears 1956; AFL: Hou. 1961–62; Oak. 1967–69, 72, 74

Most Points After Touchdown, Lifetime
  943 George Blanda, Chi. Bears 1949–58; Balt. 1950; AFL: Hou. 1960–66; Oak. 1967–75

Most Points After Touchdown, Season
  64 George Blanda, Hou. 1961 (AFL)

Most Points After Touchdown, Game
  9 Marlin (Pat) Harder, Chi. Cards vs N. Y., Oct. 17, 1948
     Bob Waterfield, L. A. vs Balt., Oct. 22, 1950
     Charlie Gogolak, Wash. vs N. Y., Nov. 27, 1966

Most Consecutive Points After Touchdown
  234 Tommy Davis, S. F. 1959–65

Most Points After Touchdown (no misses), Season
  56 Danny Villanueva, Dall. 1966

Most Points After Touchdown (no misses), Game
  9 Marlin (Pat) Harder, Chi. Cards vs N. Y., Oct. 17, 1948
     Bob Waterfield, L. A. vs Balt., Oct. 22, 1950

Field Goals

Most Seasons Leading League
5   Lou Groza, Cleve., 1950, 52–54,
    57

Most Field Goals, Lifetime
335   George Blanda, Chi. Bears 1949–
      58; Balt. 1950; AFL: Hou.
      1960–66; Oak. 1967–75

Most Field Goals, Season
34   Jim Turner, N.Y. 1968 (AFL)

Most Field Goals, Game
7   Jim Bakken, St. L. vs Pitt., Sept.
    24, 1967

Most Consecutive Games, Field Goals
31   Fred Cox, Minn. 1968–70

Most Consecutive Field Goals
16   Jan Stenerud, K.C. 1969 (AFL)
     Don Cockroft, Clev. 1974–75
     Garo Yepremian, Mia. 1978

Longest Field Goal
63 yds. Tom Dempsey, New Orl. vs Det.
        Nov. 8, 1970

Rushing

Most Seasons Leading League
8   Jim Brown, Cleve. 1957–61, 63–65

Most Yards Gained, Lifetime
12,312   Jim Brown, Cleve., 1957–65

Most Yards Gained, Season
2,003   O. J. Simpson, Buff., 1973

Most Yards Gained, Game
275   Walter Payton, Chi. vs. Minn.,
      Nov. 20, 1977

Longest Run from Scrimmage
97 yards Andy Uram, Green Bay vs
         Chi. Cards, Oct. 8, 1939 (td)
         Bob Gage, Pitt. vs Chi. Bears,
         Dec. 4, 1949 (td)

Highest Average Gain, Lifetime (700 att.)
5.2   Jim Brown, Cleve. 1957–65
      (2,359–12,312)

Highest Average Gain, Season (100 att.)
9.9   Beattie Feathers, Chi. Bears,
      1934 (101–1004)

Highest Average Gain, Game (10 att.)
17.1   Marion Motley, Cleve. vs Pitt.,
       Oct. 29, 1950 (11–188)

Most Touchdowns Rushing, Lifetime
106   Jim Brown, Cleve., 1957–65

Most Touchdowns Rushing, Season
19   Jim Taylor, Green Bay, 1962

Most Touchdowns Rushing, Game
6   Ernie Nevers, Chi. Cards vs Chi.
    Bears, Nov. 28, 1929

Passing

Most Seasons Leading League
6   Sammy Baugh, Wash., 1937, 40,
    43, 45, 47, 49

Most Passes Attempted, Lifetime
6,467   Fran Tarkenton, Minn. 1961–66,
        72–78; N.Y. Giants 1967–71
        (3,686 completions)

Most Passes Attempted, Season
572   Fran Tarkenton, Minn. 1978
      (345 completions)

Most Passes Attempted, Game
68   George Blanda, Hou. vs Buff.,
     Nov. 1, 1964 (AFL) (37 com-
     pletions)

Most Passes Completed, Lifetime
3,686   Fran Tarkenton, Minn. 1961–66,
        72–78; N.Y. Giants 1967–71
        (6,467 attempts)

Most Passes Completed, Season
345   Fran Tarkenton, Minn. 1978
      (572 attempts)

Most Passes Completed, Game
37   George Blanda, Hou. vs Buff.,
     Nov. 1, 1964 (AFL) (68
     attempts)

Most Consecutive Passes Completed
17   Bert Jones, Balt. vs. N.Y. Jets,
     Dec. 15, 1974

Passing Efficiency, Lifetime (1,500 att.)
59.6   Ken Stabler, Oak. 1970–78
       (1,983–1,182)

Passing Efficiency, Season (100 att.)
70.3   Sammy Baugh, Wash., 1945
       (182–129)

Passing Efficiency, Game (20 att.)
90.9   Ken Anderson, Cin. vs. Pitt.,
       Nov. 10, 1974 (22–20)

Shortest Pass Completion for Touchdown
2″   Eddie LeBaron (to Bielski), Dall.
     vs Wash., Oct. 9, 1960

Longest Pass Completion (all TDs)
99   Frank Filchock (to Farkas),
     Wash. vs Pitt., Oct. 15, 1939
     George Izo (to Mitchell), Wash.
     vs Cleve., Sept. 15, 1963
     Karl Sweetan (to Studstill), Det.
     vs Balt., Oct. 16, 1966
     C. A. Jurgensen (to Allen), Wash.
     vs Chi., Sept. 15, 1968

Most Yards Gained Passing, Lifetime
47,003   Fran Tarkenton, Minn. 1961–
         66, 72–78; N.Y. Giants 1967–71

Most Yards Gained Passing, Season
4,007   Joe Namath, N. Y. 1967 (AFL)

Most Yards Gained Passing, Game
554   Norm Van Brocklin, L. A. vs
      N. Y. Yanks, Sept. 28, 1951
      (41–27)

LONGEST FIELD GOAL in NFL competition (63 yards) was kicked by a man with only half a foot—Tom Dempsey of the New Orleans Saints, who wears a special shoe over his foot, and has only part of his right arm. His record kick beat the Detroit Lions, 19-17, on the last play of the game on November 8, 1970.

Most Touchdown Passes, Lifetime
  342 Fran Tarkenton, Minn. 1961–66, 72–78; N.Y. Giants 1967–71

Most Touchdown Passes, Season
  36 George Blanda, Hou. 1961 (AFL) Y. A. Tittle, N. Y. 1963

Most Touchdown Passes, Game
  7 Sid Luckman, Chi. Bears vs N. Y. Nov. 14, 1943
     Adrian Burk, Phil. vs Wash., Oct. 17, 1954
     George Blanda, Hou. vs N. Y., Nov. 19, 1961 (AFL)
     Y. A. Tittle, N. Y. vs Wash., Oct. 28, 1962
     Joe Kapp, Minn. vs Balt., Sept. 28, 1969

Most Consecutive Games, Touchdown Passes
  47 John Unitas, Balt., 1956–60

Passes Had Intercepted

Fewest Passes Intercepted, Season (Qualifiers)
  1 Joe Ferguson, Buff. 1976 (151 attempts)

Most Consecutive Passes Attempted, None Intercepted
  294 Bryan (Bart) Starr, Green Bay, 1964–65

Most Passes Intercepted, Game
  8 Jim Hardy, Chi. Cards vs Phil., Sept. 24, 1950 (39 attempts)

Lowest Percentage Passes Intercepted, Lifetime (1,500 att.)
  3.31 Roman Gabriel, L.A. 1962–72; Phil. 1973–77 (4,498–149)

Lowest Percentage Passes Intercepted, Season (Qualifiers)
  0.66 Joe Ferguson, Buff. 1976 (151–1)

Pass Receptions

Most Seasons Leading League
  8 Don Hutson, Green Bay, 1936–37, 39, 41–45

Most Pass Receptions, Lifetime
  649 Charley Taylor, Wash. 1964–75, 77

Most Pass Receptions, Season
  101 Charley Hennigan, Hou. 1964 (AFL)

TOUCHDOWN PASS RECORD RECEIVER: Elroy (Crazy Legs) Hirsch caught 17 in a season, and had an 11-game streak.

N.F.L. Records (continued)

Most Pass Receptions, Game
18 Tom Fears, L. A. vs Green Bay, Dec. 3, 1950 (189 yds.)

Longest Pass Reception (all TDs)
99 Andy Farkas (Filchock), Wash. vs Pitt., Oct. 15, 1939
Bobby Mitchell (Izo), Wash. vs Cleve., Sept. 15, 1963
Pat Studstill (Sweetan), Det. vs Balt., Oct. 16, 1966
Gerry Allen (Jurgensen), Wash. vs Chi., Sept. 15, 1968

Most Consecutive Games, Pass Receptions
105 Dan Abramowicz, N.O. 1967–73; S.F. 1973–74

Touchdowns Receiving

Most Touchdown Passes, Lifetime
99 Don Hutson, Green Bay, 1935–45

Most Touchdown Passes, Season
17 Don Hutson, Green Bay, 1942
Elroy (Crazy Legs) Hirsch, L. A., 1951
Bill Groman, Hou. 1961 (AFL)

Most Touchdown Passes, Game
5 Bob Shaw, Chi. Cards vs Balt., Oct. 2, 1950

Most Consecutive Games, Touchdown Passes
11 Elroy (Crazy Legs) Hirsch, L.A., 1950–51
Gilbert (Buddy) Dial, Pitt., 1959–60

Pass Interceptions

Most Interceptions by, Lifetime
79 Emlen Tunnell, N. Y. (74), 1948–58; Green Bay (5), 1959–61

Most Interceptions by, Season
14 Richard (Night Train) Lane, L. A., 1952

Most Interceptions by, Game
4 By many players

Interception Yardage

Most Yards Gained, Lifetime
1,282 Emlen Tunnell, N. Y., 1948–58; Green Bay, 1959–61

Most Yards Gained, Season
349 Charley McNeil, San Diego 1961 (AFL)

Most Yards Gained, Game
177 Charley McNeil, San Diego vs Hou., Sept. 24, 1961 (AFL)

Longest Gain (all TDs)
102 Bob Smith, Det. vs Chi. Bears, Nov. 24, 1949
Erich Barnes, N. Y. vs Dall., Oct. 22, 1961
Gary Barbaro, K.C. vs. Sea., Dec. 11, 1977

Touchdowns on Interceptions

Most Touchdowns, Lifetime
9 Ken Houston, Hou. 1967–72; Wash. 1973–78

Most Touchdowns, Season
4 Ken Houston, Hou. 1971
Jim Kearney, K.C. 1972

Punting

Most Seasons Leading League
4 Sammy Baugh, Wash., 1940–43
Jerrel Wilson, AFL: K.C., 1965, 68; NFL: K.C. 1972–73

LONGEST PUNTER: Steve O'Neal (N.Y. Jets) kicked 98 yards in the AFL in 1969.

MOST TOUCHDOWN PASSES: Y. A. Tittle threw a record 36 touchdown passes in 1963 and 7 in one game in 1962. Both marks have been equaled by other quarterbacks.

Most Punts, Lifetime
1,072 Jerrel Wilson, AFL: K.C. 1963–69; NFL: K.C. 1970–77; N.E. 1978

Most Punts, Season
109 John James, Atl. 1978

Most Punts, Game
14 Dick Nesbitt, Chi. Cards. vs Chi. Bears, Nov. 30, 1933
Keith Molesworth, Chi. Bears vs G.B., Dec. 10, 1933
Sammy Baugh, Wash. vs Phil., Nov. 5, 1939
John Kinscherf, N. Y. vs Det., Nov. 7, 1943
George Taliaferro, N. Y. Yanks vs L. A., Sept. 28, 1951

Longest Punt
98 yards Steve O'Neal, N. Y. Jets vs. Den., Sept. 21, 1969 (AFL)

Average Yardage Punting

Highest Punting Average, Lifetime (300 punts)
45.1 yards Sammy Baugh, Wash., 1937–52 (338)

Highest Punting Average, Season (20 punts)
51.4 yards Sammy Baugh, Wash., 1940 (35)

Highest Punting Average, Game (4 punts)
61.8 yards Bob Cifers, Det. vs. Chi. Bears, Nov. 24, 1946

Punt Returns
Yardage Returning Punts

Most Yards Gained, Lifetime
2,209 Emlen Tunnell, N.Y. Giants 1948–58; G.B. 1959–61

Most Yards Gained, Season
655 Neal Colzie, Oak. 1975

Most Yards Gained, Game
205 George Atkinson, Oak. vs. Buff., Sept. 15, 1968

Longest Punt Return (all TDs)
98 Gil LeFebvre, Cin. vs. Brk., Dec. 3, 1933
Charlie West, Minn. vs. Wash., Nov. 3, 1968
Dennis Morgan, Dall. vs. St. L., Oct. 13, 1974

Average Yardage Returning Punts

Highest Average, Lifetime (75 returns)
13.4 Billy (White Shoes) Johnson, Hou. 1974–78

Highest Average, Season (Qualifiers)
23.0 Herb Rich, Balt. 1950

Highest Average, Game (3 returns)
47.7 Chuck Latourette, St. L. vs. N.O., Sept. 29, 1968

Touchdowns Returning Punts

Most Touchdowns, Lifetime
8 Jack Christiansen, Det. 1951–58

Most Touchdowns, Season
4 Jack Christiansen, Det. 1951
Rick Upchurch, Den. 1976

Most Touchdowns, Game
2 Jack Christiansen, Det. vs. L.A., Oct. 14, 1951; vs. G.B., Nov. 22, 1951
Dick Christy, N.Y. Titans vs. Den., Sept. 24, 1961
Rick Upchurch, Den. vs Clev., Sept. 26, 1976

Kickoff Returns
Yardage Returning Kickoffs

Most Yards Gained, Lifetime
6,922 Ron Smith, Chi. 1965, 70–72; Atl. 1966–67; L.A. 1968–69; S.D. 1973; Oak. 1974

Most Yards Gained, Season
1,317 Bobby Jancik, Hou. 1963 (AFL)

Most Yards Gained, Game
294 Wally Triplett, Det. vs L. A., Oct. 29, 1950 (4)

Longest Kickoff Return for Touchdown
106 Al Carmichael, Green Bay vs. Chi. Bears, Oct. 7, 1956
Noland Smith, K.C. vs Den., Dec. 17, 1967 (AFL)

Average Yardage Returning Kickoffs

Highest Average, Lifetime (75 returns)
30.6 Gale Sayers, Chi. 1965–71

Highest Average, Season (15 returns)
41.1 Travis Williams, Green Bay, 1967 (18)

Highest Average, Game (3 returns)
73.5 Wally Triplett, Det. vs L. A., Oct. 29, 1950 (4–294)

Touchdowns Returning Kickoffs
Most Touchdowns, Lifetime
6 Ollie Matson, Chi. Cards, 1952 (2), 54, 56, 58 (2)
Gale Sayers, Chi., 1965, 66 (2), 67 (3)
Travis Williams, G.B., 1967 (4), 69, 71

Most Touchdowns, Season
4 Travis Williams, Green Bay, 1967
Cecil Turner, Chi. 1970

Most Touchdowns, Game
2 Thomas (Tim) Brown, Phil. vs Dall., Nov. 6, 1966
Travis Williams, Green Bay vs Cleve., Nov. 12, 1967

Fumbles

Most Fumbles, Lifetime
105 Roman Gabriel, L.A. 1962–72; Phil. 1973–77

Most Fumbles, Season
17 Dan Pastorini, Hou., 1973

Most Fumbles, Game
7 Len Dawson, K.C. vs San Diego, Nov. 15, 1964 (AFL)

Most Own Fumbles Recovered, Lifetime
43 Fran Tarkenton, Minn. 1961–66, 72–78; N.Y. Giants 1967–71

Most Own Fumbles Recovered, Season
8 Paul Christman, Chi. Cards, 1945; Bill Butler, Minn., 1963

Most Own Fumbles Recovered, Game
4 Otto Graham, Cleve. vs N. Y., Oct. 25, 1953
Sam Etcheverry, St. L. vs N. Y., Sept. 17, 1961
Roman Gabriel, L. A. vs S. F., Oct. 12, 1969
Joe Ferguson, Buff. vs. Miami, Sept. 18, 1977

Most Opponents' Fumbles Recovered, Lifetime
28 Jim Marshall, Clev. 1960; Minn. 1961–78

Most Opponents' Fumbles Recovered, Season
9 Don Hultz, Minn., 1963

Most Opponents' Fumbles Recovered, Game
3 Corwin Clatt, Chi. Cards vs Det., Nov. 6, 1949
Vic Sears, Phil. vs Green Bay, Nov. 2, 1952
Ed Beatty, S. F. vs L. A., Oct. 7, 1956
Ron Carroll, Hou. vs Cin., Oct. 27, 1974
Maurice Spencer, N.O. vs Atl., Oct. 10, 1976
Steve Nelson, N.E. vs. Phil., Oct. 8, 1978

Longest Fumble Run
104 Jack Tatum, Oak. vs G.B., Sept. 24, 1972

Miscellaneous

Most Drop Kick Field Goals, Game
4 John (Paddy) Driscoll, Chi. Cards vs Columbus, Oct. 11, 1925 (23, 18, 50, 35 yards)
Elbert Bloodgood, Kansas City vs Duluth, Dec. 12, 1926 (35, 32, 20, 25 yards)

Longest Drop Kick Field Goal
50 Wilbur (Pete) Henry, Canton vs Toledo, Nov. 13, 1922
John (Paddy) Driscoll, Chi. Cards vs Milwaukee, Sept. 28, 1924; vs Columbus, Oct. 11, 1925

Most Yards Returned Missed Field Goal
101 Al Nelson, Phil. vs Dall., Sept. 26, 1971 (TD)

SEASON RECORDS—OFFENSE

(Playoff games not included)

Most Seasons League Champion
11 Green Bay, 1929–31, 36, 39, 44, 61–62, 65–67

Most Consecutive Games Without Defeat (Regular Season)
24 Canton, 1922–23 (Won–21, Tied–3)
Chicago Bears, 1941–43 (Won–23, Tied–1)

Most Consecutive Victories (All Games)
18 Chicago Bears (1933–34; 1941–42)
    Miami (1972–73)

Most Consecutive Victories (Regular Season)
17 Chicago Bears, 1933–34

Most Consecutive Victories, One Season (All Games)
17 Miami, 1972

Most Consecutive Shutout Games Won
7 Detroit, 1934

Scoring

Most Seasons Leading League
9 Chicago Bears, 1934–35, 39, 41–43, 46–47, 56

Most Points, Season
513 Houston, 1961 (AFL)

Most Points, Game
72 Washington vs N. Y., Nov. 27, 1966

Most Touchdowns, Season
66 Houston, 1961 (AFL)

Most Touchdowns, Game
10 Philadelphia vs Cin., Nov. 6, 1934
    Los Angeles vs Balt., Oct. 22, 1950
    Washington vs N. Y., Nov. 27, 1966

Most Touchdowns, Both Teams, Game
16 Washington (10) vs N. Y. (6), Nov. 27, 1966

Most Points After Touchdown, Season
65 Houston, 1961 (AFL)

Most Points After Touchdown, Game
10 Los Angeles vs Balt., Oct. 22, 1950

Most Points After Touchdown, Both Teams, Game
14 Chicago Cards (9) vs N. Y. (5), Oct. 17, 1948
    Houston (7) vs Oakland (7), Dec. 22, 1963 (AFL)
    Washington (9) vs N. Y. (5), Nov. 27, 1966

Most Field Goals Attempted, Season
49 Los Angeles, 1966
    Washington, 1971

Most Field Goals Attempted, Game
9 St. Louis vs Pitt., Sept. 24, 1967

Most Field Goals Attempted, Both Teams, Game
11 St. Louis (6) vs Pitt. (5), Nov. 13, 1966
    Washington (6) vs Chi. (5), Nov. 14, 1971
    Green Bay (6) vs Det. (5), Sept. 29, 1974
    Washington (6) vs. N.Y. Giants (5), Nov. 14, 1976

Most Field Goals, Season
34 New York, 1968 (AFL)

Most Field Goals, Game
7 St. Louis vs Pitt., Sept. 24, 1967

Most Field Goals, Both Teams, Game
8 Cleveland (4) vs St. L. (4), Sept. 20, 1964
    Chicago (5) vs Phil. (3), Oct. 20, 1968
    Washington (5) vs Chi. (3), Nov. 14, 1971
    Kansas City (5) vs. Buff. (3), Dec. 19, 1971
    Detroit (4) vs G.B. (4), Sept. 29, 1974
    Cleveland (5) vs Den. (3), Oct. 19, 1975
    New England (4) vs S.D. (4), Nov. 9, 1975

Most Consecutive Games Scoring Field Goals
31 Minnesota, 1968–70

First Downs

Most Seasons Leading League
9 Chicago Bears, 1935, 39, 41, 43, 45, 47–49, 55

Most First Downs, Season
345 Seattle, 1978

Most First Downs, Game
38 Los Angeles vs N. Y., Nov. 13, 1966

Most First Downs, Both Teams, Game
58 Los Angeles (30) vs Chi. Bears (28), Oct. 24, 1954
    Denver (34) vs K.C. (24), Nov. 18, 1974

Most First Downs, Rushing, Season
181 New England, 1978

Most First Downs, Rushing, Game
25 Philadelphia vs Wash., Dec. 2, 1951

Most First Downs, Passing, Season
186 Houston, 1964 (AFL)
     Oakland, 1964 (AFL)

Most First Downs, Passing, Game
25 Denver vs K.C., Nov. 18, 1974

Net Yards Gained (Rushes and Passes)

Most Seasons Leading League
12 Chicago Bears, 1932, 34–35, 39, 41–44, 47, 49, 55–56

Most Yards Gained, Season
6,288 Houston, 1961 (AFL)

Most Yards Gained, Game
735 Los Angeles vs N. Y. Yanks, Sept. 28, 1951 (181-r, 554-p)

Most Yards Gained, Both Teams, Game
1,133 Los Angeles (636) vs N. Y. Yanks (497), Nov. 19, 1950

Rushing

Most Seasons Leading League
12 Chicago Bears, 1932, 34–35, 39–42, 51, 55–56, 68, 77

Most Rushing Attempts, Season
681 Oakland, 1977

Most Rushing Attempts, Game
72 Chicago Bears vs Brk., Oct. 20, 1935

Most Rushing Attempts, Both Teams, Game
108 Chicago Cards (70) vs Green Bay (38), Dec. 5, 1948

Most Yards Gained Rushing, Season
3,165 New England, 1978

Most Yards Gained Rushing, Game
426 Detroit vs Pitt., Nov. 4, 1934

Most Yards Gained Rushing, Both Teams, Game
595 L. A. (371) vs N. Y. Yanks (224), Nov. 18, 1951

Highest Average Gain Rushing, Season
5.7 Cleveland, 1963

Most Touchdowns Rushing, Season
36 Green Bay, 1962

Most Touchdowns Rushing, Game
7 Los Angeles vs. Atlanta, Dec. 4, 1976

Most Touchdowns Rushing, Both Teams, Game
8 Los Angeles (6) vs N. Y. Yanks (2), Nov. 18, 1951
Cleveland (6) vs L. A. (2), Nov. 24, 1957

Passing

Most Seasons Leading League
10 Washington, 1937, 39–40, 42–45, 47, 67, 74

Most Passes Attempted, Season
592 Houston, 1964 (AFL)
Minnesota, 1978

Most Passes Attempted, Game
68 Houston vs Buffalo, Nov. 1, 1964 (AFL) (37 comp.)

Most Passes Attempted, Both Teams, Game
98 Minn. (56) vs Balt. (42), Sept. 28, 1969

Most Passes Completed, Season
352 Minnesota, 1978

Most Passes Completed, Game
37 Houston vs Buffalo, Nov. 1, 1964 (AFL) (68 att.)

Most Passes Completed, Both Teams, Game
56 Minn. (36) vs Balt. (20), Sept. 28, 1969

Most Yards Gained Passing, Season
4,392 Houston, 1961 (AFL)

Most Yards Gained Passing, Game
554 Los Angeles vs N. Y. Yanks, Sept. 28, 1951

Most Yards Gained Passing, Both Teams, Game
834 Philadelphia (419) vs St. L. (415), Dec. 16, 1962

Most Seasons Leading League (Completion Pct.)
11 Washington, 1937, 39–40, 42–45, 47–48, 69-70

Most Touchdowns Passing, Season
48 Houston, 1961 (AFL)

Most Touchdowns Passing, Game
7 Chicago Bears vs N. Y., Nov. 14, 1943
Philadelphia vs. Wash., Oct. 17, 1954
Houston vs N. Y., Nov. 19, 1961 and Oct. 14, 1962 (AFL)
New York vs Wash., Oct. 28, 1962
Minnesota vs Balt., Sept. 28, 1969

Most Touchdowns Passing, Both Teams, Game
12 New Orleans (6) vs St. Louis (6), Nov. 2, 1969

Most Passes Had Intercepted, Season
48 Houston, 1962 (AFL)

Fewest Passes Had Intercepted, Season
5 Cleveland, 1960 (264-att.)
Green Bay, 1966 (318-att.)

Most Passes Had Intercepted, Game
9 Detroit vs Green Bay, Oct. 24, 1943
Pittsburgh vs Phil., Dec. 12, 1965

Punting

Most Seasons Leading League (Avg. Distance)
6 Washington, 1940–43, 45, 58

Highest Punting Average, Season
47.6 Detroit, 1961

Punt Returns

Most Seasons Leading League
8 Detroit, 1943–45, 51–52, 62, 66, 69

Most Yards Gained Punt Returns, Season
781 Chicago Bears, 1948

Most Yards Gained Punt Returns, Game
231 Detroit vs S. F., Oct. 6, 1963

Highest Average Punt Returns, Season
20.2 Chicago Bears, 1941

Most Touchdowns Punt Returns, Season
5 Chicago Cards, 1959

Most Touchdowns Punt Returns, Game
2 Detroit vs L. A., Oct. 14; vs
Green Bay, Nov. 22, 1951
Chicago Cards vs Pitt., Nov. 1;
vs N. Y., Nov. 22, 1959
New York Titans vs Den., Sept.
24, 1961 (AFL)
Denver vs. Clev., Sept. 26, 1976

Kickoff Returns

Most Seasons Leading League
6 Washington, 1942, 47, 62–63, 73–74

Most Yards Gained Kickoff Returns,
Season
1,824 Houston, 1963 (AFL)

Most Yards Gained Kickoff Returns,
Game
362 Detroit vs L. A., Oct. 29, 1950

Most Yards Gained Kickoff Returns,
Both Teams, Game
560 Detroit (362) vs L. A. (198) Oct.
29, 1950

Highest Average Kickoff Returns,
Season
29.4 Chicago, 1972

Most Touchdowns Kickoff Returns,
Season
4 Green Bay, 1967
Chicago, 1970

Most Touchdowns Kickoff Returns,
Game
2 Chicago Bears vs Green Bay,
Sept. 22, 1940–Nov. 9, 1952
Philadelphia vs Dall., Nov. 6,
1966
Green Bay vs Cleve., Nov. 12,
1967

Fumbles

Most Fumbles, Season
56 Chicago Bears, 1938
San Francisco, 1978

Fewest Fumbles, Season
8 Cleveland, 1959

Most Fumbles, Game
10 Phil/Pitts vs N. Y., Oct. 9, 1943
Detroit vs Minn., Nov. 12, 1967
Kansas City vs Hou., Oct. 12,
1969 (AFL)
San Francisco vs. Det., Dec. 17,
1978

Most Fumbles, Both Teams, Game
14 Chicago Bears (7) vs Cleve. (7),
Nov. 24, 1940
St. Louis (8) vs N. Y. (6), Sept. 17,
1961
Kansas City (10) vs Hou. (4),
Oct. 12, 1969 (AFL)

Most Opponents' Fumbles Recovered,
Season
31 Minnesota, 1963 (50 fumbles)

Most Opponents' Fumbles Recovered,
Game
8 Washington vs St. L., Oct. 25,
1976

Most Own Fumbles Recovered, Season
37 Chicago Bears, 1938 (56 fumbles)

Most Fumbles (Opponents' and Own)
Recovered, Season
58 Minnesota, 1963 (95 fumbles)

Most Fumbles (Opponents' and Own),
Recovered, Game
10 Denver vs Buff., Dec. 13, 1964
(AFL)
Pittsburgh vs Hou., Dec. 9, 1973
Washington vs St. L., Oct. 25,
1976

Penalties

Most Seasons Leading League, Fewest
Penalties
9 Pittsburgh, 1946–47, 50–52, 54,
63, 65, 68

Most Penalties, Season
133 Los Angeles, 1978

Fewest Penalties, Season
19 Detroit, 1937 (139 yards)

Most Penalties, Game
22 Brooklyn vs Green Bay, Sept. 17,
1944 (170 yards)
Chicago Bears vs Phil., Nov. 26,
1944 (170 yards)

Fewest Penalties, Game
0 By many teams

Fewest Penalties, Both Teams, Game
0 Brooklyn vs Pitt., Oct. 28, 1934;
vs Bos., Sept. 28, 1936
Cleveland Rams vs Chi. Bears,
Oct. 9, 1938
Pittsburgh vs Phil., Nov. 10, 1940

Most Yards Penalized, Season
1,274 Oakland, 1969 (AFL)

Fewest Yards Penalized, Season
139 Detroit, 1937 (19 pen.)

Most Yards Penalized, Game
209 Cleveland vs Chi. Bears, Nov. 25,
1951 (21 pen.)

DEFENSE

Fewest Points Allowed, Season (since
1932)
44 Chicago Bears, 1932

Fewest Touchdowns Allowed, Season
(since 1932)
6 Chicago Bears 1932
Brooklyn, 1933

Fewest First Downs Allowed, Season
77 Detroit, 1935

Fewest First Downs Allowed, Rushing,
Season
35 Chicago Bears, 1942

Fewest First Downs Allowed, Passing, Season
33 Chicago Bears, 1943

Fewest Yards Allowed, Season
1,539 Chicago Cards, 1934

Fewest Yards Allowed Rushing, Season
519 Chicago Bears, 1942

Fewest Touchdowns Allowed, Rushing, Season
2 Detroit, 1934
Dallas, 1968
Minnesota, 1971

Fewest Yards Allowed Punt Returns, Season
22 Green Bay, 1967

Fewest Yards Allowed Kickoff Returns, Season
225 Brooklyn, 1943

Fewest Yards Allowed Passing, Season
545 Philadelphia, 1934

Most Opponents Tackled Attempting Passes, Season
67 Oakland, 1967 (AFL)

Fewest Touchdowns Allowed, Passing, Season
1 Portsmouth, 1932
Philadelphia, 1934

Most Seasons Leading League, Interceptions Made
9 New York Giants, 1933, 1937–39, 44, 48, 51, 54, 61

Most Pass Interceptions Made, Season
49 San Diego, 1961 (AFL)

Most Yards Gained, Interceptions, Season
929 San Diego, 1961 (AFL)

Most Yards Gained, Interceptions, Game
314 Los Angeles vs S. F., Oct. 18, 1964

Most Touchdowns, Interception Returns, Season
9 San Diego, 1961 (AFL)

Most Touchdowns, Interception Returns, Game
3 Baltimore vs Green Bay, Nov. 5, 1950
Cleveland vs Chi., Dec. 11, 1960
Philadelphia vs Pitt., Dec. 12, 1965
Baltimore vs Pitt., Sept. 29, 1968
Buffalo vs N. Y., Sept. 29, 1968 (AFL)
Houston vs S.D., Dec. 19, 1971
Cincinnati vs Hou., Dec. 17, 1972
Tampa Bay vs. N.O., Dec. 11, 1977

Gambling

World's Biggest Win. The world's biggest gambling win is $2,451,549 for a bet of two cruzeiros ($.58) in the Brazilian football pools Loteria Esportiva by Miron Vieira de Sousa, 30, of Ivolandia, Brazil, on the results of 13 games in October, 1975. The first thing he bought was a set of false teeth.

By winning a state lottery in January, 1976, Eric C. Leek, of North Arlington, New Jersey, won $1,776 a week for life. Aged 26, he will receive a total of $4.6 million should he live a further 50 years.

World's Biggest Loss. An unnamed Italian industrialist was reported to have lost $1,920,000 in five hours at roulette in Monte Carlo, Monaco, on March 6, 1974. A Saudi Arabian prince was reported to have lost more than $1 million in a single session at the Metro Club, Las Vegas, Nevada, in December, 1974.

Largest Casino. The largest casino in the world is the Casino, Mar del Plata, Argentina, with average daily attendances of 14,500 rising to 25,000 during carnivals. The Casino has more than 150 roulette tables running simultaneously.

BIGGEST "BANDIT" OF ALL: When playing Super Bertha, the world's largest slot machine, eight 7's add up to much more than 56.

Bingo

Origins. Bingo is a lottery game which, as keno, was developed in the 1880's from lotto, whose origin is thought to be the 17th century Italian game *tumbule*. It has long been known in the British Army (called Housey-Housey) and the Royal Navy (called Tombola). The winner was the first to complete a random selection of numbers from 1–90. The U.S. version of Bingo differs in that the selection is from 1–75. There are six million players in the United Kingdom alone.

Largest House. The largest "house" in Bingo sessions was at the Empire Pool, Wembley, Brent, Greater London, on April 25, 1965, when 10,000 attended.

Most Cards. The highest recorded number of cards played simultaneously (with a call rate of 31.7 seconds per call) has been 346 by Robert A. Berg at Pacific Beach, California, on November 16, 1973.

Bingo-Calling Marathon. A session of 180 hours 6 minutes was held at the EMI Ritz Bingo/Social Club, Aldershot, Hampshire, England, May 13–20, 1978, with Peter Smith and George Williams calling.

Slot Machines

Largest. The world's biggest slot machine (or one-armed bandit) is Super Bertha (555 cubic feet) installed by Si Redd at the Four

LONGEST DEAL: Earl Arnall of Las Vegas spent 190 hours dealing at the blackjack table in June, 1977.

Queens Casino, Las Vegas, Nevada, in September, 1973. Once in every 25,000,000,000 plays it may yield $1 million for a $10 investment.

Biggest Win. The biggest beating handed to a "one-armed bandit" was $275,000 by James Schelich (b. 1930), a blind Korean War veteran from Washington, Missouri, at the Flamingo Hilton Hotel, Las Vegas, Nevada, on October 29, 1978.

The total gambling "take" in 1977 in Nevada casinos was estimated at $1,500,000,000.

Horse Racing

Topmost Tipster. The only recorded instance of a racing correspondent forecasting ten out of ten winners on a race card was at Delaware Park, Wilmington, Delaware, on July 28, 1974, by Charles Lamb of the *Baltimore News American*.

Most Complicated Bet. The most complicated bet is the Harlequin, a British compound wager on four horses with 2,028 possible ways of winning. It was invented by Monty H. Preston of London who has been reputed to be the fastest settler of bets in the world. He once completed 3,000 bets in a 4½-hour test.

Blackjack

Marathon. Earl Arnall, a dealer at the King 8 Casino in Las Vegas, Nevada, spent 190 hours at the blackjack table, June 22–30, 1977. Ardeth Hardy set the women's mark of 169 hours 47 minutes of continuous dealing during the same period. Both took 5-minute rest breaks within each hour.

Roulette

Longest Run. The longest run on an ungaffed (*i.e.* true) wheel reliably recorded is six successive coups (in No. 10) at El San Juan Hotel, Puerto Rico, on July 9, 1959. The odds with a double zero were 1 in 38^6 or 3,010,936,383 to 1.

Longest Marathon. The longest "marathon" on record is one of 31 days from April 10 to May 11, 1970, at The Casino de Macao, to test the validity or invalidity of certain contentions in 20,000 spins.

Games and Pastimes

Bridge (Contract)

Earliest References. Bridge (corruption of Biritch) is thought to be of Levantine origin, similar games having been played there in the early 1870's. The game was known in London in 1886 under the title of "Biritch or Russian Whist." Whist, first referred to in 1529, was the world's premier card game until 1930. Its rules had been standardized in 1742.

Auction bridge (highest bidder names trump) was introduced in 1904, but was swamped by contract bridge, which was devised by Harold S. Vanderbilt (U.S.) in 1925, and first played on a Caribbean voyage in 1926. The new version became a world-wide craze after the U.S. vs. Great Britain challenge match between Ely Culbertson (born in Rumania, 1891) and Lt.-Col. Walter Thomas More Buller (1886–1938) at Almack's Club, London, September, 1930. The U.S. won the 200-hand match by 4,845 points.

Perfect Deals. The mathematical odds against dealing 13 cards of one suit are 158,753,389,899 to 1, while the odds against receiving a "perfect hand" consisting of all 13 spades are 635,013,559,596 to 1. The odds against each of the 4 players receiving a complete suit (a "perfect deal") are 2,235,197,406,895,366,368,301,559,999 to 1.

Highest Possible Scores (excluding penalties for rules infractions)

Opponents bid 7 of any suit or no trump, doubled and redoubled and vulnerable. Opponents make no trick.		Bid 1 no trump, doubled and redoubled, vulnerable	
Above Line 1st undertrick	400	*Below Line* 1st trick (40×4)	160
12 subsequent under-tricks at 600 each	7,200	*Above Line* 6 overtricks (400×6)	2,400
All Honors	150	2nd game of 2-Game Rubber	*350
		All Honors (4 aces)	150
		Bonus for making redoubled contract	50
	7,750	(Highest Possible Positive Score)	3,110

* In practice, the full bonus of 700 points is awarded after the completion of the second game, rather than 350 after each game.

World Titles. The World Championship (Bermuda Bowl) has been won most often by Italy's "Blue Team" (Squadra Azzurra)

(1957–58–59, 1961–62–63, 1965–66–67, 1969, 1973–74–75), which also won the Olympiad in 1964, 1968 and 1972. Giorgio Belladonna was on all 16 winning teams.

Most Master Points. In 1971, a new World Ranking List based on Master Points was instituted. The leading male player is Giorgio Belladonna (see above) with 1,712 points as of March, 1978, followed by 5 more Italians. The world's leading woman player is Mrs. Rixi Markus (G.B.) with 269 points to March, 1978.

Bridge Marathon. The longest recorded bridge session is one of 180 hours by four students at Edinburgh University, Scotland, April 21–28, 1972.

Checkers

Origins. Checkers, known as draughts in some countries, has origins earlier than chess. It was played in Egypt in the second millenium B.C. The earliest book on the game was by Antonio Torquemada of Valencia, Spain in 1547.

There have been three U.S. *vs.* Great Britain international matches. The earliest, in 1905, was won by the Scottish Masters, 73–34, with 284 draws. The U.S. won in 1927 in New York, 96–20 with 364 draws, and won again in the most recent match, in 1973.

The only man to win 5 British Championships has been Jim Marshall (Fife, Scotland) in 1948–50–52–54–66. The longest tenure of invincibility in freestyle play was that of Melvin Pomeroy (U.S.), who was internationally undefeated from 1914 until his death in 1933.

Longest and Shortest Games. In competition, the prescribed rate of play is not less than 30 moves per hour with the average game lasting about 90 minutes. In 1958 a match between Dr. Marian Tinsley (U.S.) and Derek Oldbury (G.B.) lasted 7½ hours.

The shortest possible game is one of 20 moves composed by Alan M. Beckerson (G.B.) on November 2, 1977.

Most Opponents. Newell W. Banks (b. Detroit, October 10, 1887) played 140 games simultaneously, winning 133 and drawing 7 in Chicago in 1933. His playing time was 145 minutes so averaging about one second per move.

Chess

Origins. The name chess is derived from the Persian word *shah*. It is a descendant of the game *Chaturanga*. The earliest reference is from the Middle Persian Karnamak (*c.* 590–628), though there are grounds for believing its origins are from the 2nd century, owing to the discovery, announced in December, 1972, of two ivory chessmen, in the Uzbek Soviet Republic, datable to that century. The game reached Britain in *c.* 1255. The *Fédération Internationale des Echecs* was established in 1924. There were an estimated 7,000,000 registered players in the U.S.S.R. in 1973.

World Champions. François André Danican, *alias* Philidor (1726–95), of France claimed the title of "world champion" from 1747 until his death. World champions have been generally recognized since 1886. The longest undisputed tenure was 27 years by Dr. Emanuel Lasker (1868–1941) of Germany, from 1894 to 1921. Robert J. (Bobby) Fischer (b. Chicago, March 9, 1943) is reckoned on the officially adopted Elo system to be the greatest Grandmaster of all time. He has an I.Q. of 187 and became at 15 the youngest ever International Grandmaster.

The women's world championship has been most often won by Vera Menchik-Stevenson (1906–44) (G.B.) from 1927 till her death, and was successfully defended a record 7 times. Nona Gaprindashvili (U.S.S.R.) has held the title since 1962, and defended 4 times.

Winning Streak. Bobby Fischer (see above) won 20 games in succession in grandmaster chess from December 2, 1970 (*vs.* Jorge Rubinetti of Argentina) to September 30, 1971 (*vs.* Tigran Petrosian of the U.S.S.R.). Anatoli Karpov (U.S.S.R.) lost only 4.3 per cent of his 597 games to December, 1977.

Longest Games. The most protracted master game on record was one drawn on the 191st move between H. Pilnik (Argentina) and Moshe Czerniak (Israel) at Mar del Plata, Argentina, in April, 1950. The total playing time was 20 hours. A game of 21½ hours, but drawn on the 171st move (average over 7½ minutes per move), was played between Makagonov and Chekhover at Baku, U.S.S.R., in 1945.

The slowest recorded move (before modern rules) was one of 11 hours between Paul Morphy (1837–84), the U.S. champion 1852–1862, and the chessmaster Louis Paulsen.

Marathon. The longest recorded session is one of 158 hours 24 minutes by Lori Daulton, Marian Selby, Charlotte Rugar and Gayle Fields (two separate pairs) from Dinwiddie County Junior High School, Dinwiddie, Virginia, on December 17–23, 1977.

Shortest Game. The shortest recorded game between masters was one of four moves when Lazard (Black) beat Gibaud in a Paris chess café in 1924. The moves were: 1. P–Q4, N–KB3; 2. N–Q2, P–K4; 3. PxP, N–N5; 4. P–KR3, N–K6. White then resigned because if he played 5. PxN there would have followed Q–KR5 check and the loss of his Queen for a Knight by any other move.

Most Opponents. The record for most opponents tackled (with replacements as they are defeated) is held by Branimir Brebrich (Canada) who played 575 games (winning 533, drawing 27 and losing 15) in Edmonton, Alberta, Canada, January 27–28, 1978 in 28 hours of play.

Georges Koltanowski (Belgium, later of U.S.) tackled 56 opponents "blindfold" and won 50, drew 6, lost 0 in 9¾ hours at the Fairmont Hotel, San Francisco, on December 13, 1960.

Cribbage

Origins. The invention of this game (once called "Cribbidge") is credited to the English dramatist John Suckling (1609–42). It is played by an estimated 10 million people in the U.S. alone.

Combinations. Alex E. Cakebread of Welwyn Garden City, England, has computed 12,994,800 different possible crib hands (four cards and turn-up).

Rare Hands. F. Art Skinner of Alberta, Canada, is reported to have had five maximum 29-point hands. Paul Nault of Athol, Massachusetts, had two such hands within eight games in a tournament on March 19, 1977. At Blackpool, England, Derek Hearne dealt two hands of six clubs with the remaining club being the turn-up on February 8, 1976.

Darts

Origins. Darts date from the use by archers of heavily weighted 10-inch throwing arrows for self-defense in close fighting. "Dartes" were used in Ireland in the 16th century, and darts was played on the *Mayflower* by the Pilgrims in 1620. Today, more people in Great Britain (6,000,000) play darts than any other single sport.

Lowest Possible Scores. Under English rules, the lowest number of darts needed to achieve standard scores are: 201, four darts; 301, six darts; 401, seven darts; 501, nine darts; 1,001, seventeen darts. The four- and six-dart "possibles" have been achieved many times, the nine-dart 501 occasionally, but the seventeen-dart 1,001 has never been accomplished. The lowest number of darts thrown for a score of 1,001 is 19 by Cliff Inglis at the Bromfield Men's Club, Devon, England, on November 11, 1975.

Fastest Match. The fastest time taken for a match of 3 games of 301 is 1 minute 58 seconds by Ricky Fusco at the Perivale Residents Association Club, Middlesex, England, on December 30, 1976.

Million-and-One. Eight players from the Highbridge Darts Organisation in England scored 1,000,001 with 43,291 darts in one session on August 26-28, 1978.

Marathon. Ron McFarland, Jim Mote, Bob Scott, and Robin Davis played non-stop (in shifts) for 725 hours 6 minutes at the Rose and Crown Pub, Santa Ana, California, from May 12 to June 12, 1976.

Dominoes

Origins. The National Museum in Baghdad, Iraq, contains artifacts from Ur called "dominoes" dated *c.* 2450 B.C. The game remains unstandardized. Eskimos play with 148 pieces, while the European game uses only 28.

Marathon. The longest session by 2 players is 123 hours 4 minutes by Alan Mannering and David Harrison of Stoke-on-Trent, England, on February 8-13, 1978.

Tiddlywinks

Origins. This game was first espoused by adults in 1955, when Cambridge University (England) issued a challenge to Oxford.

Speed Records. The record for potting 24 winks from a distance of 18 inches is 21.8 seconds by Stephen Williams in May, 1966. Allen R. Astles of the University of Wales potted 10,000 winks in 3 hours 51 minutes 46 seconds in February, 1966.

Marathons. The most protracted game on record is one of 240 hours by six players from St. Anselm's College, Birkenhead, Merseyside, England, August 2-12, 1977.

Gliding

Emanuel Swedenborg (1688-1772) of Sweden made sketches of gliders *c.* 1714.

The earliest man-carrying glider was designed by Sir George Cayley (1773-1857) and carried his coachman (possibly John Appleby) about 500 yards across a valley near Brompton Hall, Yorkshire, England, in the summer of 1853. Gliders now attain speeds of 168 m.p.h. and the Jastrzab acrobatic sailplane is designed to withstand vertical dives at up to 280 m.p.h.

Most World Titles

World individual championships (instituted 1948) have been won 5 times by West Germans.

Hang-Gliding

In the 11th century, the monk Elmer is reported to have flown from the 60-foot-tall tower of Malmesbury Abbey, Wiltshire,

England. The earliest modern pioneer was Otto Lilienthal (1848–96) of Germany who made numerous flights between 1893 and 1896. Professor Francis Rogallo of the U.S. National Space Agency developed a "wing" in the 1950's from his research into space capsule re-entries.

The farthest distance covered in free flight is 103 miles by Gerry Katz (U.S.) in a Pacific Gull Alpine 2 over California, on July 24, 1977.

The greatest height gain was 9,950 feet, recorded by Gerry Katz (U.S.) over Serro Gordo, California, on July 24, 1977.

The greatest altitude from which a hang-glider has descended is 31,600 feet by Bob McCaffrey, 18, who was released from a balloon over the Mojave Desert, California, on November 21, 1976.

Parasailing

The longest reported flight being towed is 15 hours 22 minutes by Douglas Wray (G.B.) over Lake Windermere, England, on May 2, 1977.

GLIDING WORLD RECORDS
(Single-Seaters)

DISTANCE	907.7 miles	Hans-Werner Grosse (W. Germany) in an ASW–12 on April 25, 1972.
DECLARED GOAL FLIGHT	799 miles*	Bruce Drake, David Speight, S. H. "Dick" Georgeson (all N.Z.) all in Nimbus 2s, from Te Anau to Te Ararou, January 14, 1978.
ABSOLUTE ALTITUDE	46,266 feet	Paul F. Bikle, Jr. (U.S.) in a Schweizer SGS-1-23E over Mojave, Calif. (released at 3,963 feet) on Feb. 25, 1961 (also record altitude gain—42,303 feet).
GOAL AND RETURN	1,015.7 miles	Karl H. Striedieck (U.S.) in an ASW–17 from Lock Haven, Penn. to Tennessee on May 9, 1977.
SPEED OVER TRIANGULAR COURSE		
100 km.	102.74 m.p.h.	K. Briegleb (U.S.) in a Kestrel 17 over the U.S. on July 18, 1974.
300 km.	95.95 m.p.h.	Walter Neubert (W. Germany) in a Kestrel 604 over Kenya on March 3, 1972.
500 km.	88.82 m.p.h.	Edward Pearson (G.B.) in a Nimbus 2 over Namibia on November 27, 1976.
750 km.	86.99 m.p.h.*	G. Eckle (W. Germany) in a Nimbus 2 over South Africa on January 8, 1978.
1,000 km.	68.04 m.p.h.*	Hans-Werner Grosse (W. Germany) in an ASW–17 over Australia, on February 17, 1978.

*Awaiting official confirmation

Golf

Origins. Although a stained glass window in Gloucester Cathedral, Scotland, dating from 1350 portrays a golfer-like figure, the earliest mention of golf occurs in a prohibiting law passed by the Scottish Parliament in March, 1457, under which "golff be utterly cryit doune." The Romans had a cognate game called *paganica*, which may have been carried to Britain before 400 A.D. The Chinese National Golf Association claims the game is of Chinese origin from the 3rd or 2nd century B.C. Gutta percha balls succeeded feather balls in 1848, and were in turn succeeded in 1902 by rubber-cored balls, invented in 1899 by Haskell (U.S.). Steel shafts were authorized in 1929.

Clubs

Oldest. The oldest club of which there is written evidence is the Gentleman Golfers (now the Honourable Company of Edinburgh Golfers) formed in March, 1744—10 years prior to the institution of the Royal and Ancient Club of St. Andrews, Fife, Scotland. The oldest existing club in North America is the Royal Montreal Club (1873) and the oldest in the U.S. is St. Andrews, Westchester County, New York (1888). An older claim is by the Foxbury Country Club, Clarion County, Pennsylvania (1887).

Largest. The only club in the world with 15 courses is the Eldorado Golf Club in California. The club with the highest membership in the world is the Wentworth Club, Virginia Water, Surrey, England, with 1,850 members, compared with 1,750 members of the Royal and Ancient Golf Club at St. Andrews (see above).

Courses

Highest. The highest golf course in the world is the Tuctu Golf Club in Morococha, Peru, which is 14,335 feet above sea level at its lowest point. Golf has, however, been played in Tibet at an altitude of over 16,000 feet.

Lowest. The lowest golf course in the world was that of the Sodom and Gomorrah Golfing Society at Kallia, on the northeastern shores of the Dead Sea, 1,250 feet below sea level. The clubhouse was burnt down in 1948 but the game is now played on the nearby Kallia Hotel course.

Longest Hole. The longest hole in the world is the 17th hole (par 6) of 745 yards at the Black Mountain Golf Club, North Carolina. It was opened in 1964. In August, 1927, the 6th hole at Prescott Country Club in Arkansas measured 838 yards.

Largest Green. Probably the largest green in the world is the 5th green at International G.C., Bolton, Massachusetts, with an area greater than 28,000 square feet.

Biggest Bunker. The world's biggest trap is Hell's Half Acre on the 7th hole of the Pine Valley course, New Jersey, built in 1912 and generally regarded as the world's most trying course.

Longest Course. The world's longest course is the 8,101-yard Dub's Dread Golf Club course (par 78) in Piper, Kansas.

Longest "Course." Floyd Satterlee Rood used the whole United States as a course when he played from the Pacific surf to the Atlantic surf from September 14, 1963 to October 3, 1964, in 114,737 strokes. He lost 3,511 balls on the 3,397.7-mile trip.

Lowest Scores

9 holes and 18 holes—Men. The lowest recorded score on any 18-hole course with a par of 70 or more is 55 first achieved by A. E. Smith, the English professional, at Woolacombe on January 1, 1936. The course measured 4,248 yards. The detail was 4, 2, 3, 4, 2, 4, 3, 4, 3=29 out, and 2, 3, 3, 3, 3, 2, 5, 4, 1=26 in.

E. F. Staugaard (U.S.) also carded a 55 on the 6,419-yard Montebello Park (California) Golf Club in 1935.

Nine holes in 25 (4, 3, 3, 2, 3, 3, 1, 4, 2) was recorded by A. J. "Bill" Burke in a round of 57 (32+25) on the 6,389-yard par 71 Normandie course in St. Louis on May 20, 1970. This equalled the score of Daniel E. Cavin (3, 3, 3, 3, 3, 3, 2, 3, 2) on the par 36 2,880-yard Bill Brewer Course, Greggton, Texas, on September 27, 1959.

The United States P.G.A. tournament record for 18 holes is 59 by Al Geiberger (b. September 1, 1937) in the second round of the Danny Thomas Classic, on the 72-par 7,249-yard course at Memphis, Tennessee, on June 10, 1977.

In non-P.G.A. tournaments, Sam Snead had 59 in the Greenbrier Open (now called the Sam Snead Festival), at White Sulphur Springs, West Virginia, on May 16, 1959, and Gary Player (South Africa) (born November 1, 1935) also carded 59 in the second round of the Brazilian Open in Rio de Janeiro on November 29, 1974.

36 holes. The record for 36 holes is 122 (59 + 63) by Sam Snead in the 1959 Greenbrier Open (now called the Sam Snead Festival) (non-P.G.A.) (see above) May 16–17, 1959. Horton Smith (see below) scored 121 (63+58) on a short course on December 21, 1928.

72 holes. The lowest recorded score on a first-class course is 257 (27 under par) by Mike Souchak (born May 10, 1927) in the Texas Open at Brackenridge Park, San Antonio in February, 1955, made up of 60 (33 out and 27 in), 68, 64, 65 (average 64.25 per round), exhibiting, as one critic said, his "up and down form." Horton Smith (1908–63), twice U.S. Masters Champion, scored 245 (63, 58, 61 and 63) for 72 holes on the 4,700-yard course (par 64) at Catalina Country Club, California, to win the Catalina Open on December 21–23, 1928.

The lowest 72 holes in a national championship is 262 by Percy Alliss (1897–1975) of Britain, with 67, 66, 66 and 63 in the Italian Open Championship at San Remo in 1932, and by Liang Huan Lu (b. 1936) (Taiwan) in the 1971 French Open at Biarritz. Kelvin D. G. Nagle (b. December 21, 1920) of Australia shot 261 in the Hong Kong Open in 1961.

Women. The lowest recorded score on an 18-hole course (over 6,000 yards) for a woman is 62 (30+32) by Mary (Mickey) Kathryn Wright (born February 14, 1935), of Dallas, on the Hogan Park Course (6,282 yards) at Midland, Texas, in November, 1964.

Wanda Morgan (b. March 22, 1910) recorded a score of 60 (31 + 29) on the Westgate-on-Sea and Birchington Golf Club course (England) over 18 holes (5,002 yards) on July 11, 1929.

LOW SCORER: In the non-P.G.A. Greenbrier Open in 1959, Sam Snead carded records for 18 holes (59 strokes) and 36 holes (122 strokes).

Highest Round Score. It is recorded that Chevalier von Cittern went round 18 holes at Biarritz, France, in 1888 in 316 strokes—an average of 17.55 shots per hole.

Steven Ward took 222 strokes for the 6,212-yard Pecos Course, Reeves County, Texas, on June 18, 1976—but he was only aged 3 years 286 days.

Highest Single-Hole Scores. The highest score recorded for a single hole in the British Open is 21 by a player in the inaugural meeting at Prestwick in 1860. Double figures have been recorded on the card of the winner only once, when Willie Fernie (1851–1924) scored a 10 at Musselburgh, Lothian, Scotland, in 1883. Ray Ainsley of Ojai, California, took 19 strokes for the par-4 16th hole during the second round of the U.S. Open at Cherry Hills Country Club, Denver, Colorado, on June 10, 1938. Most of the strokes were used in trying to extricate the ball from a brook. Hans Merrell of Mogadore, Ohio, took 19 strokes on the par-3 16th (222 yards) during the third round of the Bing Crosby National Tournament at the Cypress Point course, Del Monte, California, on January 17, 1959.

Most Shots—Women. A woman player in the qualifying round of the Shawnee Invitational for Ladies at Shawnee-on-Delaware, Pennsylvania, in c. 1912, took 166 strokes for the 130-yard 16th hole. Her tee shot went into the Binniekill River and the ball floated. She put out in a boat with her exemplary, but statistically minded, husband at the oars. She eventually beached the ball 1½ miles downstream, but was not yet out of the woods. She had to play through a forest on the home stretch.

Most Rounds in a Day

The greatest number of rounds played on foot in 24 hours is 22 rounds plus 5 holes (401 holes) by Ian Colston, 35, at Bendigo G.C., Victoria, Australia (6,061 yards) on November 27–28, 1971. He covered more than 100 miles.

The most holes played on foot in a week (168 hours) is 1,102 by David Shepardson (U.S.), 17, at Maple Grove Golf Club, Wisconsin, in August, 1976.

Fastest and Slowest Rounds

With such variations in the lengths of courses, speed records, even for rounds under par, are of little comparative value.

Bob Williams at Eugene, Oregon, completed 18 holes (6,010 yds.) in 27 minutes 48.2 seconds in 1971, but this test permitted him to stroke the ball while it was still moving. The record for a still ball is 31 minutes 22 seconds by Len Richardson, the South African Olympic athlete, at Mowbray, Capetown, over a 6,248-yard course in November, 1931.

On June 11, 1976, forty-three players representing Borger High School, Huber, Texas, completed the 18-hole 6,109-yard Huber Golf Course in 10 minutes 11.4 seconds.

The slowest stroke-play-tournament round was one of 6 hours 45 minutes by South Africa in the first round of the 1972 World Cup at the Royal Melbourne Golf Club, Australia. This was a 4-ball medal round, everything holed out.

Longest Drive

In long-driving contests 330 yards is rarely surpassed at sea level.

The world record is 392 yards by a member of the Irish P.G.A., Tommie Campbell, made at Dun Laoghaire, Co. Dublin, in July, 1964.

The United States P.G.A. record is 341 yards by Jack William Nicklaus (born Columbus, Ohio, January 21, 1940), then weighing 206 lbs., in July, 1963.

Bill Calise, 32, won the McGregor contest at Wayne Country Club, New Jersey, on June 20, 1954, with 365 yards.

Valetin Barrios (Spain) drove a ball 568½ yards on an airport runway at Palma, Majorca, on March 7, 1977.

The longest on an ordinary course is 515 yards by Michael Hoke Austin (born February 17, 1910) of Los Angeles, in the U.S. National Seniors Open Championship at Las Vegas, Nevada, on September 25, 1974. Aided by an estimated 35-m.p.h. tailwind, the 6-foot-2-inch 210-lb. golfer drove the ball on the fly to within a yard of the green on the par-4 450-yard 5th hole of the Winterwood Course. The ball rolled 65 yards past the hole.

Arthur Lynskey claimed a drive of 200 yards out and 2 miles down off Pikes Peak, Colorado, on June 28, 1968.

A drive of 2,640 yards (1½ miles) across ice was achieved by an Australian meteorologist named Nils Lied at Mawson Base, Antarctica, in 1962. On the moon, the energy expended on a mundane 300-yard drive would achieve, craters permitting, a distance of a mile.

LONGEST DRIVE (left): Tommie Campbell hit a 392-yard drive in July, 1964.
MOST WINS (right): Byron Nelson won 19 out of 31 tournaments in the 1945 season.

Longest Hitter. The golfer regarded as the longest consistent hitter the game has ever known is the 6-foot-5-inch-tall, 230-lb. George Bayer (U.S.), the 1957 Canadian Open Champion. His longest measured drive was one of 420 yards at the fourth in the Las Vegas Invitational in 1953. It was measured as a precaution against litigation since the ball struck a spectator. Bayer also drove a ball pin high on a 426-yard hole in Tucson, Arizona. Radar measurements show that an 87-m.p.h. impact velocity for a golf ball falls to 46 m.p.h. in 3.0 seconds.

Longest Putt

The longest recorded holed putt in a major tournament was one of 86 feet on the vast 13th green at the Augusta National, Georgia, by Cary Middlecoff (b. January, 1921) in the 1955 Masters Tournament.

Bobby Jones was reputed to have holed a putt in excess of 100 feet on the 5th green in the first round of the 1927 British Open at St. Andrews, Scotland.

Most Tournament Wins

The record for winning tournaments in a single season is 19 (out of 31) by Byron Nelson (born February 4, 1912), of Fort Worth, Texas, in 1945. Of these, 11 were consecutive, including the U.S. Open, P.G.A., Canadian P.G.A. and Canadian Open, from March 16 to August 15. He was a money prize winner in 113 consecutive tournaments.

Mickey Wright (U.S.) won 82 professional tournaments up to June, 1978.

Jack Nicklaus (U.S.) is the only golfer who has won five major titles, including the U.S. Amateur, twice, and a record total 17 major tournaments (1962–78). His remarkable record in the British Open is three firsts, five seconds and two thirds.

Most Titles

U.S. Open	Willie Anderson (1880–1910)	4	1901–03–04–05
	Robert Tyre Jones, Jr. (1902–71)	4	1923–26–29–30
	Ben W. Hogan (b. Aug. 13, 1912)	4	1948–50–51–53
U.S. Amateur	R. T. Jones, Jr.	5	1924–25–27–28–30
British Open	Harry Vardon (1870–1937)	6	1896–98–99, 1903, 1911, 1914
British Amateur	John Ball (1861–1940)	8	1888–90–92–94–99, 1907–10, 1912
P.G.A. Championship (U.S.)	Walter C. Hagen (1892–1969)	5	1921–24–25–26–27
Masters Championship (U.S.)	Jack W. Nicklaus (b. Jan. 21, 1940)	5	1963–65–66–72–75
U.S. Women's Open	Miss Elizabeth (Betsy) Earle-Rawls (b. May 4, 1928)	4	1951–53–57–60
	Miss "Mickey" Wright (b. Feb. 14, 1935)	4	1958–59–61–64
U.S. Women's Amateur	Mrs. Glenna Vare (née Collett) (b. June 20, 1903)	6	1922–25–28–29–30–35

U.S. Open

This championship was inaugurated in 1894. The lowest 72-hole aggregate is 275 (71, 67, 72 and 65) by Jack Nicklaus on the Lower Course (7,015 yards) at Baltusrol Golf Club, Springfield, New Jersey, on June 15–18, 1967, and by Lee Trevino (b. Horizon City, Texas, December 1, 1939) at Oak Hill Country Club, Rochester, New York, on June 13–16, 1968. The lowest score for 18 holes is 63 by Johnny Miller (b. April 29, 1947) of California on the 6,921-yard, par-71 Oakmont (Pennsylvania) course on June 17, 1973.

U.S. Masters

The lowest score in the U.S. Masters (instituted at the 6,980-yard Augusta National Golf Course, Georgia, in 1934) was 271 by Jack Nicklaus in 1965 and Raymond Floyd (born 1942) in 1976. The lowest rounds have been 64 by Lloyd Mangrum (1914–74) (1st round, 1940), Jack Nicklaus (3rd round, 1965), Maurice Bembridge (G.B.) (b. February 21, 1945) (4th round, 1974), and Gary Player (S. Africa) (4th round, 1978).

U.S. Amateur

This championship was inaugurated in 1893. The lowest score for 9 holes is 30 by Francis D. Ouimet (1893–1967) in 1932.

The Open (British)

The Open Championship was inaugurated in 1860 at Prestwick, Strathclyde, Scotland. The lowest score for 9 holes is 29 by Tom Haliburton (Wentworth) and Peter W. Thomson (Australia), in the

LOWEST SCORER (left): Gary Player has scored a record 59 in the non-PGA Brazilian Open (1974), and became the fourth man to shoot 64 in the U.S. Masters (1978). **MOST P.G.A. VICTORIES** (right): Walter Hagen took this title five times from 1921 to 1927.

first round at the Open on the Royal Lytham and St. Anne's course at Lytham St. Anne's, Lancashire, England, on July 10, 1963. Tony Jacklin (G.B., b. July, 1944) also shot a 29 in the first round of the 1970 Open at St. Andrews, Scotland.

The lowest scoring round in the Open itself is 63 by Mark Hayes (U.S., b. July 12, 1949) at Turnberry, Strathclyde, Scotland, in the second round on July 7, 1977. Henry Cotton (G.B.) at Royal St. George's, Sandwich, Kent, England, completed the first 36 holes in 132 (67+65) on June 27, 1934.

The lowest 72-hole aggregate is 268 (68, 70, 65, and 65) by Tom Watson (U.S.) (b. September 4, 1949) at Turnberry, Scotland, on July 9, 1977.

British Amateur

The lowest score for nine holes in the British Amateur Championship (inaugurated in 1885) is 29 by Richard Davol Chapman (born March 23, 1911) of the U.S. at Sandwich in 1948. Michael Francis Bonallack (b. 1934) shot a 61 (32+29) on the 6,905-yard par-71 course at Ganton, Yorkshire, on July 27, 1968, on the 1st 18 of the 36 holes in the final round.

World Cup (formerly Canada Cup)

The World Cup (instituted 1953) has been won most often by the U.S. with 12 victories in 1955–56, 1960–61–62–63–64–66–67–69–71–73. The only men on six winning teams have been Arnold Palmer (b. Sept. 10, 1929) (1960, 62–63–64, 66–67) and Jack Nicklaus (1963–4, 66–67, 71, 73). The only man to take the individual title three times is Jack Nicklaus (U.S.) in 1963–64–71. The lowest aggregate score for 144 holes is 545 by Australia (Bruce Devlin and David Graham) at San Isidro, Buenos Aires, Argentina, on November 12–15, 1970, and the lowest score by an individual winner was 269 by Roberto de Vicenzo, 47, on the same occasion.

Walker Cup

The U.S. versus Great Britain–Ireland series instituted in 1921 (for the Walker Cup since 1922), now biennial, has been won by the U.S. 24½–2½ to date (July, 1978). Joe Carr (G.B.–I.) played in 10 contests (1947–67).

Ryder Trophy

The biennial Ryder Cup (instituted 1927) professional match between the U.S. and G.B., has been won by the U.S. 18½–3½ to date (July, 1978). Billy Casper has the record of winning most matches, with 20 won (1961–75).

Biggest Victory Margin

Randall Colin Vines (b. June 22, 1945) of Australia won the Tasmanian Open in 1968 with a score of 274, with a margin of 16 strokes over the second-place finisher.

Longest Tie

The longest delayed result in any National Open Championship occurred in the 1931 U.S. Open at Toledo, Ohio. George von Elm and Billy Burke tied at 292, then tied the first playoff at 149. Burke won the second playoff by a single stroke after 72 extra holes.

Highest Earnings

The greatest amount ever won in official U.S. P.G.A. golf prizes is $3,349,393 by Jack Nicklaus to the end of 1978.

The record for a year is $362,429 by Tom Watson (U.S.) in 1978.

The highest career earnings by a woman is $813,213 by Kathy Whitworth (b. September 27, 1939) through the end of 1978.

Nancy Lopez (b. January 6, 1957) won a record $189,814 in the 1978 season.

Youngest and Oldest Champions. The youngest winner of the British Open was Tom Morris, Jr. (b. 1850, d. December 25, 1875) at Prestwick, Ayrshire, Scotland, in 1868, aged 18. The youngest winners of the British Amateur title were John Charles Beharrel (b. May 2, 1938) at Troon, Strathclyde, Scotland, on June 2, 1956, and Robert (Bobby) Cole (S. Africa) (b. May 11, 1948) at Carnoustie, Tayside, Scotland on June 11, 1966, both aged 18 years 1 month. The oldest winner of the British Amateur was the Hon. Michael Scott at Hoylake, Cheshire, England, in 1933, when 54. The oldest British Open Champion was "Old Tom" Morris (b. 1821) who was aged 46 when he won in 1867. In modern times, the 1967 champion Roberto de Vicenzo (b. Buenos Aires, Argentina, April 14, 1923) was aged 44 years 93 days. The oldest U.S. Amateur Champion was Jack Westland (born 1905) at Seattle, Washington, in 1952, aged 47.

TOP MONEY WINNER: In 1978, only her second year on the LPGA tour, Nancy Lopez won a record $189,814.

Shooting Your Age

Sam Snead holds the record for shooting the lowest score in professional competition less than the player's age in years with a 64 on the Onion Creek Golf Club, Austin, Texas (par 70) of 6,585 yards in April, 1978, when he was one month short of his 66th birthday.

The oldest player to score his age is C. Arthur Thompson (1869–1975) of Victoria, British Columbia, Canada, who scored 103 on the Uplands course of 6,215 yards when aged 103 in 1973.

The youngest player to score his age is Robert Leroy Klingaman (born October 22, 1914) who shot a 58 when aged 58 on the 5,654-yard course at the Caledonia Golf Club, Fayetteville, Pennsylvania, on August 31, 1973. Bob Hamilton, age 59, shot 59 on the 6,233-yard blue course, Hamilton Golf Club, Evansville, Indiana, on June 3, 1975.

Throwing the Golf Ball

The lowest recorded score for throwing a golf ball around 18 holes (over 6,000 yards) is 82 by Joe Flynn, 21, at the 6,228-yard Port Royal Course, Bermuda, on March 27, 1975.

Most Peripatetic Golfer

George S. Salter of Carmel, California, has played in 116 different "countries" around the world from 1964 to 1977.

Richest Prize

The greatest first place prize money was $100,000 (total purse $500,000) in the 144-hole "World Open" played at Pinehurst, North Carolina, on November 8–17, 1973, won by Miller Barber, 42, of Texas. The World Series of Golf also carries a prize of $100,000.

ACE GOLFER (left): Professional Art Wall, Jr. holds a record for having hit 41 holes-in-one in his career. OLDEST TO SHOOT HIS AGE: C. Arthur Thompson (right) shot a round of 103 in 1973, at age 103.

Largest Tournament

The annual Ford Amateur Golf Tournament in Great Britain had a record 91,000 competitors in 1977.

Holes-in-One

In 1975, *Golf Digest* was notified of 26,267 holes-in-one, so averaging over 71 per day.

Longest. The longest straight hole shot in one is the 10th hole (444 yards) at Miracle Hills Golf Club, Omaha, Nebraska. Robert Mitera achieved a hole-in-one there on October 7, 1965. Mitera, aged 21 and 5 feet 6 inches tall, weighed 165 lbs. A two-handicap player, he normally drove 245 yards. A 50-m.p.h. gust carried his shot over a 290-yard drop-off. The group in front testified to the remaining 154 yards.

The longest dogleg achieved in one is the 480-yard 5th hole at Hope Country Club, Arkansas, by L. Bruce on November 15, 1962.

The women's record is 393 yards by Marie Robie of Wollaston, Massachusetts, on the first hole of the Furnace Brook Golf Club, September 4, 1949.

Most. The greatest number of holes-in-one in a career is 41 by Art Wall, Jr. (born November 23, 1923).

Douglas Porteous, 28, aced 4 holes over 36 consecutive holes—the 3rd and 6th on September 26 and the 5th on September 28 at Ruchill Golf Club, Glasgow, Scotland, and the 6th at the Clydebank and District Golf Club Course on September 30, 1974. Robert Taylor holed the 188-yard 16th hole at Hunstanton, Norfolk, England, on three successive days—May 31, June 1 and 2, 1974. Joe Lucius, 59, aced the 138-yard 15th at the Mohawk Golf Club, Tiffin, Ohio, for the eighth time on November 16, 1974.

Consecutive. There is no recorded instance of a golfer performing three consecutive holes-in-one, but there are at least 15 cases of "aces" being achieved in two consecutive holes of which the greatest was Norman L. Manley's unique "double albatross" on two par-4 holes (330-yard 7th and 290-yard 8th) on the Del Valle Country Club course, Saugus, California, on September 2, 1964.

The only woman ever to card consecutive aces is Sue Prell, on the 13th and 14th holes at Chatswood Golf Club, Sydney, Australia, on May 29, 1977.

The closest recorded instances of a golfer getting 3 consecutive holes-in-one were by the Rev. Harold Snider (b. July 4, 1900) who aced the 8th, 13th and 14th holes of the par-3 Ironwood course in Phoenix, Arizona, on June 9, 1976, and Dr. Joseph Boydstone on the 3rd, 4th and 9th at Bakersfield G.C., California on October 10, 1962.

Youngest and Oldest. The youngest golfer recorded to have shot a hole-in-one was Tommy Moore (6 years 36 days) of Hagerstown, Maryland, on the 145-yard 4th at the Woodbrier Golf Course, Martinsburg, West Virginia, on March 8, 1968. The oldest golfers to have performed the feat were George Miller, 93, at the 11th at Anaheim Golf Club, California, on December 4, 1970, and Charles Youngman, 93, at the Tam O'Shanter Club, Toronto, in 1971.

Greyhound Racing

Earliest Meeting. In September, 1876, a greyhound meeting was staged at Hendon, North London, England, with a railed hare operated by a windlass. Modern greyhound racing originated with the perfecting of the mechanical hare by Owen P. Smith at Emeryville, California, in 1919.

Fastest Dog. The highest speed at which any greyhound has been timed is 41.72 m.p.h. (410 yards in 20.1 secs.) by *The Shoe* for a track record at Richmond, New South Wales, Australia, on April 25, 1968. It is estimated that he covered the last 100 yards in 4.5 seconds or at 45.45 m.p.h. The fastest *photo*-timing is 29.16 seconds over 500 meters or 38.35 m.p.h. by *Glen Rock* on May 19, 1977, and *Balinska Band* on June 25, 1977. The fastest photo-timing over hurdles is 29.79 seconds (37.54 m.p.h.) by *Bansha Pride* in 1975.

Winning Streak. An American greyhound, *Real Huntsman*, won a world record 28 consecutive victories in 1950–51.

Gymnastics

Earliest References. A primitive form of gymnastics was widely practiced in ancient Greece during the period of the ancient Olympic Games (776 B.C. to 393 A.D.), but the modern sport developed after *c.* 1780.

World Championships. The greatest number of individual titles won by a man in the World Championships is 10 by Boris Shakhlin (U.S.S.R.) between 1954 and 1964. He was also on three winning teams. The women's record is 10 individual wins and 5 team titles by Larissa Semyonovna Latynina (born December 27, 1934, retired 1966) of the U.S.S.R., between 1956 and 1964.

Olympic Games. Japan has won the most men's titles with 5 victories (1960, 1964, 1968, 1972, 1976). The U.S.S.R. has won 7 women's team titles (1952–1976).

The only man to win six individual gold medals is Boris Shakhlin (U.S.S.R.), with one in 1956, four (two shared) in 1960 and one in 1964. He was also a member of the winning Combined Exercises team in 1956.

The most successful woman has been Vera Caslavska-Odlozil (Czechoslovakia), with seven individual gold medals, three in 1964 and four (one shared) in 1968. Larissa Latynina of the U.S.S.R. won six individual and three team gold medals, five silver, and four bronze for an all-time record total of 18 Olympic medals.

Nadia Comaneci (b. 1961, Rumania) became the first gymnast to be awarded a perfect score of 10.00 in the Olympic Games, in the 1976 Montreal Olympics. She ended the competition with a total of seven such marks (four on the uneven parallel bars, three on the balance beam). Nelli Kim (U.S.S.R., b. July 29, 1957) was also awarded two perfect scores during the same competition.

Youngest International Competitor. Anita Jokiel (Poland) was aged 11 years 2 days when she competed at Brighton, East Sussex, England, on December 6, 1977.

World Cup. In the first World Cup Competition in London in 1975, Ludmilla Tourisheva (now Mrs. Valery Borzov) (born October 7, 1952) of the U.S.S.R. won all five available gold medals.

MOST MEDALS: Boris Shakhlin (left) is the only man ever to win 6 Olympic individual gold medals.

GYMNASTIC PERFECTION: Nelli Kim (left) and Nadia Comaneci (right) were each awarded unprecedented perfect scores at the 1976 Olympic Games.

Chinning the Bar. The record for 2-arm chins from a dead hang position is 106 by William D. Reed (University of Pennsylvania) on June 23, 1969. William Aaron Vaught (b. 1959) did 20 one-arm chin-ups at Finch's Gymnasium, Houston, Texas, on January 3, 1976. The women's record for one-handed chin-ups is 27 in Hermann's Gym, Philadelphia, in 1918, by Lillian Leitzel (Mrs. Alfredo Codona) (U.S.), who was killed in Copenhagen, Denmark, on March 15, 1931. Her total would be unmatched by any male, but it is doubtful if they were achieved from a "dead hang" position. It is believed that only one person in 100,000 can chin a bar one-handed. Francis Lewis (born 1896) of Beatrice, Nebraska, in May, 1914, achieved 7 consecutive chins using only the middle finger of his left hand. His bodyweight was 158 lbs.

Rope Climbing. The U.S. Amateur Athletic Union records are tantamount to world records: 20 feet (hands alone) 2.8 secs., Don Perry, at Champaign, Illinois, on April 3, 1954; 25 feet (hands alone), 4.7 secs., Garvin S. Smith at Los Angeles, on April 19, 1947.

Parallel Bar Dips. Tommy Gildert of Burnley, Lancashire, England, performed a record 220 consecutive dips on the parallel bars on June 1, 1978.

Push-Ups. Henry C. Marshall (b. 1946) did 7,650 consecutive push-ups in 3 hours 55 minutes, on his way to 9,075 in 5 hours, in San Antonio, Texas, on September 5, 1977. Among his many push-up achievements, Marshall has done 139 push-ups on his right arm in 67 seconds and 112 on his left in 57 seconds, both on November 30, 1974.

Troy Lapic (b. March 30, 1966), of Corsicana, Texas, did 1,834 push-ups, the most in 30 minutes, on August 19, 1978. Dale Pearman of Lake Dallas, Texas, did 208 fingertip push-ups in 80 seconds on August 26, 1976. Robert Goldman of Arverne, New York, did 80 consecutive handstand push-ups in 43 seconds on August 31, 1978.

Sit-Ups. The greatest recorded number of consecutive sit-ups on a hard surface without feet pinned or knees bent is 26,000 in 11 hours 44 minutes by Angel Bustamonte (b. February 28, 1959) in Sacramento, California, on December 17, 1977. On November 20, 1975, Dr. David G. Jones recorded 123 sit-ups at Bolling A.F.B., Maryland, in 2 minutes under the same conditions.

Jumping Jacks. The greatest number of side-straddle hops is 20,088, performed in 4 hours 30 minutes (more than 1 per sec.) by Chris B. Luther (b. 1947) at Beechwood School, Fort Lewis, Washington on November 12, 1977.

Vertical Jump. The greatest height reached in a vertical jump (the difference between standing and jumping fingertip reach) is 42 inches by David Thompson (6 feet 4 inches) of North Carolina in 1972. Higher jumps reported by athletes Franklin Jacobs (U.S.) and Greg Joy (Canada) were probably made with an initial run. Olympic Pentathlon champion Mary E. Peters (G.B.) reportedly jumped 30 inches in California in 1972.

Greatest Tumbler. James Chelich (b. Fairview, Alberta, Canada, March 12, 1957) performed 8,450 forward rolls in 8.3 miles on September 21, 1974.

Ian Michael Miles (born July 6, 1960) of Corsham, Wiltshire, England, made a successful diving front somersault with a tuck over 33 men at Harrogate, North Yorkshire on July 27, 1977.

Rope Jumping. The greatest number of turns ever performed without a break or fault is 50,180 in 6 hours by Rabbi Barry Silberg in Milwaukee, Wisconsin on July 30, 1978.

Other rope-jumping records made without a break:

Most turns in one jump	5	Katsumi Suzuki	Saitama, Japan May 29, 1975
Most turns in 1 minute	290	Brian D. Christensen	East Ridge, Tenn. May 30, 1978
Most turns in 10 seconds	108	A. Rayner	Wakefield, Eng. June 28, 1978
Most doubles (with cross)	56	K. A. Brooks	Gosford, N.S.W., Aust. Jan. 16, 1976
Double turns	6,851	Katsumi Suzuki (Japan)	Tokyo July 4, 1976
Treble turns	381	Katsumi Suzuki (Japan)	Saitama May 29, 1975
Quadruple turns	51	Katsumi Suzuki (Japan)	Saitama May 29, 1975
Duration	1,264 miles	Tom Morris (Aust.)	Brisbane-Cairns 1963
Most children, single rope (11 turns)	52	Ogallala Girls Team	Nebraska May 14, 1977

SUNDAY THE RABBI JUMPED ROPE: Rabbi Barry Silberg of Milwaukee jumped 50,180 times without a break or a fault on July 30, 1978.

Largest Gymnasium. The world's largest gymnasium is Yale University's Payne Whitney Gymnasium at New Haven, Connecticut, completed in 1932 and valued at $18,000,000. The building, known as the "Cathedral of Muscle," has nine stories with wings of five stories each. It is equipped with 4 basketball courts, 3 rowing tanks, 28 squash courts, 12 handball courts, a roof jogging track and a 25-yard by 14-yard swimming pool on the first floor and a 55-yard-long pool on the third floor.

Largest Crowd. The largest recorded crowd was some 18,000 people who packed the Forum, Montreal, Canada for the finals of the women's individual apparatus competitions at the XXI Olympic Games on July 22, 1976.

Comparable audiences are reported at the Shanghai Stadium, People's Republic of China.

Handball (Court)

Origin. Handball is a game of ancient Celtic origin. In the early 19th century only a front wall was used, but later side and back walls were added. The court is now standardized 60 feet by 30 feet in Ireland, Ghana and Australia, and 40 feet by 20 feet in Canada, Mexico and the U.S. The game is played with both a hard and soft ball in Ireland, and a soft ball only elsewhere.

The earliest international contest was in New York City in 1887, between the champions of the U.S. and Ireland.

HANDBALL MASTER:
Jim Jacobs of New York
City has won a total of 12
U.S. National titles.

Championship. World championships were inaugurated in New York in October, 1964, with competitors from Australia, Canada, Ireland, Mexico and the U.S. The U.S. is the only nation to have won twice, with victories in 1964 and 1967 (shared).

In November, 1967, Canada and the U.S. shared the team title and in October, 1970, it was won by Ireland.

Most Titles. The most successful player in the U.S.H.A. National Four-Wall Championships has been James Jacobs (U.S.), who won a record 6 singles titles (1955–56–57–60–64–65) and shared in 6 doubles titles (1960–62–63–65–67–68). Martin Decatur has also shared in 6 doubles titles (1962–63–65–67–68–75), 5 of these with Jacobs as his partner.

Handball (Field)

Origins. Field handball was first played c. 1895. The earliest international match was when Sweden beat Denmark on March 8, 1935. It was introduced into the Olympic Games at Berlin in 1936 as an 11-a-side outdoor game, but when reintroduced in 1972 it was an indoor game with 7-a-side, which has been the standard team size since 1952. Field handball is played somewhat like soccer but with hands instead of feet.

By 1977 there were some 70 countries affiliated with the International Handball Federation, a World Cup competition, and an estimated 10,000,000 participants.

Olympic Games. The U.S.S.R. won both men's and women's titles at the competition in Montreal in 1976.

World Titles. The most victories in the world championship (instituted 1938) competition are by Rumania with four men's and three women's titles from 1956 to 1974.

Harness Racing

Origins. Trotting races were held in Valkenburg, Netherlands, in 1554. In England the trotting gait (the simultaneous use of the diagonally opposite legs) was first recorded in England *c.* 1750. The sulky first appeared in harness racing in 1829. Pacers thrust out their fore and hind legs simultaneously on one side.

Highest Price. The highest price paid for a trotter is $3,000,000 for *Nevele Pride* by the Stoner Creek Stud of Lexington, Kentucky, from Louis Resnick and Nevele Acres in 1969. The highest for a pacer is $3,600,000 for *Nero* in March, 1976.

Greatest Winnings. The greatest amount won by a trotting horse is $1,960,945 by *Bellino II* (France) to retirement in 1977. The record for a pacing horse is $1,201,470 by *Albatross*, who was retired to stud in December, 1972.

RECORDS AGAINST TIME

TROTTING

World (mile track)	1:54.8	Nevele Pride (U.S.), Indianapolis	Aug. 31, 1969

PACING

World (mile track)	1:52.0	Steady Star (Canada), Lexington, Ky.	Oct. 1, 1971

RECORDS SET IN RACES

Trotting	1:55.6	Noble Victory (U.S.) at Du Quoin, Ill.	Aug. 31, 1966
	1:55.6	Green Speed (U.S.) at Du Quoin, Ill.	Sept. 3, 1977
Pacing	1:53.2	Warm Breeze (U.S.) at Sacramento, California	June, 1977

Most Successful Driver

The most successful sulky driver in North America has been Herve Filion (Canada) (b. Quebec, February 1, 1940) who reached a record of 6,282 wins by the end of the 1977 season, after a record 637 victories in the 1974 season. Filion won the North American championship for the ninth time in 1977.

William Haughton has won a record $25,400,000 in his career to the end of 1977.

Hockey

Origins. There is pictorial evidence of hockey being played on ice in the Netherlands in the 17th century. The game probably was first played in 1855 at Kingston, Ontario, Canada, but Halifax also lays claim to priority.

The International Ice Hockey Federation was founded in 1908. The National Hockey League was inaugurated in 1917. The World Hockey Association was formed in 1971.

Olympic Games. Canada has won the Olympic title six times (1920–24–28–32–48–52) and the world title 19 times, the last being at Geneva in 1961. The longest Olympic career is that of Richard Torriani (Switzerland) from 1928 to 1948. The most gold medals won by any player is three; this was achieved by four U.S.S.R. players in the 1964–68–72 Games—Vitaliy Davidov, Aleksandr Ragulin, Anatoliy Firssov and Viktor Kuzkin. Davidov and Ragulin had played on nine World Championship teams prior to the 1972 Games.

Stanley Cup. This cup, presented by the Governor-General Lord Stanley (original cost $48.67), became emblematic of world professional team supremacy 33 years after the first contest at Montreal in 1893. It has been won most often by the Montreal Canadiens, with 21 wins in 1916, 1924, 1930, 1931, 1944, 1946, 1953, 1956, 1957, 1958, 1959, 1960, 1965, 1966, 1968, 1969, 1971, 1973, 1976, 1977 and 1978. Henri Richard played in his eleventh finals in 1973.

Longest Match. The longest match was 2 hours 56 minutes 30 seconds when the Detroit Red Wings eventually beat the Montreal Maroons 1–0 in the 17th minute of the sixth period of overtime at the Forum, Montreal, at 2:25 a.m. on March 25, 1936.

Longest Career. Gordie Howe skated a record 25 years for the Detroit Red Wings from 1946–47 through the 1970–71 season, playing in a record total of 1,687 N.H.L. games. During that time he also set records for most career goals, assists, and scoring points, and collected 500 stitches in his face. After leaving the Red Wings, he has played for 5 more seasons with the Houston Aeros and the New England Whalers of the World Hockey Association.

Most Consecutive Games. Garry Unger, playing for Toronto, Detroit and St. Louis, has skated in 803 consecutive games without a miss—10 complete seasons from 1968–69 through the end of 1977–78. The most consecutive complete games by a goaltender is 502, set by Glenn Hall (Detroit, Chicago), beginning in 1955 and ending when he suffered a back injury in a game against Boston on November 7, 1962.

Longest Season. The only man ever to play 82 games in a 78-game season is Ross Lonsberry. He began the 1971–72 season with the Los Angeles Kings where he played 50 games. Then, in January, he was traded to the Philadelphia Flyers (who had played only 46 games at the time) where he finished out the season (32 more games).

Dennis Owchar (with Pittsburgh and Colorado) and Jerry Butler (with St. Louis and Toronto) played 82 games in an 80-game season in 1977–78.

Most Wins and Losses

The Montreal Canadiens had the winningest season in N.H.L. history in 1976–77. They ended the regular 80-game season with a record 132 points earned, with an all-time record of 60 victories and 12 ties against only 8 losses.

The Washington Capitols set the record for seasonal losses with 67 in their maiden season in the league (1974–75). They won only 8 games.

Longest Winning Streak. In the 1929–30 season, the Boston Bruins won 14 straight games. The longest a team has ever gone without a defeat is 28 games, set by Montreal from December 18, 1977, to February 20, 1978 (23 wins, 5 ties).

Longest Losing Streak. The Washington Capitols went from February 18 to March 26, 1975, without gaining a point—a total of 17 straight defeats. The longest time a team has gone without a win was when the Kansas City Scouts played 27 games before scoring a victory. Starting February 12, 1976, they lost 21 games and tied 6 games before ending the drought on April 4, 1976.

Team Scoring

Most Goals. The greatest number of goals recorded in a World Championship match has been 47–0 when Canada beat Denmark on February 12, 1949.

The Boston Bruins set all-time records for goal production in the 1970–71 season with a total of 399. Added to a record 697 assists they tallied a record total of 1,096 points. One line alone (Esposito, Hodge, Cashman) accounted for 336 points—a record itself.

Guy Lafleur, Steve Shutt, and Jacques Lemaire of the Montreal Canadiens produced a total of 150 goals in the 1976–77 season—a record for a single line.

The N.H.L. record for both teams is 21 goals, scored when the Montreal Canadiens beat the Toronto St. Patricks at Montreal 14–7 on January 10, 1920. The most goals ever scored by one team in a single game was set by the Canadiens, when they defeated the Quebec Bulldogs on March 3, 1920 by a score of 16–3.

The Detroit Red Wings scored 15 consecutive goals without an answering tally when they defeated the New York Rangers 15–0 on January 23, 1944.

Fastest Scoring. Toronto scored 8 goals against the New York Americans in 4 minutes 52 seconds on March 19, 1938.

The fastest goals that have ever been scored from the opening whistle both came at 6 seconds of the first period: by Henry Boucha of the Detroit Red Wings on January 28, 1973, against Montreal; and by Jean Pronovost of the Pittsburgh Penguins on March 25, 1976, against St. Louis. Claude Provost of the Canadiens scored a goal against Boston after 4 seconds of the opening of the second period on November 9, 1957.

Kim D. Miles scored a goal after only 3 seconds of play for the University of Guelph, playing the University of Western Ontario on February 11, 1975.

The fastest scoring record is held by Bill Mosienko (Chicago) who scored 3 goals in 21 seconds against the New York Rangers on March 23, 1952.

Gus Bodnar (Toronto Maple Leafs) scored a goal against the New York Rangers at 15 seconds of the first period of *his first N.H.L. game* on October 30, 1943. Later in his career, while with Chicago, Bodnar again entered the record book when he assisted on all 3 of Bill Mosienko's quick goals.

HIGH SCORING CENTER: Phil Esposito (left) (Boston Bruins) put in a record 76 goals in the 1970–71 regular season. Added to his 76 assists, he totaled 152 points, also an N.H.L. record.

Individual Scoring

Most Goals and Points. The career record in the N.H.L. for goals is 786 by Gordie Howe of the Detroit Red Wings. Howe scored 1,809 points in his N.H.L. career, with 1,023 assists.

Reggie Leach (Philadelphia Flyers) scored a total of 80 goals in the 1975–76 season including the playoffs.

Phil Esposito (Boston Bruins) scored 76 goals on a record 550 shots in the 1970–71 regular season. Esposito also holds the record for most points in a season at 152 (76 goals, 76 assists), set in the same season.

Phil Esposito has also scored 100 or more points in 6 different seasons, and 50 or more goals in 5 consecutive years. Bobby Orr had 6 *consecutive* 100-or-more-point seasons from 1969–70 to 1974–75. Bobby Hull (Chicago) had five 50-or-more-goal years when he left the N.H.L.

Anders Hedberg (born in Sweden, February 25, 1951) set a W.H.A. mark, scoring 83 goals for the Winnipeg Jets in 1976–77.

The most goals ever scored in one game is 7 by Joe Malone of the Quebec Bulldogs against the Toronto St. Patricks on January 31, 1920. Four different men have scored 4 goals in one period—Harvey Jackson (Toronto), Max Bentley (Chicago), Clint Smith (Chicago), and Red Berenson (St. Louis).

The most points scored in one N.H.L. game is 10, a record set by Darryl Sittler of the Toronto Maple Leafs, on February 7, 1976, against the Boston Bruins. He had 6 goals and 4 assists.

Jim Harrison, playing for Alberta, set a W.H.A. record for points with 10 (3 goals, 7 assists) against Toronto on January 30, 1973.

In 1921–22, Harry (Punch) Broadbent of the Ottawa Senators scored 25 goals in 16 consecutive games to set an all-time "consecutive game goal-scoring streak" record.

Most Assists. Bobby Orr of Boston assisted on 102 goals in the 1970–71 season for a record. His average of 1.31 assists per game is also a league record.

The most assists recorded in one game is 7 by Billy Taylor of Detroit on March 16, 1947 against Chicago. Detroit won 10–6.

Most 3-Goal Games. In his 15-year N.H.L. career, Bobby Hull of Chicago scored 3 or more goals in 28 games. Four of these were 4-goal efforts. The term "hat-trick" properly applies when 3 goals are scored consecutively by one player in a game without interruption by either an answering score by the other team or a goal by any other player on his own team. In general usage, a "hat-trick" is any 3-goal effort by a player in one game.

Goaltending

The longest any goalie has gone without a defeat is 33 games, a record set by Gerry Cheevers of Boston in 1971–72. The longest a goalie has ever kept successive opponents scoreless is 461 minutes 29 seconds by Alex Connell of the Ottawa Senators in 1927–28. He registered 6 consecutive shutouts in this time.

The most shutouts ever recorded in one season is 22 by George Hainsworth of Montreal in 1928–29 (this is also a team record). This feat is even more remarkable considering that the season was only 44 games long at that time, compared to the 80-game season currently used.

Terry Sawchuk registered a record 103 career shutouts in his 20 seasons in the N.H.L. He played for Detroit, Boston, Toronto, Los Angeles, and the New York Rangers during that time. He also appeared in a record 971 games.

Most Penalties

The most any team has been penalized in one season is the 1,980 minutes assessed against the Philadelphia Flyers in 1975–76.

A record total of 48 different penalties were whistled on March 31,

MOST ASSISTS: Bobby Orr, star defenseman of the Boston Bruins, assisted on 102 goals in 1970–71. This was an average of 1.31 assists per game.

1976 when Detroit played Toronto at Detroit. A record number of minutes were assessed against the New York Rangers and the St. Louis Blues in St. Louis on December 14, 1974. New York was penalized 113 minutes (9 minors, 7 majors, 4 misconducts and 2 game misconducts). St. Louis received 143 minutes in penalties (9 minors, 7 majors, 6 misconducts and 3 game misconducts).

Bryan Watson (Montreal, Detroit, California, Pittsburgh, St. Louis and Washington) has amassed a record total of 2,176 penalty minutes in 858 games over 13 seasons, and he is still playing.

Dave Schultz of Philadelphia was called for a record 472 minutes in the 1974–75 season. Schultz averaged a record 346 minutes per year in penalties from 1972–73 through 1975–76 (1,386 minutes total).

Jim Dorey of the Toronto Maple Leafs set an all-time record in Toronto on October 16, 1968, in a game against the Pittsburgh Penguins. He was whistled down for a total of 9 penalties in the game, 7 of which came in the second period (also a record). The 4 minor penalties, 2 major penalties, 2 10-minute misconducts, and 1 game misconduct added up to a record total of 48 minutes for one game.

Penalty Shots. Armand Mondou of the Montreal Canadiens was the first player in the N.H.L. to attempt a penalty shot on November 10, 1934. He did not score. Since then, about 40 per cent of those awarded have resulted in goals. The most penalty shots called in a single season was 29 in 1934–35.

Fastest Player. The highest speed measured for any player is 29.7 m.p.h. for Bobby Hull (Chicago Black Hawks) (b. January 3, 1939). The highest puck speed is also attributed to Hull, whose left-handed slap shot has been measured at 118.3 m.p.h.

FAST-MOVING SCORER: In addition to his career record 28 "hat-tricks," Bobby Hull has also been hailed as the fastest man on ice at 29.7 m.p.h. His slap shot has been clocked at 118.3 m.p.h.

Horse Racing

Origins. Horsemanship was an important part of the Hittite culture of Anatolia, Turkey, dating from about 1400 B.C. The 33rd ancient Olympic Games of 648 B.C. featured horse racing. The earliest horse race recorded in England was one held in *c.* 210 A.D. at Netherby, Yorkshire, among Arabians brought to Britain by Lucius Septimius Severus (146–211 A.D.), Emperor of Rome. The oldest race still being run annually is the Lanark Silver-Bell, instituted in Scotland by William Lion (1143–1214). Organized horse racing began in New York State at least as early as March, 1668.

The original Charleston Jockey Club, Virginia, was the first in the world, organized in 1734. Racing colors (silks) became compulsory in 1889.

Racecourses. The world's largest racecourse is the Newmarket course in England (founded 1636), on which the Beacon Course, the longest of the 19 courses, is 4 miles 397 yards long and the Rowley Mile is 167 feet wide. The border between Suffolk and Cambridgeshire runs through the Newmarket course. The world's largest racecourse grandstand was opened in 1968 at Belmont Park, Long Island, N.Y., at a cost of $30,700,000. It is 110 feet tall, 440 yards long and contains 908 mutuel windows. The greatest seating capacity at any racetrack is 40,000 at the Atlantic City Audit, New Jersey. The world's smallest is the Lebong racecourse, Darjeeling, West Bengal, India (altitude 7,000 feet), where the complete lap is 481 yards. It was laid out *c.* 1885 and used as a parade ground.

Longest Race

The longest recorded horse race was one of 1,200 miles in Portugal, won by *Emir*, a horse bred from Egyptian-bred Blunt Arab stock. The holder of the world's record for long distance racing and speed is *Champion Crabbet*, who covered 300 miles in 52 hours 33 minutes, carrying 245 lbs., in 1920.

In 1831, Squire George Osbaldeston (1787–1866), M.P. of East Retford, England, covered 200 miles in 8 hours 42 minutes at Newmarket, using 50 mounts, so averaging 22.99 m.p.h.

Most Entrants. The most horses entered in a single race was 66, in the Grand National Steeplechase of March 22, 1929, held at Aintree, England. The record for flat racing is 58 in the Lincolnshire Handicap in England, on March 13, 1948.

Victories. The horse with the best recorded win-loss record was *Kincsem*, a Hungarian mare foaled in 1874, who was unbeaten in 54 races (1876–79), including the English Goodwood Cup of 1878.

Camarero, owned by Don José Coll Vidal of Puerto Rico, foaled in 1951, had a winning streak of 56 races, 1953–55, and 73 wins in 77 starts altogether.

Greatest Winnings. The greatest amount ever won by a horse is $1,977,896 by *Kelso* (foaled in 1957) in the U.S., between 1959 and his retirement on March 10, 1966. In 63 races he won 39, came in second in 12 and third in 2.

TALLEST RACEHORSE: "Fort d'Or" stands 18.2 hands. He is owned by Lady Elizabeth Nugent of England (who was born in Ireland).

The most won by a mare is $1,535,443 by *Dahlia*, from 1972 to 1976.

The most won in a year is $860,404 by *Secretariat* in 1973. His total winnings were $1,316,808 in two seasons.

Triple Crown. Eleven horses have won all three races in one season which constitute the American Triple Crown (Kentucky Derby, Preakness Stakes and the Belmont Stakes). This feat was first achieved by *Sir Barton* in 1919, and most recently by *Seattle Slew* in 1977 and *Affirmed* in 1978.

The only Triple Crown winner to sire another winner was *Gallant Fox*, the 1930 winner, who sired *Omaha*, who won in 1935.

Tallest. The tallest horse ever to race is *Fort d'Or*, owned by Lady Elizabeth (Eliza) Nugent (*née* Guinness) of Berkshire, England, which stands 18.2 hands. He was foaled in April, 1963.

Most Valuable Horse

The most expensive horse ever is Triple Crown winner *Seattle Slew* (foaled 1974). A half share in *Slew* was sold for $6,000,000 in February, 1978.

In February, 1973, the 3-year-old colt *Secretariat* was syndicated in 32 shares, valued at $190,000 each. It has been estimated that, had the syndication taken place on his retirement in late 1973, he could have been sold at nearly $13,000,000.

The highest price for a yearling is $1,500,000 for a colt by *Secretariat* out of *Charming Alibi*, subsequently named *Canadian Bound*, bought at Keeneland, Kentucky, on July 20, 1976.

Horses

Speed Records

Distance	Time	m.p.h.	Name	Course	Date
¼ mile	20.8s.	43.26	Big Racket (Mex.)	Mexico City, Mex.	Feb. 5, 1945
½ mile	44.4s.	40.54	Sonido (Ven.)	‡Caracas, Ven.	June 28, 1970
⅝ mile	53.6s.	41.98†	Indigenous (G.B.)	‡*Epsom, England	June 2, 1960
	53.89s.	41.75††	Raffingora (G.B.)	‡*Epsom, England	June 5, 1970
	55.4s.	40.61	Zip Pocket (U.S.)	Phoenix, Arizona	Apr. 22, 1967
¾ mile	1m. 06.2s.	40.78	Broken Tendril (G.B.)	*Brighton, England	Aug. 6, 1929
Mile	1m. 07.2s.	40.18	Grey Papa (U.S.)	Longacres, Wash.	Sept. 4, 1972
	1m. 31.8s.	39.21	Soueida (G.B.)	*Brighton, England	Sept. 19, 1963
	1m. 31.8s.	39.21	Loose Cover (G.B.)	*Brighton, England	June 9, 1966
	1m. 32.2s.	39.04	Dr. Fager (U.S.)	Arlington, Ill.	Aug. 24, 1968
1¼ miles	1m. 57.4s.	38.33	Double Discount	Arcadia, Calif.	Oct. 9, 1977
1½ miles	2m. 23.0s.	37.76	Fiddle Isle (U.S.)	Arcadia, Calif.	Mar. 21, 1970
2 miles**	3m. 15.0s.	36.93	Polazel (G.B.)	Salisbury, England	July 8, 1924
2¼ miles	4m. 14.6s.	35.35	Miss Grillo (U.S.)	Pimlico, Md.	Nov. 12, 1948
3 miles	5m. 15.0s.	34.29	Farragut (Mex.)	Aguascalientes, Mex.	Mar. 9, 1941

* Course downhill for ¼ of a mile.

** A more reliable modern record is 3m. 16.75 secs. by *Il Tempo* (N.Z.) at Trentham, Wellington, New Zealand, on January 17, 1970.

† Hand-timed.

†† Electrically-timed.

‡ Straight courses.

Dead Heats

There is no recorded case in turf history of a quintuple dead heat. The nearest approach was in the Astley Stakes, at Lewes, England, on August 6, 1880, when *Mazurka, Wandering Nun* and *Scobell* triple dead-heated for first place, just ahead of *Cumberland* and *Thora*, who dead-heated for fourth place. Each of the five jockeys thought he had won. The only three known examples of a quadruple dead heat were between *Honest Harry, Miss Decoy*, a filly by *Beningbrough* (later named *Young Daffodil*) and *Peteria* at Bogside, England, on June 7, 1808; between *Defaulter, The Squire of Malton, Reindeer* and *Pulcherrima* in the Omnibus Stakes at The Hoo, England, on April 26, 1851; and between *Overreach, Lady Go-Lightly, Gamester* and *The Unexpected* at the Houghton Meeting at Newmarket, England, on October 22, 1855.

Since the introduction of the photo-finish, the highest number of horses in a dead heat has been three, on several occasions.

Funeral Wreath. The largest floral piece honoring a horse was the tribute to the racehorse *Ruffian*, an 8½-foot-high, 8-foot-wide horseshoe made of 1,362 white carnations. It was made by Jay W. Becker Florist Inc. of Floral Park, New York, and decorated the grave of the horse in the infield at Belmont Race Track where she was buried in July, 1975.

Jockeys

The most successful jockey of all time is Willie Shoemaker (b. weighing 2½ lbs. on August 19, 1931) now weighing 98 lbs. and standing 4 feet 11½ inches, who beat Johnny Longden's lifetime record of 6,032 winners on September 7, 1970. From April, 1949, to the end of 1977 he rode 7,331 winners from some 30,939 mounts. His winnings have aggregated some $64,789,155.

MOST SUCCESSFUL RIDER: Willie Shoemaker in a familiar position—first across the finish line at the Kentucky Derby.

Chris McCarron (U.S.), 19, won a total of 546 races in 1974.

The greatest amount ever won by any jockey in a year is $6,188,353 by Darrel McHargue (b. 1954) in the U.S. in 1978.

The oldest jockey was Levi Barlingame (U.S.), who rode his last race at Stafford, Kansas, in 1932, aged 80. The youngest jockey was Frank Wootton (English Champion jockey 1909–12), who rode his first winner in South Africa aged 9 years 10 months. The lightest recorded jockey was Kitchener (died 1872), who won the Chester Cup in England on *Red Deer* in 1844 at 49 lbs. He was said to have weighed only 40 lbs. in 1840.

Victor Morley Lawson won his first race at Warwick, England, on *Ocean King*, October 16, 1973, aged 67.

The most winners ridden on one card is 8 by Hubert S. Jones, 17, out of 13 mounts at Caliente, California, on June 11, 1944 (of which 5 were photo-finishes), and by Oscar Barattuci at Rosario City, Argentina, on December 15, 1957.

The longest winning streak is 12 races by Sir Gordon Richards (G.B.) who won the last race at Nottingham, England, on October 3, 1933, six out of six at Chepstow on October 4, and the first five races the next day at Chepstow.

Trainers. The greatest number of wins by a trainer in one year is 494 by Jack Van Berg in 1976. He also won a record $2,972,218 in prize money.

Owners. The most winners by an owner in one year is 494 by Dan R. Lasater (U.S.) in 1974, when he also won a record $3,022,960 in prize money.

Shortest Odds

The shortest odds ever quoted for any racehorse are 1 to 10,000 for *Dragon Blood*, ridden by Lester Piggott (G.B.) in the Premio Naviglio in Milan, Italy, on June 1, 1967. He won. Odds of 1 to 100 were quoted for the American horse *Man o' War* (foaled March 29, 1917, died November 1, 1947) on three separate occasions in 1920. In 21 starts in 1919–20 he had 20 wins and one second (on August 13, 1919, in the Sanford Memorial Stakes).

Pari-Mutuel Record

The U.S. pari-mutuel record pay-off is $941.75 to $1 on *Wishing Ring* at Latonia track, Kentucky, in 1912.

Largest Prizes. The richest race ever held is the All-American Futurity, a race for quarter-horses over 440 yards at Ruidoso Downs, New Mexico. The prizes in 1978 totaled $1,280,000.

The richest first prize was $437,500, won by *Moon Lark*, the winner of the 1978 All-American Futurity.

Horseshoe Pitching

Origin. This sport was derived by military farriers and is of great antiquity. The first formal World Championships were staged at Bronson, Kansas, in 1909.

Most Titles. The record for men's titles is 10 by Ted Allen (Boulder, Colorado) in 1933–34–35–40–46–53–55–56–57–59. The women's record is 9 titles by Vicki Chapelle Winston (LaMonte, Missouri) in 1956–58–59–61–63–66–67–69–75.

Highest Percentage. The record for percentage of ringers in one game is 95 by Ruth Hangen (Getzville, N.Y.) in 1973. The record for consecutive ringers is 72 by Ted Allen in 1951 for men, and 42 by Ruth Hangen in 1974 for women.

Most Ringers. The most ringers in a single game is 175 by Glen Henton of Maquoketa, Iowa, in 1965.

Marathon. The longest continuous session is 120 hours by a team of 6 playing in shifts in South Gate, California, June 7–12, 1977.

Ice Skating

Origins. The earliest reference to ice skating is in Scandinavian literature of the 2nd century, although its origins are believed, on archeological evidence, to be 10 centuries earlier still. The earliest English account of 1180 refers to skates made of bone. The earliest known illustration is a Dutch woodcut of 1498. The earliest skating club was the Edinburgh Skating Club, Scotland, formed in 1742. The earliest artificial ice rink in the world was the "Glaciarium," built in Chelsea, London, in 1876. The International Skating Union was founded in 1892.

DANCING FEAT:
Ludmilla Pakhomova and
Aleksandr Gorshkov have
won six ice dance
titles since 1970.

Longest Race. The longest race regularly held is the "Elfsteden-tocht" ("Tour of the Eleven Towns") in the Netherlands. It covers 200 kilometers (124 miles 483 yards) and the fastest time is 7 hours 35 minutes by Jeen van den Berg (born January 8, 1928) on February 3, 1954.

Largest Rink. The world's largest artificial ice rink is the quadruple rink at Burnaby, British Columbia, Canada, completed in December, 1972, which has an ice area of 68,000 sq. ft. The largest artificial outdoor rink is the Fujikyu Highland Promenade Rink, Japan, opened at a cost of $938,000 in 1967 with an area of 165,750 square feet (3.8 acres).

Figure Skating

World. The greatest number of individual world men's figure skating titles (instituted 1896) is ten by Ulrich Salchow (1877–1949), of Sweden, in 1901–05 and 1907–11. The women's record (instituted 1906) is also ten individual titles, by Sonja Henie (April 8, 1912–October 12, 1969), of Norway, between 1927 and 1936. Irina Rodnina (born September 12, 1949), of the U.S.S.R., has won ten pairs titles (instituted 1908)—four with Aleksiy Ulanov (1969–72) and six with her husband Aleksandr Zaitsev (1973–77). The most ice dance titles (instituted 1950) won is six by Aleksandr Gorshkov (born December 8, 1946) and Ludmilla Pakhomova (born December 31, 1946), both of the U.S.S.R., in 1970–71–72–73–74 and 1976.

Olympic. The most Olympic gold medals won by a figure skater is three by Gillis Grafstrom (1893–1938), of Sweden, in 1920, 1924, and 1928 (also silver medal in 1932); and by Sonja Henie (see above) in 1928, 1932 and 1936.

Most Difficult Jump. The first ever triple Axel performed in competition was by Vern Taylor (b. 1958) (Canada) in the World Championships at Ottawa on March 10, 1978.

MOST DIFFICULT JUMPS: Sergei Shakrai and Marina Tcherkasova (left) are the only pair ever to perform the quadruple twist lift. Vern Taylor (right) performed the first triple Axel in competition in March 1978.

A quadruple twist lift has been performed by only one pair, Sergei Shakrai (b. 1957) and Marina Tcherkasova (b. 1962) of the U.S.S.R., in an international competition at Helsinki, Finland, on January 26, 1977. They were also the first skaters to accomplish simultaneous triple jumps in international competition, at Strasbourg, France, on February 1, 1978.

Highest Marks. The highest number of maximum six marks awarded for one performance in an international championship was 11 to Aleksandr Zaitsev and Irina Rodnina (U.S.S.R.) in the European pairs competition in Zagreb, Yugoslavia, in 1974.

MOST WORLD PAIRS TITLES: Irina Rodnina has won a total of 10 world pairs titles—six with her husband Aleksandr Zaitsev (shown here). Rodnina and Zaitsev were also awarded a record 11 perfect marks for a performance in 1974.

Donald Jackson (Canada) was awarded 7 "sixes" in the world men's championship at Prague, Czechoslovakia, in 1962.

Most Titles Speed Skating

World. The greatest number of world speed skating titles (instituted 1893) won by any skater is five by Oscar Mathisen (Norway) in 1908–09 and 1912–14, and Clas Thunberg (born April 5, 1893) of Finland, in 1923, 1925, 1928–29 and 1931. The most titles won by a woman is four by Mrs. Inga Voronina, *née* Artomonova (1936–66) of Moscow, U.S.S.R., in 1957, 1958, 1962 and 1965, and Mrs. Atje Keulen-Deelstra of the Netherlands (b. 1938) in 1970 and 1972–73–74.

SPEED SKATER:
Sheila Young set
a record mark for
500 meters in 1976.

WORLD SPEED SKATING RECORDS
(Ratified by the I.S.U. as of June 1, 1978.)

Distance	min. sec.	Name and Nationality	Place	Date
Men				
500 meters	37.00	Evgeni Kulikov (U.S.S.R.)	Medeo, U.S.S.R.	Mar. 29, 1975
1,000 meters	1:14.99	Eric Heiden (U.S.)	Salavan, Norway	Mar. 12, 1978
1,500 meters	1:55.18	Jan Egil Storholt (Norway)	Medeo, U.S.S.R.	Mar. 20, 1977
3,000 meters	4:07.01	Eric Heiden (U.S.)	Inzell, W. Ger.	Mar. 2, 1978
5,000 meters	6:56.90	Kay Stenshjemmel (Norway)	Medeo, U.S.S.R.	Mar. 19, 1977
10,000 meters	14:34.33	Viktor Leskine (U.S.S.R.)	Medeo, U.S.S.R.	Apr. 3, 1977
Women				
500 meters	40.68	Sheila Young (U.S.)	Inzell, W. Ger.	Mar. 13, 1976
1,000 meters	1:23.46	Tatiana Averina (U.S.S.R.)	Medeo, U.S.S.R.	Mar. 29, 1975
1,500 meters	2:07.18	Khalida Vorobyeva (U.S.S.R.)	Medeo, U.S.S.R.	Apr. 10, 1978
3,000 meters	4:31.00	Galina Stepanskaya (U.S.S.R.)	Medeo, U.S.S.R.	Mar. 23, 1976

Olympic. The most Olympic gold medals won in speed skating is six by Lidia Skoblikova (born March 8, 1939), of Chelyaminsk, U.S.S.R., in 1960 (2) and 1964 (4). The male record is held by Clas Thunberg (see above) with 5 gold (including 1 tied gold) and also 1 silver and 1 tied bronze in 1924–28.

Longest Marathon. The longest recorded skating marathon is one of 109 hours 5 minutes by Austin McKinley of Christchurch, New Zealand, June 21–25, 1977.

FASTEST SAND YACHT: "Coronation Year Mk. II" has been piloted to a speed of 57.69 m.p.h.

Ice and Sand Yachting

Origin. The sport originated in the Low Countries (earliest patent is dated 1600) and along the Baltic coast. The earliest authentic record is Dutch, dating from 1768. The largest ice yacht built was *Icicle*, built for Commodore John E. Roosevelt for racing on the Hudson River, New York, *c.* 1870. It was 68 feet 11 inches long and carried 1,070 square feet of canvas.

Highest Speed. The highest speed officially recorded is 143 m.p.h. by John D. Buckstaff in a Class A stern-steerer on Lake Winnebago, Wisconsin, in 1938. Such a speed is possible in a wind of 72 m.p.h.

Sand Yachting. Land or sand yachts of Dutch construction were first reported on beaches (now in Belgium) in 1595. The earliest international championship was staged in 1914.

The fastest recorded speed for a sand yacht is 57.69 m.p.h. (measured mile in 62.4 secs.) by *Coronation Year Mk. II*, owned by R. Millett Denning and crewed by J. Halliday, Bob Harding, J. Glassbrook and Cliff Martindale at Lytham St. Anne's, England, in 1956.

A speed of 77.47 m.p.h. was attained by Jan Paul Lowe (born April 15, 1936) (U.S.) in *Sunkist*, at Ivanpaugh Dry Lake, California, on March 25, 1975.

Jai-Alai *(Pelota)*

The game, which originated in Italy as *longue paume* and was introduced into France in the 13th century, is said to be the fastest of all ball games. Gloves were introduced *c.* 1840 and the *chistera* (basket-like glove) was invented *c.* 1860 by Jean "Gantchiki" Dithurbide of Ste. Pée. The long *grand chistera* was invented by Melchior Curuchague of Buenos Aires, Argentina, in 1888.

Various games are played in a *fronton* (enclosed stadium) the most popular being *main mie, remonte, rebot, pala, grand chistera* and *cesta punta*. The sport is governed by the Federacion Internacional de Pelota Vasca in Madrid, Spain.

The world's largest *fronton* is the World Jai-Alai in Miami, Florida, which had a record attendance of 15,052 on December 27, 1975.

The fastest throw of a (*pelota*) ball was made by José Ramon Areitio at an electronically measured speed of 180 m.p.h., recorded at the Palm Beach Jai-Alai, Florida, on February 2, 1978.

Longest Domination. The longest domination as the world's No. 1 player was enjoyed by Chiquito de Cambo (*né* Joseph Apesteguy) (France) (b. May 10, 1881–d. 1955), from the beginning of the century until succeeded in 1938 by Jean Urruty (France) (b. October 19, 1913).

Judo

Origin. Judo is a modern combat sport which developed out of an amalgam of several old Japanese fighting arts, the most popular of which was *ju-jitsu* (*jiu jitsu*), which is thought to be of pre-Christian Chinese origin. Judo has developed greatly since 1882, when it was first devised by Dr. Jigoro Kano (1860–1938). World Championships were inaugurated in Tokyo on May 5, 1956.

Highest Grades. The efficiency grades in Judo are divided into pupil (*kyu*) and master (*dan*) grades. The highest awarded is the extremely rare red belt *Judan* (10th *dan*), given only to seven men. The Judo protocol provides for a *Juichidan* (11th *dan*), who also would wear a red belt, and even a *Junidan* (12th *dan*), who would wear a white belt twice as wide as an ordinary belt, and even a *Shihan* (the highest of all), but these have never been bestowed.

Marathon. The longest recorded Judo marathon with continuous play by two of six Judoka in 5-minute stints is 200 hours by the Dufftown and District Judo Club, Banffshire, Scotland on July 9–17, 1977.

Champion. The only man to have won 4 world titles is Willem Ruska of the Netherlands who won the 1967 and the 1971 heavyweight and the 1972 Olympic heavyweight and Open titles.

Karate

Origins. Originally *karate* (empty hand) is known to have been developed by the unarmed populace as a method of attack on, and defense against, armed Japanese aggressors in Okinawa, Ryukyu

Islands, based on techniques devised from the 6th century Chinese art of *Chuan-fa* (Kempo). Transmitted to Japan in the 1920's by Funakoshi Gichin, the founder of modern *karate*, this method of combat was further refined and organized into a sport with competitive rules.

The five major schools of *karate* in Japan are *Shotokan*, *Wado-ryu*, *Goju-ryu*, *Shito-ryu*, and *Kyokushinkai*, each of which places different emphasis on speed, power, etc. Other styles include *Gojukai*, *Shotokai* and *Shukokai*. The military form of *Tae-kwan-do* with 9 *dans* is a Korean equivalent of *karate*. *Kung fu* is believed to have originated in Nepal or Tibet but was adopted within Chinese temples *via* India.

Wu shu is a comprehensive term embracing all Chinese martial arts.

Most Titles. The only winner of 3 All-Japanese titles has been Takeshi Oishi, who won in 1969–70–71.

The highest *dan* among karatekas is Yamaguchi Gogen (b. 1907), a 10th *dan* of the *Goju-ryu* Karate Do.

Greatest Force. Considerably less emphasis is placed on *Tamashiwara* (wood breaking, etc.) than is generally supposed. Most styles use it only for demonstration purposes. However, the force needed to break a brick with the abductor *digiti quinti* muscle of the hand is normally 130–140 lbs. The highest measured impact is 196 lbs. force.

Lacrosse

Origin. The game is of American Indian origin, derived from the inter-tribal game *baggataway*, and was played by Iroquois Indians in lower Ontario, Canada, and upper New York State, before 1492. The game was included in the Olympic Games of 1908, and featured as an exhibition sport in the 1928 and 1948 Games.

World Championship. Of the three World Tournaments held to date, the United States has won two. Canada won the most recent, held in Stockport, England, on July 9, 1978.

Longest Throw. The longest recorded throw is 162.86 yards, by Barney Quinn of Ottawa, Canada, on September 10, 1892.

Highest Score. The highest score in any international match was U.S. over Canada, 28–4, at Stockport, England, on July 3, 1978.

Modern Pentathlon

The Modern Pentathlon (Riding, Fencing, Shooting, Swimming and Running) was inaugurated into the Olympic Games at Stockholm in 1912.

Point scores in riding, fencing, cross country and hence overall scores have no comparative value between one competition and another. In shooting and swimming (300 meters), where measurements are absolute, the point scores are of record significance.

MODERN PENTATHLON CHAMPIONS: András Balczó (left) won 6 world titles and 5 Olympic medals, 3 of them gold. Lars Hall (right) is the only man to win 2 individual championships.

	Points		
Shooting	1,088 Mario Medda (Italy)	Munich, W. Germany	Aug. 29, 1972
	1,088 Jiri Adam (Czech.)	Montreal, Canada	July 20, 1976
	1,088 Alexei Palianov (U.S.S.R.)	London, England	Sept. 8, 1977
Swimming	1,324 Robert Nieman (U.S.)	Montreal, Canada	July 21, 1976

Most World Titles. The record number of world titles won is 6 by András Balczó (Hungary) in 1963, 1965, 1966, 1967 and 1969, and the Olympic title in 1972, which also rates as a world title.

Olympic Titles. The greatest number of Olympic gold medals won is three by Balczó, a member of Hungary's winning team in 1960 and 1968, and the 1972 individual champion. Lars Hall (Sweden) uniquely has won two individual championships (1952 and 1956). Balczó has won a record number of five medals (3 gold and 2 silver).

Motorcycling

Earliest Races. The first motocycle race was held on an oval track at Sheen House, Richmond, Surrey, England, on November 29, 1897, won by Charles Jarrott (1877–1944) on a Fournier. The oldest motorcycle races in the world are the Auto-Cycle Union Tourist Trophy (T.T.) series, first held on the 15.81-mile "Peel" ("St. John's") course on the Isle of Man on May 28, 1907, and still run on the island, on the "Mountain" circuit (37.73 miles).

Longest Circuits. The 37.73-mile "Mountain" circuit, over which the two main T.T. races have been run since 1911, has 264 curves and corners and is the longest used for any motorcycle race.

Fastest Circuit. The highest average lap speed attained on any closed circuit is 160.288 m.p.h. by Yvon du Hamel (Canada) on a modified 903-c.c. four-cylinder Kawasaki 21 on the 31-degree banked 2.5-mile Daytona International Speedway, Florida, in March, 1973. His lap time was 56.149 seconds.

The fastest road circuit is the Francorchamps circuit near Spa, Belgium. It is 14.12 kilometers (8 miles 1,340 yards) in length and was lapped in 3 minutes 50.3 seconds (average speed of 137.150 m.p.h.) by Barry S. F. Sheene (born Holborn, London, England, September 11, 1950) on a 495-c.c. four-cylinder Suzuki during the Belgian Grand Prix on July 3, 1977.

Fastest Race. The fastest race in the world was held at Grenzlandring, West Germany, in 1939. It was won by Georg Meier (b. Germany, 1910) at an average speed of 134 m.p.h. on a supercharged 495-c.c. flat-twin B.M.W.

The fastest road race is the 500-c.c. Belgian Grand Prix on the Francorchamps circuit (see above). The record time for this 10-lap 87.74-mile race is 38 minutes 58.5 seconds (average speed of 135.068 m.p.h.) by Barry Sheene (U.K.) on a 495-c.c. four-cylinder Suzuki on July 3, 1977.

Longest Race. The longest race is the Liège 24 hours. The greatest distance ever covered is 2,761.9 miles (average speed 115.08 m.p.h.) by Jean-Claude Chemarin and Christian Leon of France on a 941-c.c. four-cylinder Honda on the Francorchamps circuit (8 miles 1,340 yards) near Spa, Belgium, August 14–15, 1976.

World Championships. Most world championship titles (instituted by the Fédération Internationale Motorcycliste in 1949) won are 15 by Giacomo Agostini (Italy) in the 350-c.c. class 1968, 69, 70, 71, 72, 73, 74 and in the 500-c.c. class 1966, 67, 68, 69, 70, 71, 72, 75. Agostini (b. 1942) is the only man to win two world championships in five consecutive years (350- and 500-c.c. titles in 1968–69–70–71–72). Agostini won 122 races in the world championship series between April 24, 1965, and August 29, 1976, including a record 19 in 1970, also achieved by Stanley Michael Bailey "Mike" Hailwood, M.B.E., G.M. (b. Oxford, England, April 2, 1940) in 1966.

Alberto "Johnny" Cecotto (born Caracas, Venezuela, January, 1956) was the youngest person to win a world championship. He was aged 19 years 211 days when he won the 350-c.c. title on August 24, 1975.

The oldest was Hermann-Peter Müller (1909–76) of West Germany, who won the 250-c.c. title in 1955, aged 46.

Most Successful Machines. Italian M.V.-Agusta motorcycles won 37 world championships between 1952 and 1973 and 276 world championship races between 1952 and 1976. Japanese Honda machines won 29 world championship races and five world championships in 1966. In the seven years Honda contested the championship (1961–67) its annual average was 20 race wins.

FASTEST 440: Russ Collins drove his 2000-c.c. nitro-burning Honda over a 440-yard course in 7.62 seconds, reaching a terminal velocity of 199.55 m.p.h.

Speed Records

Official world speed records must be set with two runs over a measured distance within a time limit (one hour for F.I.M. records, two hours for A.M.A. records).

Donald Vesco (born 1939) of El Cajon, California, recorded an average speed of 303.810 m.p.h. over the measured mile at Bonneville Salt Flats, Utah, on September 28, 1975, to establish an A.M.A. record. Riding a 21-foot-long *Silver Bird* Streamliner powered by two 750-c.c. Yamaha TZ750 4-cylinder engines developing 180 b.h.p., he covered the first mile in 11.817 seconds (304.646 m.p.h.). On the second run his time was 11.882 seconds (302.979 m.p.h.). The average time for the two runs was 11.8495 (303.810 m.p.h.) for the A.M.A. record. On the same day, he set an F.I.M. record at an average speed of 302.928 m.p.h. Also on the same day, he covered a flying quarter mile in 2.925 seconds (307.692 m.p.h.), the highest speed ever achieved on a motorcycle.

The world record average speed for two runs over one kilometer (1,093.6 yards) from a standing start is 16.68 seconds by Henk Vink (Netherlands) on his supercharged 984-c.c. 4-cylinder Kawasaki, at Elvington Airfield, Yorkshire, England, on July 24, 1977. The faster run was made in 16.09 seconds.

The world record for two runs over 440 yards from a standing start is 8.805 seconds by Henk Vink on his supercharged 1,132-c.c. 4-cylinder Kawasaki, at Elvington Airfield, Yorkshire, England, on July 23, 1977. The faster run was made in 8.55 seconds.

The fastest time for a single run over 440 yards from a standing start is 7.62 seconds by Russ Collins of Gardena, California, riding his nitro-burning 2000-c.c. 8-cylinder Honda *Sorcerer* at the National

Hot Rod Association's World Finals at Ontario Motor Speedway on October 7, 1978. The highest terminal velocity recorded at the end of a 440-yard run from a standing start is 7.62 seconds by Russ Collins in the same run.

Marathon. The longest time a solo motorcycle has been kept in continuous motion is 500 hours by Owen Fitzgerald, Richard Kennett, and Don Mitchell in Western Australia, on July 10–31, 1977. They covered 8,432 miles.

Mountaineering

Origins. Although bronze-age artifacts have been found on the summit (9,605 feet) of the Riffelhorn, Switzerland, mountaineering, as a sport, has a continuous history dating back only to 1854. Isolated instances of climbing for its own sake exist back to the 14th century. The Atacamenans built sacrificial platforms near the summit of Llullaillaco in South America (22,058 feet) in late pre-Columbian times, c. 1490.

Rock Climbing. The world's most demanding free climbs are in the Yosemite Valley, California, with a severity rating of 5.12.

Warren Harding and Dean Caldwell averaged 80 vertical feet a day in their record 27 days on the Wall of the Early Morning Light on Yosemite's El Capitan in November, 1971.

Greatest Wall. The highest final stage in any wall climb is that on the south face of Annapurna I (26,545 feet). It was climbed by the British expedition led by Christian Bonington April 2–May 27, 1970, when Donald Whillans, 36, and Dougal Haston, 27, scaled to the summit. They used 18,000 feet of rope.

The longest wall climb is on the Rupal-Flank from the base camp at 11,680 feet to the South Point (26,384 feet) of Nanga Parbat—a vertical ascent of 14,704 feet. This was scaled by the Austro-Germano-Italian Expedition led by Dr. Herrligkoffer in April, 1970.

Mount Everest. Mount Everest (29,028 feet) was first climbed at 11:30 a.m. on May 29, 1953, when the summit was reached by Edmund Percival Hillary (born July 20, 1919), of New Zealand, and the Sherpa, Tenzing Norgay (born, as Namgyal Wangdi, in Nepal in 1914, formerly called Tenzing Khumjung Bhutia). The successful expedition was led by Col. (later Hon. Brigadier) Henry Cecil John Hunt (born June 22, 1910).

Since the first ascent, another 79 climbers have succeeded, the latest being George Ritter and Bernd Cullmann of West Germany, who completed their climb on October 17, 1978.

Subsequent ascents of Mount Everest are as follows:

Climbers	Date
Ernst Schmidt, Jurg Marmet (Switz.)	May 23, 1956
Hans Rudolf von Gunten, Adolf Reist (Switz.)	May 24, 1956
Wang Fu-chou, Chu Yin-hua (China), Konbu	May 25, 1960
James Warren Whittaker (U.S.), Sherpa Nawang Gombu	May 1, 1963
Barry C. Bishop, Luther G. Jerstad (U.S.)	May 22, 1963
Dr. William F. Unsoeld, Dr. Thomas F. Hornbein (U.S.)	May 22, 1963
Capt. A. S. Cheema (India), Sherpa Nawang Gombu	May 20, 1965
Sonam Gyaltso, Sonam Wangyal	May 22, 1965
C. P. Vohra (India), Sherpa Ang Kami	May 24, 1965
Capt. H. P. S. Ahluwalia, H. C. S. Rawat (India), Phu Dorji	May 29, 1965
Nomi Uemura, Tero Matsuura (Japan)	May 11, 1970
Katsutoshi Harabayashi (Japan) and Sherpa Chotari	May 12, 1970
Sgt. Mirko Minuzzo, Sgt. Rinaldo Carrel (Italy) with Lapka Tenzing and Samba Tamang	May 5, 1973
Capt. Fabrizio Innamorati, W. O. Virginio Epis and Sgt. Maj. Claudio Benedetti (Italy) with Sonam Gallien	May 7, 1973
Hisashi Ishiguro, Yasuo Kato (Japan)	Oct. 26, 1973
Mrs. Junko Tabei, Ang Tserang	May 16, 1975
Mrs. Phanthog, Sodnam Norbu, Lotse Samdrub, Darphuntso, Kunga Pasang, Tsering Tobgyal, Ngapo Khyen (Tibet), Hou Sheng-Fu (China)	May 27, 1975
Doug Scott, Dougal Haston (U.K.)	Sept. 24, 1975
Peter Boardman (U.K.), Pertemba (Nepal)	Sept. 26, 1975
Sgt. John Stokes, Cpl. Michael Lane (U.K.)	May 17, 1976
Robert McCormack, Dr. Chris Chandler (U.S.)	Oct. 15, 1976
Ko Sang Don (S. Korea) and Sherpa Perma Norbu	Sept. 15, 1977
Wolfgang Nairz, Robert Schaur, Horst Bergman (Austria), Ang Phu (Nepal)	May 3, 1978
Reinhold Messner (Italy), Peter Habler (Austria)	May 8, 1978
Karl Reinhard, Oswald Olz (Austria)	May 11, 1978
Franz Oppurg (Austria) (first solo climb)	May 14, 1978
Hubert Hillmaier, Josef Mack, Hans Engl (W. Germany) and 3 Sherpas	Oct. 14, 1978
Pierre Mazeaud, Jean Afanassief, Nicolas Jaeger (France), Kurt Diemberger (Austria)	Oct. 15, 1978
Wanda Rutkiewicz (Poland), Wilhelm Klimek, Siegfried Hupfauer (W. Ger.), Robert Allenbach (Switz.), Sherpas Mingma, Ang Dorje and Ang Kami	Oct. 16, 1978
George Ritter and Bernd Cullmann (W. Ger.)	Oct. 17, 1978

Olympic Games

Note: These records now include the un-numbered Games held at Athens in 1906, which some authorities ignore. Although inserted between the regular IIIrd Games in 1904 and the IVth Games in 1908, the 1906 Games were both official and were of a higher standard than all three of those that preceded them.

Origins. The earliest celebration of the ancient Olympic Games of which there is a certain record is that of July, 776 B.C. (when Coroibos, a cook from Elis, won a foot race), though their origin probably dates from *c.* 1370 B.C. The ancient Games were terminated by an order issued in Milan in 393 A.D. by Theodosius I, "the Great" (*c.* 346–395), Emperor of Rome. At the instigation of Pierre de Fredi, Baron de Coubertin (1863–1937), the Olympic Games of the modern era were inaugurated in Athens on April 6, 1896.

Most Medals

In the ancient Olympic Games, victors were given a chaplet (head garland) of olive leaves. Leonidas of Rhodes won 12 running titles from 164–152 B.C.

MODERN OLYMPIC GAMES began in 1896 through the efforts of Baron de Coubertin.

Individual. The most individual gold medals won by a male competitor in the modern Games is 10 by Raymond Clarence Ewry (U.S.) (b. October 14, 1874, at Lafayette, Indiana; d. September 27, 1937), a jumper (see *Track and Field*). The female record is seven by Vera Caslavska-Odlozil (b. May 3, 1942) of Czechoslovakia (also see *Gymnastics*).

The only Olympian to win 4 consecutive individual titles in the same event has been Alfred A. Oerter (b. September 19, 1936, New York City) who won the discus title in 1956–60–64–68.

Most Olympic Gold Medals at One Games. Mark Spitz (U.S.), the swimmer who won 2 relay golds in Mexico in 1968, won 7 more (4 individual and 3 relay) at Munich in 1972. The latter figure is an absolute Olympic record for one celebration at any sport.

National. The total figures for most medals and most gold medals for all Olympic events (including those now discontinued) for the Summer (1896–1976) and Winter Games (1924–1976) are:

	Gold	Silver	Bronze	Total
1. U.S.A.	658*	511½	438½	1,608
2. U.S.S.R. (formerly Russia)	311	255	244	810
3. G.B. (including Ireland to 1920)	165½	202½	178	546

* The A.A.U. (U.S.) reinstated James F. Thorpe (1888–1953), the disqualified high scorer in the 1912 decathlon and pentathlon events on October 12, 1973, but no issue of medals has yet been authorized by the International Olympic Committee. If allowed, this would give the U.S. 2 more gold medals.

Youngest and Oldest Gold Medalists. The youngest woman to win a gold medal is Marjorie Gestring (U.S.) (b. November 18, 1922) aged 13 years 9 months, in the 1936 women's springboard event. The youngest winner ever was a French boy (whose name is not recorded) who coxed the Netherlands coxed pair in 1900. He was not more than 10 and may have been as young as 7. He substituted for Dr. Hermanus Brockmann, who coxed in the heats but proved too heavy.

Oscar G. Swahn was a member of the winning Running Deer shooting team in 1912, aged 65 years 258 days.

Longest Span. The longest competitive span of any Olympic competitor is 40 years by Dr. Ivan Osiier (Denmark) (1888–1965), who competed as a fencer in 1908, 1912 (silver medal), 1920, 1924, 1928, 1932 and 1948, and by Magnus Konow (Norway) (1887–1972) in yachting, 1908–20 and 1936–48. The longest span for a woman is 24 years (1932–56) by the Austrian fencer Ellen Müller-Preiss. Raimondo d'Inzeo (born February 8, 1925) competed for Italy in equestrian events in a record eight celebrations (1948–1976), gaining one gold medal, two silver and three bronze medals. Janice Lee York Romary (born August 6, 1928), the U.S. fencer, competed in all six Games from 1948 to 1968, and Lia Manoliu (Rumania) (born April 25, 1932) competed from 1952 to 1972, winning the discus title in 1968.

Largest Crowd. The largest crowd at any Olympic site was 150,000 at the 1952 ski-jumping at the Holmenkollen, outside Oslo, Norway. Estimates of the number of spectators of the marathon race through Tokyo, Japan, on October 21, 1964, have ranged from 500,000 to 1,500,000.

Most Competitors. The greatest number of competitors in any summer Olympic Games has been 7,147 at Munich in 1972. A record 122 countries competed in the 1972 Munich Games. The fewest was 311 competitors from 13 countries in 1896. In 1904 only 12 countries participated. The largest team was 880 men and 4 women from France at the 1900 Games in Paris.

Most Participations. Five countries have never failed to be represented at the 19 Celebrations of the Games: Australia, Greece, Great Britain, Switzerland and the United States of America.

Pigeon Racing

Earliest References. Pigeon Racing was the natural development of the use of homing pigeons for the carrying of messages—a quality utilized in the ancient Olympic Games (776 B.C.–393 A.D.). The sport originated in Belgium. The earliest major long-distance race was from Crystal Palace, South London, England, in 1871. The earliest recorded occasion on which 500 miles was flown in a day was by "Motor," owned by G. P. Pointer of Thurso, Scotland, which was released on June 30, 1896, and covered 501 miles at an average speed of 49½ m.p.h.

Longest Flights. The greatest recorded homing flight by a pigeon was made by one owned by the 1st Duke of Wellington (1769–1852). Released from a sailing ship off the Ichabo Islands,

West Africa, on April 8, it dropped dead a mile from its loft at Nine Elms, London, England, on June 1, 1845, 55 days later, having flown an airline route of 5,400 miles, but an actual distance of possibly 7,000 miles to avoid the Sahara Desert.

Highest Speeds. In level flight in windless conditions it is very doubtful if any pigeon can exceed 60 m.p.h. The highest race speed recorded is one of 3,229 yards per minute (110.07 m.p.h.) in East Anglia, England, on May 8, 1965, when 1,428 birds were backed by a powerful south southwest wind. The winner was owned by A. Vidgeon & Son.

The highest race speed recorded over a distance of more than 1,000 kilometers is 82.93 m.p.h. by a hen pigeon in the Central Cumberland Combine Race over 683 miles 147 yards from Murray Bridge, South Australia, to North Ryde, Sydney, on October 2, 1971.

The world's longest reputed distance in 24 hours is 803 miles (velocity 1,525 yards per minute) by E. S. Peterson's winner of the 1941 San Antonio (Texas) Racing Club event.

Lowest Speed. *Blue Chip*, a pigeon belonging to Harold Hart, released in Rennes, France, arrived home in its loft in Leigh, England, on September 29, 1974, 7 years 2 months later. It had covered the 370 miles at an average speed of 0.00589 m.p.h., which is slower than the world's fastest snail.

Most First Prizes. Owned by R. Green, of Walsall Wood, West Midlands, England, *Champion Breakaway* had won a record 53 first prizes from 1972 to June, 1978.

Highest-Priced Bird. Louis Massarella of Leicester, England, paid 850,000 Belgian francs ($24,150) for *De Bliksem* on December 31, 1975.

Polo

Earliest Games. Polo is usually regarded as being of Persian origin, having been played as *Pulu c.* 525 B.C. Other claims have come from Tibet and the Tang dynasty of China 250 A.D.

Stone goalposts (probably 12th century), 8 yards wide and 300 yards apart, still stand at Isfahan, Iran. The earliest club of modern times was the Kachar Club (founded in 1859) in Assam, India. The game was introduced into England from India in 1869 by the 10th Hussars at Aldershot, Hampshire, and the earliest match was one between the 9th Lancers and the 10th Hussars on Hounslow Heath, west of London, in July, 1871. The earliest international match between England and the U.S. was in 1886.

Playing Field. The game is played on the largest field of any ball game in the world. The ground measures 300 yards long by 160 yards wide with side-boards or, as in India, 200 yards wide without boards.

Highest Handicap. The highest handicap based on eight $7\frac{1}{2}$-minute "chukkas" is 10 goals, introduced in the U.S. in 1891 and in the United Kingdom and in Argentina in 1910. The most recent additions to the select ranks of the 38 players to have received 10-goal handicaps are A. Heguy and A. Harriot of Argentina.

Highest Score. The highest aggregate number of goals scored in an international match is 30, when Argentina beat the U.S. 21–9 at Meadowbrook, Long Island, New York, in September, 1936.

Most Olympic Medals. Polo has been part of the Olympic program on five occasions: 1900, 1908, 1920, 1924 and 1936. Of the 21 gold medalists, a 1920 winner, John Wodehouse, the 3rd Earl of Kimberly (b. 1883–d. 1941) uniquely also won a silver medal (1908).

Most Internationals. Thomas Hitchcock, Jr. (1900–44) played five times for the U.S. vs. England (1921–24–27–30–39) and twice vs. Argentina (1928–36).

Most Expensive Pony. The highest price ever paid for a polo pony was $22,000, paid by Stephen Sanford for Lewis Lacey's *Jupiter* after the 1928 U.S. vs. Argentina international.

Oldest Pony. *Rustum*, a Barb gelding from Stourhead, England, was still playing regularly at the age of 36.

Largest Trophy. Polo claims the world's largest sporting trophy —the Bangalore Limited Handicap Polo Tournament Trophy. This massive cup standing on its plinth is 6 feet tall and was presented in 1936 by the Indian Raja of Kolanka.

Largest Crowd. Crowds of more than 50,000 have watched flood-lit matches at the Sydney, Australia, Agricultural Shows.

A crowd of 40,000 watched a game played at Jaipur, India, in 1976, when elephants were used instead of ponies. The length of the polo sticks used has not been ascertained.

Powerboat Racing

Origins. The earliest application of the gasoline engine to a boat was by Jean Joseph Etienne Lenoir (1822–1900) on the River Seine, Paris, in 1865. The sport was given impetus by the presentation of a championship cup by Sir Alfred Harmsworth of England in 1903, which was also the year of the first offshore race from Calais to Dover.

Harmsworth Cup. Of the 25 contests from 1903 to 1961, the U.S. has won the most with 16.

The greatest number of wins has been achieved by Garfield A. Wood (U.S.) with 8 (1920–21, 1926, 1928–29–30, 1932–33). The only boat to win three times is *Miss Supertest III*, owned by James G. Thompson (Canada), driven by Jack Regas (Canada), in 1959–60–

LONGEST POWERBOAT JUMP: Jerry Comeaux jumped his boat 110 feet in the air for the film "Live and Let Die."

61. This boat also achieved the record speed of 119.27 m.p.h. at Picton, Ontario, Canada, in 1961. The trophy is now awarded to the British Commonwealth driver with the highest points in the World Offshore Championships.

Gold Cup. The Gold Cup (instituted 1903) has been won 7 times by Bill Muncey (1956–57–61–62–72–77–78). The record speed attained is 128.338 m.p.h. for a 2½-mile lap by the unlimited hydroplane *Atlas Van Lines*, driven by Bill Muncey in a qualifying round on the Columbia River, Washington, in July, 1977, and again in July, 1978.

Highest Speeds. The Class I offshore record, as recognized by the Union Internationale Motonautique, is 92.17 m.p.h. by *Yellow-drama II*, driven by Ken Cassir, on The Solent, Hampshire, England, on April 13, 1978.

The R6 inboard engine record of 128.375 m.p.h. was set by the hydroplane *Vladivar I*, driven by Tony Fahey (G.B.) on Lake Windermere, Cumbria, England, on May 23, 1977.

The Class OD record is 110.25 m.p.h. by Wayne Baldwin (U.S.) on the Fox River, Wisconsin, in 1976.

Longest Race. The longest race has been the Port Richborough (London) to Monte Carlo Marathon Offshore International Event. The race extended over 2,947 miles in 14 stages on June 10–25, 1972. It was won by *H.T.S.* (G.B.), driven by Mike Bellamy, Eddie Chater and Jim Brooks in 71 hours 35 minutes 56 seconds (average 41.15 m.p.h.).

Longest Jump. The longest jump achieved by a powerboat has been 110 feet by Jerry Comeaux, 29, in a Glastron GT-150 with a 135-h.p. Evinrude Starflite off a greased ramp on an isolated waterway in Louisiana, in mid-October, 1972. The take-off speed was 56 m.p.h. The jump was required for a sequence in the eighth James Bond film *Live and Let Die.*

Dragsters. The first drag boat to attain 200 m.p.h. was Sam Kurtovich's *Crisis* which attained 200.44 m.p.h. in California in October, 1969, at the end of a one-way run. *Climax* has since been reported to have attained 205.19 m.p.h.

Longest Journey. The Dane, Hans Tholstrup, 25, circumnavigated Australia in a 17-foot Caribbean Cougar fiberglass runabout with a single 80-h.p. Mercury outboard motor from May 11 to July 25, 1971.

Rodeo

Origins. Rodeo came into being with the early days of the North American cattle industry. The earliest references to the sport are from Santa Fe, New Mexico, in 1847. Steer wrestling began with Bill Pickett (Texas) in 1900. The other events are calf roping, bull riding, saddle and bareback bronco riding.

The largest rodeo in the world is the Calgary Exhibition and Stampede at Calgary, Alberta, Canada. The record attendance has been 1,069,830, July 8–17, 1977. The record for one day is 141,670 on July 13, 1974.

Champion Bull. The top bucking bull in 1977 was *General Isomo* owned by Beutler Bros. and Mike Cervi. In 25 times out of the chute he was only ridden six times.

Champion Bronc. The bareback bronc award for 1977 was shared by *Mr. Smith*, a 16-year-old palomino owned by Christensen Bros. of Eugene, Oregon, and *Alley Cat*, a chestnut sorrel owned by D. A. Kerby. Traditionally a bronc called *Midnight* owned by Jim McNab of Alberta, Canada, was never ridden in 12 appearances at the Calgary Stampede.

Most World Titles. The record number of all-round titles is 6 by Larry Mahan (b. November 21, 1943) (1966–67–68–69–70–73). Jim Shoulders (b. 1928) of Henryetta, Oklahoma, won a record 16 world championships between 1949 and 1959. The record figure for prize money in a single season is $96,913 by Tom Ferguson, of Miami, Oklahoma, in 1976.

Youngest Champion. The youngest winner of a world title is Metha Brorsen of Oklahoma, who was only 11 years old when she won the International Rodeo Association Cowgirls barrel racing event in 1975.

Time Records. Records for timed events, such as calf roping and steer wrestling, are meaningless, because of the widely varying conditions due to the size of arenas and amount of start given the

CHAMPION COWBOY: Larry Mahan (U.S.) won the all-round world title six times.

stock. The fastest time recently recorded for roping a calf is 7.5 seconds by Junior Garrison of Marlow, Oklahoma, at Evergreen, Colorado, in 1967, and the fastest time for overcoming a steer is 2.4 seconds by James Bynum of Waxahachie, Texas, at Marietta, Oklahoma, in 1955.

The standard required time to stay on in bareback, saddle bronc and bull riding events is 8 seconds. In the now discontinued ride-to-a-finish events, rodeo riders have been recorded to have survived 90 minutes or more, until the mount had not a buck left in it.

Roller Skating

Origin. The first roller skate was devised by Joseph Merlin of Huy, Belgium, in 1760. Several "improved" versions appeared during the next century, but a really satisfactory roller skate did not materialize before 1863, when James L. Plimpton of New York City produced the present four-wheeled type, patented it, and opened the first public rink in the world at Newport, Rhode Island, in 1866. The great boom periods were 1870–75, 1908–12 and 1948–54, each originating in the U.S.

Largest Rink. The largest indoor rink ever to operate was located in the Grand Hall, Olympia, London, England. It had an actual skating area of 68,000 square feet. It first opened in 1890 for one season, then again from 1909 to 1912.

The largest rink now in operation is the Fireside Roll-Arena in Hoffman Estates, Illinois, which has a total skating surface of 29,859 square feet.

Roller Hockey. Roller hockey was first introduced in England as Rink Polo, at the old Lava rink, Denmark Hill, London, in the late 1870's. The Amateur Rink Hockey Association was formed in 1905, and in 1913 became the National Rink Hockey (now Roller Hockey) Association. Britain won the inaugural World Championship in 1936, and since then Portugal has won the most with 11 titles from 1947 to 1973.

Most Titles. Most world speed titles have been won by Alberta Vianello (Italy) with 16 between 1953 and 1965. Most world pair titles have been taken by Dieter Fingerle (W. Germany) with four in 1959–65–66–67. The records for figure titles are 5 by Karl Heinz Losch in 1958–59–61–62–66 and 4 by Astrid Bader, also of West Germany, in 1965 to 1968.

Speed Records. The fastest speed (official world's record) is 25.78 m.p.h. by Giuseppe Cantarella (Italy) who recorded 34.9 seconds for 440 yards on a road at Catania, Italy, on September 28, 1963. The mile record on a rink is 2 minutes 25.1 seconds by Gianni Ferretti (Italy). The greatest distance skated in one hour on a rink by a woman is 21.995 miles by Marisa Danesi at Inzell, West Germany, on September 28, 1968. The men's record on a track is 23.133 miles by Alberto Civolani (Italy) at Inzell, West Germany, on September 28, 1968. He went on to skate 50 miles in 2 hours 20 minutes 33.1 seconds.

Marathon Record. The longest recorded continuous roller skating marathon was one of 322 hours 20 minutes by Randy Reed of Springfield, Oregon, June 12–26, 1977.

The longest reported skate was by Clinton Shaw (Canada) from Victoria, British Columbia, to St. John's, Newfoundland (4,900 miles) on the Trans-Canadian Highway *via* Montreal from April 1 to November 11, 1967. On May 4, 1974, he started his New York–California skate, arriving in Santa Monica, California, on July 20, 1974, after 3,100 miles. His longest stint in a day was 106 miles from Clines Corners to Laguna, both in New Mexico.

Rowing

Oldest Race. The earliest established sculling race is the Doggett's Coat and Badge, first rowed on August 1, 1716, on a 5-mile course from London Bridge to Chelsea. It is still being rowed every year over the same course, under the administration of the Fishmongers' Company. The first English regatta probably took place on the Thames by the Ranelagh Gardens, near Putney, London, in 1775. Boating began at Eton, England, in 1793. The oldest club, the Leander Club, was formed in *c.* 1818.

Olympic Games. Since 1900 there have been 119 Olympic finals of which the U.S. has won 26, Germany (now West Germany) 15 and Great Britain 14. Four oarsmen have won 3 gold medals: John B. Kelly (U.S.) (1889–1960), father of Princess Grace of Monaco, in the sculls (1920) and double sculls (1920 and 1924); his cousin Paul V. Costello (U.S.) (b. December 27, 1899) in the double sculls (1920, 1924 and 1928); Jack Beresford, Jr. (G.B.) (1899-1977) in the sculls (1924), coxless fours (1932) and double sculls (1936) and Vyacheslav Ivanov (U.S.S.R.) (b. July 30, 1938) in the sculls (1956, 1960 and 1964). Beresford competed in five games, winning an additional two silver medals.

Sculling. The record number of wins in the Wingfield Sculls (instituted 1830) is seven by Jack Beresford, Jr., from 1920 to 1926. The fastest time (Putney to Mortlake) has been 21 minutes 11 seconds by Leslie Southwood in 1933. The record number of world professional sculling titles (instituted 1831) won is seven by William Beach (Australia) between 1884 and 1887. Stuart A. Mackenzie (Great Britain and Australia) performed the unique feat of winning the Diamond Sculls at Henley for the sixth consecutive occasion on July 7, 1962. In 1960 and 1962 he was in Leander colors.

Highest Speed. Speeds in tidal or flowing water are of no comparative value. The highest recorded speed for 2,000 meters on non-tidal water by an eight is 5 mins. 32.17 secs. (13.46 m.p.h.) by East Germany at the Montreal Olympics on July 18, 1976. A team from the Penn A.C. (U.S.) was timed in 5 minutes 18.8 seconds (14.03 m.p.h.) in the F.I.S.A. Championships on the Meuse River, Liege, Belgium, on August 17, 1930.

Cross-Channel Row. The fastest row across the English Channel is 3 hours 50 minutes by Rev. Sidney Swann (b. 1862) in 1911.

WORLD RECORDS

MEN—Fastest times over 2,000 m course

	min sec	Country	Place	Date
Single Sculls	6:52.46	Sean Drea (Ireland)	Montreal, Canada	July 23, 1976
Double Sculls	6:12.48	Norway	Montreal, Canada	July 23, 1976
Coxed Pairs	6:56.94	East Germany	Copenhagen, Denmark	Aug. — 1971
Coxless Pairs	6:33.02	East Germany	Montreal, Canada	July 23, 1976
Coxed Fours	6:09.28	U.S.S.R.	Montreal, Canada	July 23, 1976
Coxless Fours	5:53.65	East Germany	Montreal, Canada	July 23, 1976
Quadruple Sculls	5:47.83	U.S.S.R.	Montreal, Canada	July 18, 1976
Eights	5:32.17	East Germany	Montreal, Canada	July 18, 1976

WOMEN—Fastest times over 1,000 m course

	min sec	Country	Place	Date
Single Sculls	3:34.31	Christine Scheiblich (East Germany)	Amsterdam, Netherlands	Aug. 21, 1977
Double Sculls	3:09.29	East Germany	Prague, Czech.	Sept. 10, 1978
Coxless Pairs	3:26.32	East Germany	Amsterdam, Netherlands	Aug. 21, 1977
Coxed Fours	3:20.59	East Germany	Amsterdam, Netherlands	Aug. 21, 1977
Quadruple Sculls	3:03.29	East Germany	Prague, Czech.	Sept. 10, 1978
Eights	2:59.20	U.S.S.R.	Hamilton, New Zealand	Nov. 1, 1978

Shooting

Earliest Club. A target shooting club in Geneva, Switzerland, has records since 1474, and the first shooting match was held at Eichstädt, Germany, in 1477.

		Possible Score			
Free Pistol	50 m. 6 × 10 shot series	600—	577	Moritze Minder (Switz.)	Seoul, Korea, 1978
Free Rifle	300 m. 3 × 40 shot series	1,200—	1,159	Lones W. Wigger, Jr. (U.S.)	Mexico City, 1977
Small-Bore Rifle	50 m. 3 × 40 shot series	1,200—	1,167	Lones W. Wigger, Jr. (U.S.)	Mexico City, 1973
Small-Bore Rifle	50 m. 60 shots prone	600—	599	Ho Jun Li (N. Korea)	Munich, 1972
				Karel Bulan (Czech.)	Thun, Switzerland, 1974
				Mircea Ilca (Rumania)	Bucharest, 1975
				Karl Heinz Smieszek (W. Ger.)	Montreal, 1976
				Alister Millar Allan (U.K.)	Seoul, Korea, 1978
Rapid-Fire Pistol	25 m. silhouettes 60 shots	600—	598	Giovanni Liverzani (Italy)	Phoenix, Ariz., 1970
Running (Boar) Target	50 m. 60 shots "normal runs"	600—	579	Alexander Gazov (U.S.S.R.)	Montreal, 1976
Trap	200 birds	200—	199	Angelo Scalzone (Italy)	Munich, 1972
				Michel Carrega (France)	Thun, Switzerland, 1974
Skeet	200 birds	200—	200	Yevgeniy Petrov (U.S.S.R.)	Phoenix, Ariz., 1970
				Yuri Tzuranov (U.S.S.R.)	Bologna, Italy, 1971
				Tariel Zhgenti (U.S.S.R.)	Turin, Italy, 1973
				Kield Rasmussen (Denmark)	Vienna, 1975
				Wieslaw Gawlikowski (Poland)	Vienna, 1975
Center-Fire Pistol	25 m. 60 shots	600—	597	Thomas D. Smith (U.S.)	Sao Paulo, Brazil, 1963

Olympic Games. The record number of gold medals won is five by seven marksmen: Carl Osburn (U.S.) (1912–1924); Konrad Stäheli (Switz.) (1900 and 1906); Willis Lee (U.S.) (1920); Louis Richardet (Switz.) (1900 and 1906); Ole Andreas Lilloe-Olsen (Norway) (1920–1924); Alfred Lane (U.S.) (1912 and 1920) and Morris Fisher (U.S.) (1920 and 1924). Osburn also won 4 silver and 2 bronze medals to total 11. The only marksman to win 3 individual gold medals has been Gulbrandsen Skatteboe (Norway) (b. July 18, 1875) in 1906–1908–1912.

Record Heads. The world's finest head is the 23-pointer stag head in the Maritzburg collection, Germany. The outside span is 75½ inches, the length 47½ inches and the weight 41½ lbs. The greatest number of points is probably 33 (plus 29) on the stag shot in 1696 by Frederick III (1657–1713), the Elector of Brandenburg, later King Frederick I of Prussia.

Largest Shoulder Guns. The largest bore shoulder guns made were 2 bores. Less than a dozen of these were made by two English wildfowl gunmakers in *c.* 1885. Normally the largest guns made are double-barrelled 4-bore weighing up to 26 lbs. which can be handled only by men of exceptional physique. Larger smooth-bore guns have been made, but these are for use as punt-guns.

Bench Rest Shooting. The smallest group on record at 1,000 yards is 6.125 inches by Kenneth A. Keefer, Jr., with a 7 m.m.-300 Remington Action in Williamstown, Pennsylvania, on September 22, 1974.

Block Tossing. Using a pair of auto-loading Remington Nylon 66 .22 caliber guns, Tom Frye (U.S.) tossed 100,010 blocks (2½-inch pine cubes) and hit 100,004—his longest run was 32,860—on October 5–17, 1959.

Clay Pigeon Shooting. The record number of clay birds shot in an hour is 1,904 by Tom Kreckman, 36, at Cresco, Pennsylvania, on September 28, 1975. He used five guns and four loaders.

Most world titles have been won by S. De Lamniczer (Hungary) in 1929, 1933 and 1939. The only woman to win two world titles has been Gräfin von Soden (West Germany) in 1966–67.

Biggest Bag. The largest animal ever shot by any big game hunter was a bull African elephant (*Loxodonta africana africana*) shot by E. M. Nielsen of Columbus, Nebraska, 25 miles north-northeast of Mucusso, Angola, on November 7, 1974. The animal, brought down by a Westley Richards 0.425, stood 13 feet 8 inches at the shoulder.

In November, 1965, Simon Fletcher, 28, a Kenyan farmer, claims to have killed two elephants with one 0.458 bullet.

The greatest recorded lifetime bag is 556,000 birds, including 241,000 pheasants, by the 2nd Marquess of Ripon (1852–1923) of England. He himself dropped dead on a grouse moor after shooting his 52nd bird on the morning of September 22, 1923.

Revolver Shooting. The greatest rapid-fire feat was that of Ed McGivern (U.S.), who twice fired from 15 feet in 0.45 of a second 5 shots which could be covered by a silver half dollar piece at the Lead Club Range, South Dakota, on August 20, 1932.

McGivern also, on September 13, 1932, at Lewiston, Montana, fired 10 shots in 1.2 seconds from two guns at the same time double action (no draw), all 10 shots hitting two 2¼ by 3½ inch playing cards at 15 feet.

Air Weapons. The individual world record for air rifle (40 shots at 10 meters) is 393 by Olegario Vazquez (Mexico) at Mexico City in 1973, and for air pistol (40 shots at 10 meters) is 393 by Harald Vollmar (East Germany) at Paris in February, 1976.

Rapid Firing. Using a Soper single-loading rifle, Private John Warrick, 1st Berkshire Volunteers, loaded and fired 60 rounds in one minute at Basingstoke, England, in April, 1870.

Fast Draw. Due to the lack of standardization of competitions, guns and timing devices, there are a variety of claims to the title of World's Fastest Gun. The most well-known is Bob Munden (b.

Kansas City, Mo., February 8, 1942), who has drawn and fired in 0.0175 seconds. His other single-shot records include Walk and Draw Level Blanks in 15/100ths sec. at Arcadia, California, on June 4, 1972, and Standing Reaction Blanks (4-inch balloons at 8 feet) in 16/100ths sec. at Norwalk, California, on January 21, 1973, and Self Start Blanks in 2/100ths sec. at Baldwin Park, California, on August 17, 1968. Munden also shot 5 balloons at 8 feet in a record 1.06 seconds.

Trick Shooting. The most renowned trick shot of all time was Annie Oakley (*née* Mozee) (1860–1926). She demonstrated the ability to shoot 100 ex 100 in trap shooting for 35 years, aged between 27 and 62. At 30 paces she could split a playing card end-on, hit a dime in mid-air or shoot a cigarette from the lips of her husband—one Frank Butler.

Skateboarding

Highest Speed. "World" skateboard championships have been staged intermittently since 1966. The highest speed recorded on a skateboard is 66.5 m.p.h. over 50 yards under South African Skateboard Association surveillance on a course at Natarina near Johannesburg, flat on his back, by Peter Clark, 14, on December 19, 1977. The stand-up record is 53.45 m.p.h. by John Hutson, 23, at Signal Hill, Long Beach, California, on June 11, 1978. The high jump record is 5 feet by Bryan Beardsly (U.S.) at Signal Hill, September 24-25, 1977.

Barrel Jumping. At the U.S. Skateboard Association championships, Tony Alva, 19, of Santa Monica, California, took off from a moving skateboard, jumped over 17 barrels (12-inch diameters) and landed on another skateboard.

Skiing

Origins. The most ancient ski in existence was found well preserved in a peat bog at Höting, Sweden, dating from *c.* 2500 B.C. A rock carving of a skier at Rodoy, northern Norway, dates from 2000 B.C. The earliest recorded military use was in Norway, in 1199, though it did not grow into a sport until 1843 at Tromsø. The Trysil Shooting and Skiing Club (founded 1861), in Norway, claims to be the world's oldest. Skiing was not introduced in the Alps until 1883, though there is some evidence of earlier use in the Carniola district. The earliest formal downhill race was staged at Montana, Switzerland, in 1911. The first Slalom event was run at Mürren, Switzerland, on January 21, 1922. The International Ski Federation (F.I.S.) was founded on February 2, 1924. The Winter Olympics were inaugurated on January 25, 1924.

OLYMPIC SPEEDSTER: Franz Klammer of Austria won the downhill medal in 1976 at 63.894 m.p.h.

Highest Speed. The highest speed ever claimed for any skier is 124.412 m.p.h. by Steve McKinney (U.S.) (b. 1953) at Portillo, Chile, on October 1, 1978.

The average race speed by 1976 Olympic Downhill champion Franz Klammer (born December 3, 1953) of Austria on the Iglis-Patscherkofel course, Innsbruck, Austria, was 63.894 m.p.h. on February 5, 1976.

Duration. The longest non-stop Nordic skiing marathon was one that lasted 48 hours by Onni Savi, aged 35, of Padasjoki, Finland, who covered 305.9 kilometers (190.1 miles) between noon on April 19 and noon on April 21, 1966.

Ahti Nevada (Finland) covered 174.5 miles in 24 hours at Rovaniemi, Finland, on March 30, 1977.

Ian Smith and David Brown (U.S.) completed 54 hours of Alpine skiing at Vernon Valley, Great Gorge Ski Area, McAfee, New Jersey, on January 27–29, 1978.

Most World Titles. The World Alpine Championships were inaugurated at Mürren, Switzerland, in 1931. The greatest number of titles won is 12 by Christel Cranz (born July 1, 1914), of Germany, with four Slalom (1934–37–38–39), three Downhill (1935–37–39) and five Combined (1934–35–37–38–39). She also won the gold medal for the Combined in the 1936 Olympics. The most titles won by a man is seven by Anton ("Toni") Sailer (born November 17, 1935), of Austria, who won all four in 1956 (Giant Slalom, Slalom, Downhill and the non-Olympic Alpine Combination) and the Downhill, Giant Slalom and Combined in 1958.

In the Nordic events Sixten Jernberg (Sweden) (b. February 6, 1929) won eight titles, 4 at 50 km., one at 30 km., and 3 in relays, in 1956–64. Johan Grottumsbraaten (1899–1942), of Norway, won six individual titles (two at 18 kilometers and four Combined) in 1926–32. The most by a woman is nine by Galina Koulakova (U.S.S.R.) (b. April 29, 1942) from 1968 to 1978. The record for a jumper is five by Birger Ruud (b. August 23, 1911), of Norway, in 1931–32 and 1935–36–37.

The World Cup, instituted in 1967, has been won four times by Gustavo Thoeni (Italy) (b. February 28, 1931) in 1971–72–73–75. The women's cup has been won five times by the 5-foot-6-inch 150-lb. Annemarie Moser (*née* Proell) (Austria) in 1971–72–73–74–75. In 1973, she completed a record sequence of 11 consecutive downhill victories, and in nine seasons, 1970–1978, has won a total of 52 individual events. The most individual events won by a man is 29 by Ingemar Stenmark (Sweden) in 1974–78.

Most Olympic Victories. The most Olympic gold medals won by an individual for skiing is four (including one for a relay) by Sixten Jernberg (born February 6, 1929), of Sweden, in 1956–60–64. In addition, Jernberg has won three silver and two bronze medals. The only woman to win four gold medals is Galina Koulakova (b. 1942) of U.S.S.R., who won the 5 kilometers and 10 kilometers (1972) and was a member of the winning 3×5 kilometers relay team in 1972 and the 4×5 kilometers team in 1976. Koulakova also has won one silver and two bronze medals, in 1968 and 1976.

The most Olympic gold medals won in men's alpine skiing is three, by Anton ("Toni") Sailer in 1956 and Jean-Claude Killy in 1968.

Longest Jump. The longest ski jump ever recorded is one of 181 meters (593 feet 10 inches) by Bogdan Norcic (Yugoslavia) who fell on landing at Planica, Yugoslavia, in February 1977.

The official record is 176 meters (577 feet 5 inches) by Toni Innauer (Austria) (b. April 1, 1958) at Oberstdorf, West Germany, on March 6, 1976.

The women's record is 321 feet 6 inches by Anita Wold of Norway, at Okura, Sapporo, Japan, on January 14, 1975.

WINNER OF 9 OLYMPIC MEDALS AND 8 WORLD TITLES: Sixten Jernberg of Sweden, cross-country skier, is here winning his seventh Swedish championship in a row.

WORLD CUP: Annemarie Moser (née Proell) of Austria has won the women's competition 5 times, and, in 1973, won a record 11 consecutive downhill races.

Cross-Country. The world's greatest Nordic ski race is the "Vasa Lopp," which commemorates an event of 1521 when Gustavus Vasa (1496–1560), later King of Sweden, skied 85.8 kilometers (53.3 miles) from Mora to Sälen, Sweden. The re-enactment of this journey in the reverse direction is an annual event, with a record 11,596 starters on March 5, 1978. The record time is 4 hours 9 minutes 7 seconds by Matti Kuosku on March 7, 1976.

Steepest Descent. Sylvain Saudan (b. Lausanne, Switzerland, September 23, 1936) achieved a descent of Mont Blanc on the northeast side down the Couloir Gervasutti from 13,937 feet on October 17, 1967, skiing gradients in excess of 60 degrees.

STEEPEST DESCENT: Sylvain Saudan has skied down hills with a gradient in excess of 60 degrees.

NINETEEN AT ONCE: This "Hot Dog" stunt was accomplished in Wyoming.

Greatest Descent. The greatest reported elevation descended in 12 hours is 416,000 feet by Sarah Ludwig, Scott Ludwig, and Timothy B. Gaffney, at Mt. Brighton, Michigan, on February 16, 1974.

Highest Altitude. Yuichiro Miura (Japan) skied 1.6 miles down Mt. Everest on May 6, 1970, starting from 26,200 feet. In a run from a height of 24,418 feet he reached speeds of 93.6 m.p.h. Sylvain Saudan (Switzerland) became the first man to ski down Mount McKinley (20,320 feet) on June 10, 1972. He took 7 hours to reach the 7,000 foot level and made 2,700 jump turns on the 50-55° top slopes.

Longest Run. The longest all-downhill ski run in the world is the Weissfluhjoch-Küblis Parsenn course (7.6 miles long), near Davos, Switzerland. The run from the Aiguille du Midi top of the Chamonix lift (vertical lift 8,176 feet) across the Vallée Blanche is 13 miles.

Backflip on Skis. Nineteen members of the Sunset Sports Center's "Hot Dog" team at Grand Targhee Ski Resort, Wyoming, performed a simultaneous back somersault while holding hands on February 9, 1975.

Longest Lift. The longest chair lift in the world is the Alpine Way to Kosciusko Châlet lift above Thredbo, near the Snowy Mountains, New South Wales, Australia. It takes from 45 to 75 minutes to ascend the 3.5 miles, according to the weather. The highest is at Chacaltaya, Bolivia, rising to 16,500 feet. The longest gondola ski lift, at Killington, Vermont, is 3.4 miles long.

Skijoring. The record speed reached in aircraft skijoring (being towed by an aircraft) is 109.23 m.p.h. by Reto Pitsch on the Silsersee, St. Moritz, Switzerland, in 1956.

Ski Parachuting. The greatest recorded vertical descent in parachute ski-jumping is 3,300 feet by Rick Sylvester, 29 (U.S.), who on July 28, 1976, skied off the 6,600-foot summit of Mt. Asgard in Auyuittuq National Park, Baffin Island, Canada, landing on the Turner Glacier. The jump was made for a sequence in the James Bond film "The Spy Who Loved Me."

Ski-Bob. The ski-bob was invented by a Mr. Stevens of Hartford, Connecticut, and patented (No. 47334) on April 19, 1892, as a "bicycle with ski-runners." The Fédération Internationale de Skibob was founded on January 14, 1961, in Innsbruck, Austria. The first World Championships were held at Bad Hofgastein, Austria, in 1967.

The highest speed has been 103.4 m.p.h. by Erich Brenter (Austria) at Cervinia, Italy, in 1964. The only ski-bobbers to retain world championships are Gerhilde Schiffkorn (Austria) who won the women's title in 1967 and 1969, Gertrude Geberth, who won in 1971 and 1973 and Alois Fischbauer (Austria) who won the men's title in 1973 and 1975.

Snowmobiling. The record speed for a snowmobile was increased to 135.93 m.p.h. by Donald J. Pitzen (U.S.) at Union Lake, Michigan, on February 27, 1977.

Soccer

Origins. A game with some similarities termed *Tsu-chu* was played in China in the 3rd and 4th centuries B.C. The earliest clear representation of the game is in a print from Edinburgh, Scotland, dated 1672–73. The game became standardized with the formation of the Football Association in England on October 26, 1863. A 26-a-side game, however, existed in Florence, Italy, as early as 1530, for which rules were codified in *Discorsa Calcio* in 1580. The world's oldest club is Sheffield F.C. of England, formed on October 24, 1857. Eleven on a side was standardized in 1870.

Highest Scores

Teams. The highest score recorded in any first-class match is 36. This occurred in the Scottish Cup match between Arbroath and Bon Accord on September 5, 1885, when Arbroath won 36–0 on their home ground. But for the lack of nets, the playing time might have been longer and the score possibly even higher.

The highest goal margin recorded in any international match is 17. This occurred in the England vs. Australia match at Sydney on June 30, 1951, when England won 17–0. This match is not listed by England as a *full* international.

Individuals. The most goals scored by one player in a first-class match is 16 by Stanis for Racing Club de Lens vs. Aubry-Asturies, in Lens, France, on December 13, 1942.

The record number of goals scored by one player in an international match is 10 by Gottfried Fuchs for Germany, which beat Russia 16–0 in the 1912 Olympic tournament in Sweden.

Artur Friedenreich (b. 1892) is believed to have scored an undocumented 1,329 goals in Brazilian football, but the greatest total of goals scored in a specified period is 1,216 by Edson Arantes do

Nascimento (b. Baurú, Brazil, October 23, 1940), known as Pelé, the Brazilian inside left, from September 7, 1956, to October 2, 1974 (1,254 games). His best year was 1958 with 139. His *milesimo* (1,000th) came in a penalty for his club, Santos, in the Maracaña Stadium, Rio de Janeiro, on November 19, 1969, when he was playing in his 909th first-class match. He came out of retirement in 1975 to add to his total with the New York Cosmos of the North American Soccer League. By his retirement on October 1, 1977 his total had reached 1,281 in 1,363 games. Franz ("Bimbo") Binder (b. 1911) scored 1,006 goals in 756 games in Austria and Germany between 1930 and 1950.

Fastest Goals

The record for an international match is 3 goals in 3½ minutes by Willie Hall (Tottenham Hotspur) for England against Ireland on November 16, 1938, at Old Trafford, Manchester, England.

Most Appearances

Robert ("Bobby") Moore of West Ham United and Fulham set a new record of full international appearances by playing in his 108th game for England vs. Italy on November 14, 1973 at Wembley, London. His first appearance was vs. Peru on May 20, 1962, and he retired on May 14, 1977, on his 1,000th appearance.

Most Successful National Coach

Helmut Schoen (born 1915) of West Germany coached his teams to victory in the 1972 European championship and the 1974 World Cup, as well as finishing second in the 1966 World Cup and 1976 European championships, and third in the 1970 World Cup.

MOST CAREER GOALS: For the greater part of his 20-year career, Pelé averaged a goal a match. His total before he came to play in the United States in 1975 was 1,216.

MOST VALUABLE PLAYER: A Spanish soccer club paid more than $2.3 million for the rights to Johan Cruyff.

Longest Match

The world duration record for a first-class match was set in the Copa Libertadores championship in Santos, Brazil, on August 2–3, 1962, when Santos drew 3–3 with Penarol F.C. of Montevideo, Uruguay. The game lasted $3\frac{1}{2}$ hours (with interruptions), from 9:30 p.m. to 1 a.m.

A match between the Simon Fraser University Clansmen and the Quincy College Hawks lasted 4 hours 25 minutes (221 minutes 43 seconds playing time) at Pasadena, California, in November, 1976.

Crowds

The greatest recorded crowd at any football match was 205,000 (199,854 paid) for the Brazil vs. Uruguay World Cup final in Rio de Janeiro, Brazil, on July 16, 1950.

Transfer Fees

The world's highest reported transfer fee is £922,300 ($2,305,750) for the Amsterdam Ajax striker Johan Cruyff, signed by F.C. Barcelona of Spain, announced on August 20, 1973.

It is reported that Naples, Italy, paid Bologna, Italy, $3,220,000 for center-forward Guiseppe Savoldi on July 11, 1975. Two other players were included in this deal.

World Cup

The *Fédération Internationale de Football* (F.I.F.A.) was founded in Paris on May 21, 1904, and instituted the World Cup Competition in 1930, in Montevideo, Uruguay.

The only country to win three times has been Brazil (1958–1962–1970). Brazil was also third in 1938 and second in 1950, and is the only one of the 45 participating countries to have played in all 11 competitions.

The record goal scorer has been Just Fontaine (France) with 13 goals in 6 games in the final stages of the 1958 competition. The most goals scored in a final is 3 by Geoffrey Hurst (West Ham United) for England vs. West Germany on July 30, 1966. Gerd Müller (West Germany) scored 14 goals in two World Cup finals (1970 and 1974).

Antonio Carbajal (b. 1923) played for Mexico in goal in the competitions of 1950–54–58–62 and 1966.

Receipts

The greatest receipts at a World Cup final were £204,805 ($573,454) from an attendance of 96,924 for the match between England and West Germany at the Empire Stadium, Wembley, Greater London, on July 30, 1966.

Heaviest Goalkeeper

The biggest goalie on record was Willie J. ("Fatty") Foulke of England (1874–1916) who stood 6 feet 3 inches and weighed 311 lbs. By the time he died, he tipped the scales at 364 lbs. He once stopped a game by snapping the cross bar.

Soccer (Amateur)

Most Olympic Wins. The only country to have won the Olympic football title three times is Hungary in 1952, 1964 and 1968. The United Kingdom won in 1908 and 1912 and also the unofficial tournament of 1900. These contests have now virtually ceased to be amateur. The highest Olympic score is Denmark 17 vs. France "A" 1 in 1908.

Largest Crowd. The highest attendance at any amateur match is 120,000 at Senayan Stadium, Djakarta, Indonesia, on February 26, 1976, for the Pre-Olympic Group II Final between North Korea and Indonesia.

Heading. The highest recorded number of repetitions for heading a ball is 12,100 in 54 minutes 22 seconds by Michael Helliwell, 17, of Elland, England, on December 14, 1973.

Ball Control. Luis Lopez juggled a regulation soccer ball for 3 hours 1 minute 26 seconds non-stop at San Gabriel High School, California, on August 16, 1978. He hit the ball 15,219 times with his feet, legs and head without ever letting the ball touch the ground.

Marathons. The longest recorded 11-a-side soccer marathon played without substitutes under Football Association rules is

48 hours by two teams from Muhlenberg College, Allentown, Pennsylvania, April 6–8, 1978.

The longest recorded authenticated 5-a-side games have been (outdoors) 62 hours by two teams (no substitutes) from the Duke of York's Military School, Dover, England, June 27–29, 1978, and (indoors) 91 hours 45 minutes by two teams (no substitutes) from Liverpool Polytechnic, Merseyside, England, February 16–20, 1978.

Table Football. The most protracted game of 2-a-side table football on record was one of 341 hours maintained by 6 members of Burrow upon Soar Youth Club, Leicestershire, England, April 10–24, 1976.

Softball

Origins. Softball, as an indoor derivative of baseball, was invented by George Hancock at the Farragut Boat Club of Chicago, in 1887. Rules were first codified in Minneapolis in 1895 as Kitten Ball. International rules were set in 1933 when the name Softball was officially adopted. The I.S.F. was formed in 1952 as governing body for both fast pitch and slow pitch (with a minimum of a 3-foot arch in trajectory). The world series for men was inaugurated in 1966 and for women in 1965.

Perfect Game. Richard Daris (Monarchs) and Michael DeMeo (Spindrift) pitched perfect games at Springfield, Mass., on May 16, 1976 and Newport, R.I., on June 16, 1977 respectively.

Marathon. The longest fast-pitch marathon is 54 hours by two teams of nine (no substitutes) from North Otago Softball Association, South Island, New Zealand, February 4–6, 1978. The longest for slow pitch is 72 hours 3 seconds by two teams of 10 players from the U.S. Navy in Singapore, December 28–30, 1977.

Squash

(Note: "1971," for example, refers to the 1971–72 season.)

Earliest Champion. Although racquets with a soft ball was evolved in *c.* 1850 at Harrow School (England), there was no recognized champion of any country until J. A. Miskey of Philadelphia won the American Amateur Singles Championship in 1906.

World Title. The inaugural Amateur International Federation championships were staged in Australia in August, 1967. Australia has won the team title four times. Geoffrey B. Hunt (Australia) took the individual title in 1967, 1969 and 1971.

The World Open championship, instituted in 1976, has been won twice by Geoffrey B. Hunt (Australia), in 1976 and 1977.

Most Victories

Open Championship. The most wins in the Open Championship (amateur or professional), held annually in Britain, is seven by

Hashim Khan (Pakistan) in 1950–51–52–53–54–55 and 1957. He also won the Vintage title in 1977.

Amateur Championship. The most wins in the Amateur Championship is six by Abdel Fattah Amr Bey (Egypt), later appointed Ambassador in London, who won in 1931–32–33 and 1935–36–37.

Longest and Shortest Championship Matches. The longest recorded match was one of 2 hours 35 minutes in the British Amateur Championships at Wembley, England, on December 12, 1976, when Murray Lilley (New Zealand) beat Barry O'Connor (G.B.) 9–3, 10–8, 2–9, 7–9, 10–8. The second game lasted 58 minutes and there were a total of 98 lets called in the match.

Sue Cogswell beat Teresa Lawes in only 16 minutes in a British Women's title match at Dallington, North Hampshire, on December 12, 1977.

Most Victories in the Women's Championship. The most wins in the Women's Squash Rackets Championship is 16 by Heather McKay (*née* Blundell) of Australia, 1961 to 1976.

Marathon Record. In squash marathons a rest interval of 1 minute is allowed between games and 2 minutes between the 4th and 5th games with 5 minutes additional rest per hour. The rate of play must not exceed 11 games per hour.

OPEN SQUASH CHAMPION: Hashim Khan of Pakistan has won 7 times.

WOMEN'S SQUASH CHAMPION: Heather McKay won 16 titles in the annual women's championships.

The longest recorded squash marathon (under these competition conditions) has been one of 95 hours 1 minute by Brian Moffett and Mike Sitton at the Shell Research Centre, Sittingbourne, Kent, England, on September 9–13, 1977. Robert Southall of Brisbane, Queensland, Australia, completed 102 hours 37 minutes against 66 opponents, June 22–27, 1978.

Surfing

Origins. The traditional Polynesian sport of surfing in a canoe (*ehorooe*) was first recorded by the British explorer, Captain James Cook (1728–79) on his third voyage to Tahiti in December, 1771. Surfing on a board (*Amo Amo iluna ka lau oka nalu*) was first described ("most perilous and extraordinary . . . altogether astonishing, and is scarcely to be credited") by Lt. (later Capt.) James King of the Royal Navy in March, 1779, at Kealakekua Bay, Hawaii Island. A surfer was first depicted by this voyage's official artist John Webber. The sport was revived at Waikiki by 1900. Australia's first club, the Bondi Surf Bathers Lifesaving Club, was formed in February, 1906. Hollow boards came in in 1929 and the plastic-foam type in 1956.

Highest Waves Ridden. Makaha Beach, Hawaii, provides reputedly the best consistently high waves for surfing, often reaching the rideable limit of 30–35 feet. The highest wave ever ridden was the *tsunami* of "perhaps 50 feet," which struck Minole, Hawaii, on April 3, 1868, and was ridden to save his life by a Hawaiian named Holua.

Longest Ride. About 4 to 6 times each year rideable surfing waves break in Matanchen Bay near San Blas, Nayarit, Mexico, which make rides of *c.* 5,700 feet possible.

World Champions. World Championships were inaugurated in 1964 at Sydney, Australia. The first surfer to win two titles has been Joyce Hoffman (U.S.) in 1965 and 1966.

Swimming

Earliest References. Swimming in schools in Japan was ordered by Imperial edict of Emperor Go-Yoozei as early as 1603, but competition was known from 36 B.C. Sea water bathing was fashionable at Scarborough, North Yorkshire, England, as early as 1660. Competitive swimming originated in London *c.* 1837, at which time there were five or more pools, the earliest of which had been opened at St. George's Pier Head, Liverpool, in 1828.

Largest Pools. The largest swimming pool in the world is the salt-water Orthlieb Pool in Casablanca, Morocco. It is 480 meters (1,547 feet) long and 75 meters (246 feet) wide, an area of 8.9 acres.

The largest land-locked swimming pool with heated water was the Fleishhacker Pool on Sloat Boulevard, near Great Highway, San Francisco. It measures 1,000 feet by 150 feet (3.44 acres), is up to 14 feet deep, and can contain 7,500,000 gallons of water. It was opened on May 2, 1925, but has now been abandoned to a few ducks.

The world's largest competition pool is at Osaka, Japan. It accommodates 25,000 spectators.

Fastest Swimmer. Excluding relay stages with their anticipatory starts, the highest speed reached by a swimmer is 5.19 m.p.h. by Joe Bottom (U.S.), who recorded 19.70 seconds for 50 yards in a 25-yard pool at Cleveland, Ohio, on March 24, 1977.

Most World Records. Men: 32, Arne Borg (Sweden) (b. 1901),

MOST OLYMPIC MEDALS: Mark Spitz (left) won 11 medals, including 9 gold. Shirley Babashoff (right) is one of three women who have earned 8 Olympic medals.

FASTEST SWIMMER: American Joe Bottom covered 50 yards in 19.70 seconds in March, 1977.

1921–29. Women: 42, Ragnhild Hveger (Denmark) (b. December 10, 1920), 1936–42.

World Titles. In the world swimming championships (instituted in 1973), the greatest number of medals won is ten (8 gold, 2 silver) by Kornelia Ender of East Germany. The most by a man is seven (6 gold, 1 bronze) by James Montgomery (U.S.).

Olympic Swimming Records

Most Olympic Gold Medals. The greatest number of Olympic gold medals won is 9 by Mark Andrew Spitz (U.S.) (b. February 10, 1950), as follows:

100 meter free-style	1972
200 meter free-style	1972
100 meter butterfly	1972
200 meter butterfly	1972
4 × 100 meter free-style relay	1968 and 1972
4 × 200 meter free-style relay	1968 and 1972
4 × 100 meter medley relay	1972

All but one of these performances (the 4 × 200 meter relay of 1968) were also world records at the time.

The record number of gold medals won by a woman is 4 shared by Mrs. Patricia McCormick (*née* Keller) (U.S.) (b. May 12, 1930) with the High and Springboard Diving double in 1952 and 1956 (also the women's record for individual golds); by Dawn Fraser (later Mrs. Gary Ware) (Australia) (b. September 4, 1937) with the 100 meter free-style (1956–60–64) and the 4 × 100 meter free-style relay (1956); and by Kornelia Ender (East Germany) with the 100 and 200 meter free-style (1976), the 100 meter butterfly (1976) and the 4 × 100 meter medley relay (1976). Dawn Fraser is the only swimmer to win the same event on three successive occasions.

Most Olympic Medals. The most medals won is 11 by Spitz, who in addition to his 9 golds (see above), won a silver (100 m. butterfly) and a bronze (100 m. free-style) both in 1968.

SWIMMING—WORLD RECORDS—MEN

At distances recognized by the Federation Internationale de Natation Amateur as of November 14, 1978. F.I.N.A. no longer recognizes any records made for non-metric distances. Only performances set up in 50-meter pools are recognized as World Records.

Distance	min. sec.	Name and Nationality	Place	Date
		FREE-STYLE		
100 meters	49.44	Jonty Skinner (South Africa)	Philadelphia, Pennsylvania	Aug. 14, 1976
200 meters	1:50.29	Bruce Furniss (U.S.)	Montreal, Canada	July 19, 1976
400 meters	3:51.56	Brian Goodell (U.S.)	East Berlin, E. Germany	Aug. 27, 1977
800 meters	8:01.54	Bobby Hackett (U.S.)	Long Beach, California	June 21, 1976
1,500 meters	15:02.40	Brian Goodell (U.S.)	Montreal, Canada	July 20, 1976
4 × 100 Relay	3:19.74	U.S. National Team	West Berlin, W. Germany	Aug. 22, 1978
		(Jack Babashoff, Ambrose Gaines, David McCagg, James Montgomery)		
4 × 200 Relay	7:20.82	U.S. National Team	West Berlin, W. Germany	Aug. 24, 1978
		(Bruce Furniss, William Forrester, Bobby Hackett, Ambrose Gaines)		
		BREAST STROKE		
100 meters	1:02.86	Gerald Moerken (W. Germany)	Jonkoping, Sweden	Aug. 17, 1977
200 meters	2:15.11	David Wilkie (G.B.)	Montreal, Canada	July 24, 1976
		BUTTERFLY STROKE		
100 meters	54.18	Joseph Bottom (U.S.)	East Berlin, E. Germany	Aug. 27, 1977
200 meters	1:59.23	Michael Bruner (U.S.)	Montreal, Canada	July 18, 1976
		BACK STROKE		
100 meters	55.49	John Naber (U.S.)	Montreal, Canada	July 19, 1976
200 meters	1:59.19	John Naber (U.S.)	Montreal, Canada	July 24, 1976
		INDIVIDUAL MEDLEY		
200 meters	2:03.65	Graham Smith (Canada)	West Berlin, W. Germany	Aug. 24, 1978
400 meters	4:20.05	Jesse Vassallo (U.S.)	West Berlin, W. Germany	Aug. 22, 1978
		MEDLEY RELAY		
		(Back Stroke, Breast Stroke, Butterfly Stroke, Free-Style)		
4 × 100 meters	3:42.22	U.S. National Team	West Berlin, W. Germany	Aug. 22, 1978
		(John Naber, John Hencken, Matthew Vogel, James Montgomery)		

FREE-STYLE MEDALIST: Brian Goodell won the Olympic gold medal at 1,500 meters at Montreal in world record time.

The most medals won by a woman is 8 by Dawn Fraser, who in addition to her 4 golds (see above) won 4 silvers (400 m. free-style 1956, 4×100 m. free-style relay 1960 and 1964, 4×100 m. medley relay 1960); by Shirley Babashoff (U.S.) who won 2 golds (4×100 m. free-style relay 1972 and 1976) and 6 silvers (100 m. free-style 1972, 200 m. free-style 1972 and 1976, 400 m. and 800 m. free-style 1976, and 400 m. medley 1976); and by Kornelia Ender (E. Germany) who, in addition to her 4 golds (see above) won 4 silvers (200 m-individual medley 1972, 4×100 m. medley 1972, 4×100 m. free-style 1972 and 1976).

Most Individual Gold Medals. The record number of individual gold medals won is 4 shared by four swimmers: Charles M. Daniels (U.S.) (1884–1973) (100 m. free-style 1906 and 1908,

BACK STROKE STREAK (left): John Naber set world records at 100 and 200 meters at the 1976 Olympics. FASTEST 100-METER BREAST STROKE (right): Gerald Moerken of West Germany set the new mark of 1 minute 2.86 seconds in August, 1977.

SWIMMING—WORLD RECORDS—WOMEN

(As of November 14, 1978)

Distance	min. sec.	Name and Nationality	Place	Date
		FREE-STYLE		
100 meters	55.41	Barbara Krause (E. Germany)	East Berlin, E. Germany	July 5, 1978
200 meters	1:58.53	Cynthia Woodhead (U.S.)	West Berlin, W. Germany	Aug. 22, 1978
400 meters	4:06.28	Tracey Wickham (Australia)	West Berlin, W. Germany	Aug. 24, 1978
800 meters	8:24.62	Tracey Wickham (Australia)	Edmonton, Canada	Aug. 5, 1978
1,500 meters	16:14.93	Tracey Wickham (Australia)	Brisbane, Australia	Feb. 8, 1978
4 × 100 Relay	3:43.43	U.S. National Team	West Berlin, W. Germany	Aug. 27, 1978
		(Tracy Caulkins, Stephanie Elkins, Jill Sterkel, Cynthia Woodhead)		
		BREAST STROKE		
100 meters	1:10.31	Julia Bogdanova (U.S.S.R.)	West Berlin, W. Germany	Aug. 22, 1978
200 meters	2:31.42	Lina Kachushite (U.S.S.R.)	West Berlin, W. Germany	Aug. 24, 1978
		BUTTERFLY STROKE		
100 meters	59.46	Andrea Pollack (E. Germany)	East Berlin, E. Germany	July 3, 1978
200 meters	2:09.87	Andrea Pollack (E. Germany)	East Berlin, E. Germany	July 4, 1978
200 meters	2:09.87	Tracy Caulkins (U.S.)	West Berlin, W. Germany	Aug. 27, 1978
		BACK STROKE		
100 meters	1:01.51	Ulrike Richter (E. Germany)	East Berlin, E. Germany	June 5, 1976
200 meters	2:11.93	Linda Jezek (U.S.)	West Berlin, W. Germany	Aug. 24, 1978
		INDIVIDUAL MEDLEY		
200 meters	2:14.07	Tracy Caulkins (U.S)	West Berlin, W. Germany	Aug. 20, 1978
400 meters	4:40.83	Tracy Caulkins (U.S.)	West Berlin, W. Germany	Aug. 23, 1978
		MEDLEY RELAY		
		(Back Stroke, Breast Stroke, Butterfly Stroke, Free-Style)		
4 × 100 meters	4:07.95	East German National Team	Montreal, Canada	July 18, 1976
		(Ulrike Richter, Hannelore Anke, Andrea Pollack, Kornelia Ender)		

220 yard free-style 1904, 440 yard free-style 1904); Roland Matthes (E. Germany) (b. November 17, 1950) with 100 m. and 200 m. backstroke 1968 and 1972 and Spitz and McCormick (see above).

Closest Verdict. The closest victory in the Olympic Games was in the Munich 400-meter individual medley final on August 30, 1972, when Gunnar Larsson (Sweden) won by 2/1,000ths of a second in 4 minutes 31.981 seconds over Tim McKee (U.S.)—a margin of less than ⅛ inch, or the length grown by a fingernail in 3 weeks.

DIVING MEDALIST: Klaus Dibiasi of Italy has dominated men's diving competition with 5 Olympic medals and 4 world championship medals between 1964 and 1976.

Diving

Olympic Medals. Klaus Dibiasi (Italy) won a total of 5 medals (3 gold, 2 silver) in four Games from 1964 to 1976. He is also the only diver to win the same event (highboard) at three successive Games (1968, 1972, and 1976). Pat McCormick (see above) won 4 gold medals.

World Titles. Klaus Dibiasi of Italy won 2 gold and 2 silver medals at the first two world championships held in 1973 and 1975.

Perfect Dive. In the 1972 U.S. Olympic Trials, held in Chicago, Michael Finneran (b. September 21, 1948) was awarded a score of 10 by all seven judges for a backward 1½ somersault 2½ twist free dive from the 10-meter board, an achievement without precedent.

Long Distance Swimming

A unique achievement in long distance swimming was established in 1966 by the cross-Channel swimmer Mihir Sen of Calcutta, India. These were the Palk Strait from India to Ceylon (in 25 hours 36 minutes on April 5–6); the Straits of Gibraltar (Europe to Africa in 8 hours 1 minute on August 24); the Dardanelles (Gallipoli, Europe, to Sedulbahir, Asia Minor, in 13 hours 55 minutes on September 12) and the entire length of the Panama Canal in 34 hours 15 minutes on October 29–31. He had earlier swum the English Channel in 14 hours 45 minutes on September 27, 1958.

The longest recorded ocean swim is one of 128.8 miles by Walter Poenisch (U.S.) (b. 1914) from Havana, Cuba to Little Duck Key, Florida (in a shark cage and wearing flippers) in 34 hours 15 minutes on July 11–13, 1978.

The greatest recorded distance ever swum is 1,826 miles down the Mississippi from Ford Dam, near Minneapolis, to Carrollton Avenue, New Orleans, July 6 to December 29, 1930, by Fred P. Newton, then 27, of Clinton, Oklahoma. He was in the water a total of 742 hours, and the water temperature fell as low as 47° F. He protected himself with petroleum jelly.

The longest duration swim ever achieved was one of 168 continuous hours, ending on February 24, 1941, by the legless Charles Zibbelman, *alias* Zimmy (born 1894) of the U.S., in a pool in Honolulu, Hawaii.

The longest duration swim by a woman was 87 hours 27 minutes in a salt water pool at Raven Hall, Coney Island, New York by Mrs. Myrtle Huddleston of New York City, in 1931.

The greatest distance covered in a continuous swim is 292 miles by Joe Maciag (b. March 26, 1956) from Billings to Glendive, Montana, in the Yellowstone River in 64 hours 50 minutes, July 1–4, 1976.

Channel Swimming

Earliest Man. The first man to swim across the English Channel (without a life jacket) was the merchant navy captain Matthew Webb (1848–83) (G.B.), who swam breaststroke from Dover, England, to Cap Gris Nez, France, in 21 hours 45 minutes on August 24–25, 1875. Webb swam an estimated 38 miles to make the 21-mile crossing. Paul Boyton (U.S.) had swum from Cap Gris Nez to the South Foreland in his patent lifesaving suit in 23 hours 30 minutes on May 28–29, 1875. There is good evidence that Jean-Marie Saletti, a French soldier, escaped from a British prison hulk off Dover by swimming to Boulogne in July or August, 1815. The first crossing from France to England was made by Enrique Tiraboschi, a wealthy Italian living in Argentina, who crossed in 16 hours 33 minutes on August 11, 1923, to win a $5,000 prize.

Woman. The first woman to succeed was Gertrude Ederle (U.S.) who swam from Cap Gris Nez, France, to Dover, England, on August 6, 1926, in the then record time of 14 hours 39 minutes. The first woman to swim from England to France was Florence Chadwick of California, in 16 hours 19 minutes on September 11, 1951. She repeated this on September 4, 1953, and October 12, 1955.

Youngest. The youngest conqueror is Karl Beniston (b. December 9, 1964) of Blackpool, England, who swam from Dover to Wissant, France, in 12 hours 25 minutes, when he was aged 13 years 233 days.

CHANNEL CHALLENGERS: Cindy Nicholas (left) swam the English Channel in both directions more than 10 hours faster than the previous male record holder. Gertrude Ederle (right) was the first woman to swim the Channel, on August 6, 1926.

The youngest woman was Abla Adel Khairi (b. Egypt, September 26, 1960), aged 13 years 326 days when she swam from England to France in 12 hours 30 minutes on August 17, 1974.

Oldest. The oldest conqueror of the 21-mile crossing has been William E. (Ned) Barnie, who was 55 when he swam from France to England in 15 hours 1 minute on August 16, 1951. The oldest woman to conquer the Channel was Stella Taylor (born U.S., December 20, 1929), aged 45 years 350 days when she swam it in 18 hours 15 minutes on August 26, 1975.

Fastest. The official Channel Swimming Association record is 7 hours 40 minutes by Penny Dean (b. March 21, 1955) of California, who swam from Shakespeare Beach, Dover, England to Cap Gris Nez, France on July 29, 1978.

Slowest. The slowest crossing was the third ever made, when Henry Sullivan (U.S.) swam from England to France in 26 hours 50 minutes, August 5–6, 1923.

Relays. The two-way record is 16 hours 5½ minutes by a Saudi Arabian team on August 11, 1977. They completed the return journey from France to England in a record 7 hours 58 minutes.

First Double Crossing. Antonio Abertondo (Argentina), aged 42, swam from England to France in 18 hours 50 minutes (8:35 a.m. on September 20 to 3:25 a.m. on September 21, 1961) and after about 4 minutes rest returned to England in 24 hours 16 minutes, landing at St. Margaret's Bay at 3:45 a.m. on September 22, 1961, to complete the first "double crossing" in 43 hours 10 minutes.

Fastest Double Crossing. Cynthia Nicholas, a 19-year-old from Canada, became the first woman to complete a double crossing

HUMAN POLAR BEAR: Gustave Brickner sometimes braves waters below freezing when he takes his daily dip in the Monongahela River.

of the English Channel on September 7–8, 1977. Her astonishing time of 19 hours 55 minutes was more than 10 hours faster than the previous mark.

Most Conquests. The greatest number of Channel conquests is 11 by Desmond Renford (born 1928) (Australia) from 1970 to July, 1977. Cindy Nicholas made her sixth crossing of the Channel on August 27, 1978.

Underwater. The first underwater cross-Channel swim was achieved by Fred Baldasare (U.S.), aged 38, who completed the distance from France to England with scuba in 18 hours 1 minute on July 10–11, 1962. Simon Paterson, aged 20, a frogman from Egham, Surrey, England, traveled underwater from France to England with an airhose attached to his pilot boat in 14 hours 50 minutes on July 28, 1962.

Ice Swimming

The "Human Polar Bear," Gustave A. Brickner (b. 1912) went for his daily dip in the Monongahela River of Pennsylvania on January 24, 1963, when the water temperature was 32°F., the air temperature –18°F., and the wind speed 40 m.p.h. (chill factor –85°F.). The river was ice-clogged at the time.

Most Dangerous Swim

One of the most dangerous swims on record was the unique crossing of the Potaro River in Guyana, South America, just above the 741-foot-high Kaieteur Falls by Private Robert Howatt (U.K.) (the Black Watch) on April 17, 1955. The river is 464 feet wide at the lip of the falls.

Relay Records

The longest recorded mileage in a 24-hour relay swim (team of 5) is 83 miles 620 yards by a team from the Topeka Swimming Association, Topeka, Kansas, on September 30-October 1, 1977.

The fastest time recorded for 100 miles in a pool by a team of 20 swimmers is 22 hours 47 minutes 19.5 seconds by the Menzieshill High School, Dundee, Scotland on December 17–18, 1977.

A team of 6 boys, aged 13 to 15, covered 300 miles in 230 hours 39 minutes, July 18–28, 1968, in Lake Buttermere, England.

Underground Swimming

The longest recorded underground swim is one of 3,402 yards in 87 minutes by David Stanley Gale through the Dudley Old Canal Tunnel, West Midlands, England, in August, 1967.

Treading Water

The duration record for treading water (vertical posture in an 8-foot square without touching the lane markers) is 52 hours by Norman Albert at Pennsylvania State University on November 16-18, 1977.

Table Tennis

Earliest Reference. The earliest evidence relating to a game resembling table tennis has been found in the catalogues of London sporting goods manufacturers in the 1880's. The old Ping-Pong Association was formed there in 1902, but the game proved only a temporary craze until resuscitated in 1921.

Fastest Rallying. The record number of hits in 60 seconds is 162 by Nicky Jarvis and Desmond Douglas in London, England, on December 1, 1976. This was equaled by Douglas and Paul Day at Blackpool, England, on March 21, 1977.

With a paddle in each hand, Alvin H. Getz of San Francisco completed 5,000 consecutive volleys over the net in 55 minutes in June, 1976.

Longest Rally. In a 1936 Swaythling Cup match in Prague between Alex Ehrlich (Poland) and Paneth Farcas (Rumania), the opening rally lasted 2 hours 12 minutes.

Robert Siegel and Donald Peters of Stamford, Connecticut, staged a rally lasting 8 hours 33 minutes on July 30, 1978.

Marathon. The longest recorded time for a marathon singles match by two players is 132 hours 31 minutes by Danny Price and Randy Nunes in Cherry Hill, New Jersey, August 20-26, 1978. Alan Nock of Queanbeyan, New South Wales, Australia, played a series of opponents for 125 hours 1 minute, May 15–20, 1978.

The longest doubles marathon by 4 players is 100 hours 1 minute by players from De La Salle College, Salford, England, April 12–16, 1977.

Highest Speed. No conclusive measurements have been published, but in a lecture M. Sklorz (W. Germany) stated that a smashed ball had been measured at speeds up to 105.6 m.p.h.

Youngest International. The youngest international (probably in any sport) was Joy Foster, aged 8, the 1958 Jamaican singles and mixed doubles champion.

Most Wins in Table Tennis World Championships
(Instituted 1926–27)

Event	Name and Nationality	Times	Date
Men's Singles (St. Bride's Vase)	G. Viktor Barna (Hungary)	5	1930, 32, 33, 34, 35
Women's Singles (G. Geist Prize)	Angelica Rozeanu (Rumania)	6	1950, 51, 52, 53, 54, 55
Men's Doubles	G. Viktor Barna (Hungary) with two different partners	8	1929, 30, 31, 32, 33, 34, 35, 39
Women's Doubles	Maria Mednyanszky (Hungary) with three different partners	7	1928, 30, 31, 32, 33, 34, 35
Mixed Doubles (Men)	Ferenc Sido (Hungary) with two different partners	4	1949, 50, 52, 53
(Women)	M. Mednyanszky (Hungary) with three different partners	6	1927, 28, 30, 31, 33, 34

G. Viktor Barna gained a personal total of 15 world titles, while 18 have been won by Miss Mednyanszky.

Note: With the staging of championships biennially, the breaking of the above records would now be virtually impossible.

Event	Name and Nationality	Times	Date
Men's Team (Swaythling Cup)	Hungary	11	1927, 28, 29, 30, 31, 33, 34, 35, 38, 49, 52
Women's Team (Marcel Corbillon Cup)	Japan	8	1952, 54, 57, 59, 61, 63, 67, 71

WOMEN'S TABLE TENNIS CHAMPION: Angelica Rozeanu of Rumania won 6 World Singles titles.

Tennis

Origins. The modern game of lawn tennis is generally agreed to have evolved as an outdoor form of Royal Tennis. "Field Tennis" was mentioned in an English magazine (*Sporting Magazine*) on September 29, 1793. The earliest club for such a game, variously called Pelota or Lawn Rackets, was the Leamington Club, founded

GREATEST CROWD: Billie Jean King took part in the outlandish display of the "Tennis Match of the Century" in 1973, beating Bobby Riggs in straight sets before 30,472 fans.

in 1872 by Major Harry Gem. In February, 1874, Major Walter Clopton Wingfield, of England (1833–1912) patented a form called "sphairistike," but the game soon became known as lawn tennis.

Amateurs were permitted to play with and against professionals in Open tournaments starting in 1968.

Oldest Courts. The oldest court for Royal Tennis is one built in Paris in 1496. The oldest of 17 surviving tennis courts in the British Isles is the Royal Tennis Court at Hampton Court Palace, which was built by order of King Henry VIII in 1529–30, and rebuilt by order of Charles II in 1660.

Greatest Crowd. The greatest crowd at a tennis match was the 30,472 who came to the Houston Astrodome in Houston, Texas, on September 20, 1973, to watch Billie Jean King beat Bobby Riggs, over 25 years her senior, in straight sets in the so-called "Tennis Match of the Century."

The record for an orthodox match is 25,578 at Sydney, Australia, on December 27, 1954, in the Davis Cup Challenge Round vs. the U.S. (1st day).

Most Davis Cup Victories. The greatest number of wins in the Davis Cup (instituted 1900) has been (inclusive of 1977) by the United States and Australasia/Australia, each with 24 wins.

Individual Davis Cup Performance. Nicola Pietrangeli (Italy) played 164 rubbers, 1954 to 1972, winning 120. He played 110 singles (winning 78) and 54 doubles (winning 42). He took part in 66 ties.

Greatest Domination. The "grand slam" is to hold at the same time all four of the world's major championship titles: Wimbledon, the U.S. Open, Australian and French championships. The first time this occurred was in 1935 when Frederick John Perry (U.K.) (b. 1909) won the French title, having won Wimbledon (1934), the U.S. title (1933–34) and the Australian title (1934).

The first player to hold all four titles simultaneously was J. Donald Budge (U.S.) (b. 1915), who won the championships of Wimbledon (1937), the U.S. (1937), Australia (1938), and France (1938). He subsequently retained Wimbledon (1938) and the U.S. (1938). Rodney George Laver (Australia) (b. August 9, 1938) achieved this grand slam in 1962 as an amateur and repeated as a professional in 1969 to become the first two-time grand slammer.

Two women players also have won all these four titles in the same tennis year. The first was Maureen Catherine Connolly (U.S.). She won the United States title in 1951, Wimbledon in 1952, retained the U.S. title in 1952, won the Australian in 1953, the French in 1953 and Wimbledon again in 1953. She won her third U.S. title in 1953, her second French title in 1954, and her third Wimbledon title in 1954. Miss Connolly (later Mrs. Norman Brinker) was seriously injured in a riding accident shortly before the 1954 U.S. championships; she died in June, 1969, aged only 34.

The second woman to win the "grand slam" was Margaret Smith Court (Australia) (b. July 16, 1942) in 1970.

Olympic Medals. Lawn tennis was part of the program at the first eight celebrations of the Games (including 1906). The winner of the most medals was Max Decugis (1882–1978) of France, with six (a record four gold, one silver and one bronze) in the 1900, 1906 and 1920 tournaments.

The most medals won by a woman is five by Kitty McKane (later Mrs. L. A. Godfree) of Great Britain, with one gold, two silver and two bronze in 1920 and 1924. Five different women won a record two gold medals.

Wimbledon Records

(The first Championship was in 1877. Professionals first played in 1968.) From 1971 the tie-break system was introduced, which effactually prevents sets proceeding beyond a 17th game, i.e. 9–8.

Most Appearances. Arthur W. Gore (1868–1928) of the U.K. made 36 appearances between 1888 and 1927, and was in 1909 at 41 years the oldest singles winner ever. In 1964, Jean Borotra (born August 13, 1898) of France made his 35th appearance since 1922. In 1977, he appeared in the Veterans' Doubles, aged 78.

Most Wins. Elizabeth (Bunny) Ryan (U.S.) (b. 1894) won her first title in 1914 and her nineteenth in 1934 (12 women's doubles with 5 different partners and 7 mixed doubles with 5 different partners). Her total of 19 championships was equaled by Billie Jean King (née Moffitt) (U.S.) with 6 singles, 9 women's doubles, and 4 mixed doubles, 1961–75.

The greatest number of singles wins was eight by Helen N. Moody (née Wills) (b. October 6, 1905) (U.S.), who won in 1927, 1928, 1929, 1930, 1932, 1933, 1935 and 1938.

GRAND SLAM WINNERS: The only men to win all four major titles in the same year were Rod Laver (left) of Australia who performed the feat twice in 1962 and 1969, and Don Budge (right) of the U.S. who did it once in 1937-38.

The greatest number of singles wins by a man was seven by William C. Renshaw in 1881–2–3–4–5–6–9. He also won 7 doubles titles (1880–1–4–5–6–8–9) partnered by his twin brother (James) Ernest. His total of 14 titles is also a men's record.

The greatest number of doubles wins by men was 8 by the brothers Doherty (G.B.)—Reginald Frank (1872–1910) and Hugh Lawrence (1875–1919). They won each year from 1897 to 1905 except for 1902.

The most wins in women's doubles were the 12 by Elizabeth Ryan (U.S.), mentioned above.

The greatest number of mixed doubles wins was 7 by Elizabeth Ryan (U.S.), as noted before. The men's record is four wins, shared by Elias Victor Seixas (b. August 30, 1923) (U.S.) in 1953–54–55–56, Kenneth N. Fletcher (b. June 15, 1940) (Australia) in 1963–65–66–68, and Owen Keir Davidson (Australia) (b. October 4, 1943) in 1967–71–73–74.

Youngest Champions. The youngest champion ever at Wimbledon was Charlotte Dod (1871–1960), who was 15 years 9 months old when she won in 1887.

The youngest male singles champion was Wilfred Baddeley (born January 11, 1872), who won the Wimbledon title in 1891 at the age of 19 years 175 days.

Richard Dennis Ralston (born July 27, 1942), of Bakersfield, California, was 25 days short of his 18th birthday when he won the men's doubles with Rafael H. Osuna (1938–69), of Mexico, in 1960.

The youngest ever player at Wimbledon is reputedly Miss M. Klima (Austria), who was 13 years old in the 1907 singles competi-

MOST GAMES AND LONGEST MATCHES

Note: The increasing option since 1970 by tournament organizers to use various "tie-break" systems, which are precisely designed to stop long sets, is reducing the likelihood of these records being broken and they may shortly become of mere historic interest.

	No. of Games	Players and Score	Place and Date
Any match	147	Dick Leach-Dick Dell (U. of Mich.) bt. Tommy Mozur-Lenny Schloss 3-6, 49-47, 22-20	Newport, R.I., August 18-19, 1967
Any singles	126	Roger Taylor (G.B.) bt. Wieslaw Gasiorek (Poland) 27-29, 31-29, 6-4 (4 hrs. 35 mins.)	King's Cup, Warsaw, Poland, November 5, 1966
Any women's singles	62	Kathy Blake (U.S.) bt. Elena Subirats (Mexico) 12-10, 6-8, 14-12	Piping Rock, Locust Valley, N.Y., 1966
Any women's match	81	Nancy Richey-Carole Graebner (née Caldwell) bt. Justina Bricka-Carol Hanks (all U.S.) 31-33, 6-1, 6-4	South Orange, N.J., 1964
Any mixed doubles	71	William F. Talbot-Margaret du Pont (née Osborne) bt. Robert Falkenburg-Gertrude Moran (all U.S.) 27-25, 5-7, 6-1	Forest Hills, N.Y., 1948
Any set	96	See middle set of any match above	
Longest time for any match	6 hrs. 23 mins.	Mark Cox-Robert K. Wilson (U.K.) bt. Charles M. Pasarell-Ron E. Holmburg (U.S.) 26-24, 17-19, 30-28	U.S. Indoor Championships, Salisbury, Md., August 18-19, 1967
Any Wimbledon match	112	R. A. (Pancho) Gonzales (U.S.) bt. Charles M. Pasarell (U.S.) 22-24, 1-6, 16-14, 6-3, 11-9	First round, June 24-25, 1969
Any Wimbledon doubles	98	Eugene L. Scott (U.S.)-Nicola Pilic (Yugoslavia) bt. G. Cliff Richey (U.S.)-Torben Ulrich (Denmark) 19-21, 12-10, 6-4, 4-6, 9-7	First round, June 22, 1966
Any Wimbledon set	62	Pancho Segura (Ecuador)-Alex Olmedo (Peru) bt. Abe A. Segal-Gordon L. Forbes (S. Africa) 32-30	Second round, June 1968
Longest time for any Wimbledon match	5 hrs. 12 mins.	See any Wimbledon match above	
Wimbledon men's final	58	Jaroslav Drobny (then Egypt) bt. Kenneth R. Rosewall (Australia) 13-11, 4-6, 6-2, 9-7	Final, July 1954
Wimbledon men's doubles final	70	John D. Newcombe-Anthony D. Roche (Australia) bt. Kenneth R. Rosewall-Frederick S. Stolle (Australia) 3-6, 8-6, 5-7, 14-12, 6-3	Final, July 1968
Wimbledon women's final	46	Margaret Smith Court (Australia) bt. Billie Jean Moffitt King (U.S.) 14-12, 11-9 (2 hrs. 25 mins.)	Final, July 1970
Wimbledon women's doubles final	38	Mme. Simone Mathieu (France)-Elizabeth Ryan (U.S.) bt. Freda James (now Hammersley)-Adeline Maud Yorke (both G.B.) 6-2, 9-11, 6-4	Final, July 1933
		Rosemary Casals-Billie Jean King (both U.S.) bt. Maria E. Bueno (Brazil)-Nancy Richey (U.S.) 9-11, 6-4, 6-2	Final, July 1963

Wimbledon mixed doubles final	48	Eric W. Sturgess–Mrs. Shelia Summers (S. Africa) bt. John E. Bromwich (Australia)–Alice Louise Brough (U.S.) 9–7, 9–11, 7–5	Final, July 1949
Any Davis Cup rubber	122	Stanley Smith–Erik Van Dillen (U.S.) bt. Jaime Fillol–Pat Cornejo (Chile) 7–9, 37–39, 8–6, 6–1, 6–3	American Zone Tie, 1973
Any Davis Cup singles	86	Arthur Ashe (U.S.) bt. Christian Kuhnke (Germany) 6–8, 10–12, 9–7, 13–11, 6–4	Challenge Round, Cleveland, O. 1970
Any Davis Cup tie i.e. 5 rubbers	327	India bt. Australia 3–2	East Zone Final, Calcutta, May 10–14, 1974

MOST WIMBLEDON VICTORIES: Bunny Ryan won a total of 19 Wimbledon championships (12 women's doubles, 7 mixed doubles) in 20 years of competition.

LONGEST WIMBLEDON MATCH: Pancho Gonzales (U.S.) played 112 games in 5 hours 12 minutes in 1969, and finally beat Charles Pasarell (U.S.).

A PROFITABLE RACKET: Chris Evert (left) and Guillermo Vilas (right) have had the most financially successful single years in women's and men's tennis, each netting record earnings in 1977.

tion. The youngest of modern times is Tracy Austin (U.S.) (b. December 12, 1962) who was only 14 years 7 months in the 1977 tournament.

Greatest Attendance. The record crowd for one day at Wimbledon is 38,290 on June 28, 1978. The total attendance record was set at the 1975 Championships with 338,591.

Professional Tennis

Highest Prize Money. The greatest reward for playing a single match is the $500,000 won by Jimmy Connors (U.S.) (born September 2, 1952) when he beat John Newcombe (Australia), (born May 23, 1944) in a challenge match at Caesars Palace Hotel, Las Vegas, Nevada, April 26, 1975.

The record winnings for a year, not including special restricted events and team tennis salaries, is $800,642 by Guillermo Vilas (Argentina) (born August 17, 1952) in 1977.

Christine Marie Evert (U.S.) (born December 21, 1954), the 1976 Wimbledon champion, earned a record $453,154 in 1977.

Tennis Marathons

The longest doubles is one of 73 hours by 4 players from Edmonds Senior High School, Edmonds, Washington from May 28 to June 1, 1977.

The duration record for singles is 102 hours 45 minutes by William

F. Nethercote and James F. Driscoll at Walpole, Massachusetts, June 17–21, 1978. J. Townsend Gilbert of South Burlington, Vermont, played singles against a number of opponents for 100 hours January 31–February 4, 1978.

Fastest Service. The fastest service ever *measured* was one of 163.6 m.p.h. by William Tatem Tilden (1893–1953) (U.S.) in 1931. The American professional Scott Carnahan, 22, was electronically clocked at 137 m.p.h. at Pauley Pavilion in Los Angeles, California, during the third annual "Cannonball Classic" sponsored by *Tennis* magazine, and reported in the fall of 1976.

Some players consider the service of Robert Falkenburg (U.S.) (born January 29, 1926), the 1948 Wimbledon champion, as the fastest ever produced.

Longest Career. The championship career of C. Alphonso Smith (born March 18, 1909) of Charlottesville, Virginia, extended from winning the U.S. National Boy's title at Chicago on August 14, 1924, to winning the National 65-and-over title at Aptos, California (exactly 50 years to the day later) on August 14, 1974.

Track and Field

Earliest References. Track and field athletics date from the ancient Olympic Games. The earliest accurately known Olympiad dates from July, 776 B.C., at which celebration Coroibos won the foot race. The oldest surviving measurements are a long jump of 23 feet 1½ inches by Chionis of Sparta in *c.* 656 B.C. and a discus throw of 100 cubits (*c.* 152 feet) by Protesilaus.

Oldest Race. The oldest continuously held foot race is the "Red Hose Race" held at Carnwath, Scotland, since 1507. First prize is a pair of hand-knitted knee-length red stockings.

Earliest Landmarks. The first time 10 seconds ("even time") was bettered for 100 yards under championship conditions was when John Owen recorded 9⅘ seconds in the A.A.U. Championships at Analostan Island, Washington, D.C., on October 11, 1890. The first recorded instance of 6 feet being cleared in the high jump was when Marshall Jones Brooks jumped 6 feet 0⅛ inch at Marston, near Oxford, England, on March 17, 1876. The breaking of the "4 minute barrier" in the one mile was first achieved by Dr. Roger Gilbert Bannister (born Harrow, England, March 23, 1929), when he recorded 3 minutes 59.4 seconds on the Iffley Road track, Oxford, at 6:10 p.m. on May 6, 1954.

Fastest Runners. Robert Lee Hayes (born December 20, 1942), of Jacksonville, Florida, may have reached a speed of over 27 m.p.h. at St. Louis, on June 21, 1963, in his world record 9.1 sec. 100 yards. Wyomia Tyus (U.S.) was reputed to have reached a speed of over 23 m.p.h. in Kiev, U.S.S.R., on July 31, 1965.

WORLD RECORDS—MEN

The complete list of World Records for the 32 scheduled men's events (excluding the 6 walking records, see under Walking) passed by the International Amateur Athletic Federation as of November 14, 1978. Those marked with an asterisk* are awaiting ratification. Note: On July 27, 1976, I.A.A.F. eliminated all records for races measured in yards, except for the mile (for sentimental reasons). All distances up to (and including) 400 meters must be electrically timed to be records. When a time is given to one-hundredth of a second, it represents the official, electrically timed record. In one case, a professional performance has bettered or equaled the I.A.A.F. mark, but the same highly rigorous rules as to timing, measuring and weighing are not necessarily applied.

RUNNING

Event	min. sec.	Name and Nationality	Place	Date
100 meters	9.95	James Ray Hines (U.S.)	Mexico City, Mexico	Oct. 14, 1968
200 meters (turn)	19.83	Tommie C. Smith (U.S.)	Mexico City, Mexico	Oct. 16, 1968
400 meters	43.86	Lee Edward Evans (U.S.)	Mexico City, Mexico	Oct. 18, 1968
800 meters	1:43.4	Alberto Juantorena (Cuba)	Sofia, Bulgaria	Aug. 21, 1977
1,000 meters	2:13.9	Richard Wohlhuter (U.S.)	Oslo, Norway	July 30, 1974
1,500 meters	3:32.2	Filbert Bayi (Tanzania)	Christchurch, New Zealand	Feb. 2, 1974
1 mile	3:49.4	John Walker (N.Z.)	Gothenburg, Sweden	Aug. 12, 1975
2,000 meters	4:51.4	John Walker (N.Z.)	Oslo, Norway	June 30, 1976
3,000 meters	7:32.1*	Henry Rono (Kenya)	Oslo, Norway	June 27, 1978
5,000 meters	13:08.4*	Henry Rono (Kenya)	Berkeley, California	April 8, 1978
10,000 meters	27:22.5*	Henry Rono (Kenya)	Vienna, Austria	June 11, 1978
20,000 meters	57:24.2	Jos Hermens (Netherlands)	Papendal, Netherlands	May 1, 1976
25,000 meters	1hr. 14:16.8	Pekka Paivarinta (Finland)	Oulu, Finland	May 15, 1975
30,000 meters	1hr. 31:30.4	James Noel Carroll Alder (U.K.)	Crystal Palace, London	Sept. 5, 1970
1 hour	13 miles 24⅔ yards	Jos Hermens (Netherlands)	Papendal, Netherlands	May 1, 1976

BETTERS OWN RECORD (left): Alberto Juantorena of Cuba set a record for 800 meters in the 1976 Olympics, and surpassed it on August 21, 1977. **FOUR RECORDS** fell to Henry Rono in three months, as he set new marks at 3,000, 5,000 and 10,000 meters and 3,000 meters steeplechase in spring 1978.

GREATEST HOURLY RUN: Jos Hermens of the Netherlands (number 5) ran a record 13 miles 24⅝ yards in one hour.

WORLD RECORDS—MEN (Continued)

HURDLING

Event	min. sec.	Name and Nationality	Place	Date
110 meters (3′ 6″)	13.21	Alejandro Casanas (Cuba)	Sofia, Bulgaria	Aug. 21, 1977
400 meters (3′ 0″)	47.45	Edwin Corley Moses (U.S.)	Los Angeles, California	June 11, 1977
3,000 meters Steeplechase	8:05.4	Henry Rono (Kenya)	Seattle, Washington	May 13, 1978

FIELD EVENTS

Event	ft.	in.	Name and Nationality	Place	Date
High Jump	7	8†	Vladimir Yashchenko (U.S.S.R.)	Tblisi, U.S.S.R.	June 16, 1978
Pole Vault	18	8‡	David Roberts (U.S.)	Eugene, Oregon	June 22, 1976
Long Jump	29	2‡	Robert Beamon (U.S.)	Mexico City, Mexico	Oct. 18, 1968
Triple Jump	58	8‡	Joao de Oliveira (Brazil)	Mexico City, Mexico	Oct. 15, 1975
Shot Put	72	8	Udo Beyer (East Germany)	Gothenburg, Sweden	July 6, 1978
Discus Throw	233	5	Wolfgang Schmidt (E. Germany)	East Berlin, East Germany	Aug. 9, 1978
Hammer Throw	263	6	Karl Hans Riehm (West Germany)	Heidenheim, West Germany	Aug. 6, 1978
Javelin Throw	310	4	Miklos Nemeth (Hungary)	Montreal, Canada	July 26, 1976

Note: One professional performance which was equal or superior to the I.A.A.F. marks, but where the same highly rigorous rules as to timing, measuring and weighing were not necessarily applied, was the Shot Put of 75 feet by Brian Ray Oldfield (U.S.), at El Paso, Texas, on May 10, 1975.

† Yashchenko cleared 7 feet 8¼ inches indoors in Milan, Italy, on March 12, 1978.

HURDLING RECORD HOLDER at 110 meters is Alejandro Casanas of Cuba.

World Record Breakers

Oldest. The greatest age at which anyone has broken a standard world record is 41 years 196 days in the case of John J. Flanagan (1868–1938), who set a world record in the hammer throw on July 24, 1909. The female record is 35 years 255 days for Dana Zátopkova, (*née* Ingrova) (born September 19, 1922), of Czechoslovakia, who broke the women's javelin record with 182 feet 10 inches at Prague, Czechoslovakia, on June 1, 1958.

Youngest. Ulrike Meyfarth (b. May 4, 1956) (W. Germany) equaled the world record for the women's high jump at 6 feet 3½ inches winning the gold medal at the Munich Olympics, 1972, when she was aged 16 years 4 months.

Most Records in a Day. The only athlete to have his name entered in the record book 6 times in one day was J. C. "Jesse" Owens (U.S.) who at Ann Arbor, Michigan, on May 25, 1935, equaled the 100-yard running record with 9.4 secs. at 3:15 p.m.; long-jumped 26 feet 8¼ inches at 3:25 p.m.; ran 220 yards (straight away) in 20.3 secs. at 3:45 p.m.; and 220 yards over low hurdles in 22.6 secs. at 4 p.m. The two 220-yard runs were also ratified as 200-meter world records.

Running Backwards. The fastest time recorded for running 100 yards backwards is 13.3 seconds by Paul Wilson at Hastings, New Zealand, on April 10, 1977.

WORLD RECORDS—MEN

RELAYS

Event	min. sec.	Team	Place	Date
4 × 100 meters	38.03	United States Team	Dusseldorf, West Germany	Sept. 3, 1977
		(William Collins, Steven Earl Riddick, Clifford Wiley, Steven Williams)		
4 × 200 meters	1:20.3*†	University of Southern California (U.S.)	Tempe, Arizona	May 27, 1978
		(Joel Andrews, James Sanford, William Mullins, Clancy Edwards)		
4 × 400 meters	2:56.1	United States Olympic Team	Mexico City, Mexico	Oct. 20, 1968
		(Vincent Matthews, Ronald Freeman, G. Lawrence James, Lee Edward Evans)		
4 × 800 meters	7:08.1*	U.S.S.R. Team	Podolsk, U.S.S.R.	Aug. 12, 1978
		(Vladimir Podoliakov, Nikolai Kirov, Vladimir Malosemlin, Anatoli Reschetniak)		
4 × 1,500 meters	14:38.8	West German Team	Cologne, West Germany	Aug. 17, 1977
		(Thomas Wessinghage, Harald Hudak, Michael Lederer, Karl Fleschen)		

† The time of 1:20.2 achieved by the Tobias Striders at Tempe, Arizona on May 27, 1978 was not ratified as the team was composed of varied nationalities.

DECATHLON

8,618 points		Bruce Jenner (U.S.)	Montreal, Canada	July 29–30, 1976

(First day: 100 meters, 10.94 sec.; long jump, 23 ft. 8¼ in.; shot put, 50 ft. 4½ in.; high jump, 6 ft. 8 in.; 400 meters, 47.51 sec. Second day: 110-meter hurdles, 14.84 sec.; discus, 164 ft. 2 in.; pole vault, 15 ft. 9 in.; javelin, 224 ft. 10 in.; 1,500 meters, 4 min. 12.61 sec.)

THE MARATHON

There is no official marathon record because of the varying severity of courses. The best time over 26 miles 385 yards (standardized in 1924) is 2 hours 08 minutes 33.6 seconds (av. 12.24 m.p.h.) by Derek Clayton (b. 1942 at Barrow-in-Furness, England) of Australia, at Antwerp, Belgium, on May 30, 1969.

The fastest time by a female is 2 hours 32 minutes 30 seconds (av. 10.31 m.p.h.) by Grete Waitz (Norway) (b. October 1, 1953) at New York on October 22, 1978.

Three-Legged Race. The fastest recorded time for a 100-yard three-legged race is 11.0 seconds by Harry L. Hillman and Lawson Robertson at Brooklyn, New York City, on April 24, 1909.

Ambidextrous Shot Put. Allan Feuerbach (U.S.) has put a 16-lb. shot a total of 121 feet 6¾ inches (51 feet 5 inches with his left hand and 70 feet 1¾ inches with his right) at Malmö, Sweden, in 1974.

Standing Long Jump. Joe Darby (1861–1937), the famous Victorian professional jumper from Dudley, Worcestershire, England, jumped a measured 12 feet 1½ inches *without* weights at Dudley Castle, on May 28, 1890. Johan Christian Evandt (Norway) achieved 11 feet 11¾ inches as an amateur in Reykjavik, Iceland, on March 11, 1962.

Standing High Jump. The best amateur standing high jump is 5 feet 10¾ inches by Rune Almen (Sweden) at Örebro, Sweden, on December 8, 1974. Joe Darby (see above), the professional, reportedly cleared 6 feet with his ankles tied at Church Cricket Ground, Dudley, England, on June 11, 1892.

Highest Jumper. There are several reported instances of high jumpers exceeding the official world record height of 7 feet 8 inches. The earliest of these came from unsubstantiated reports of Watusi tribesmen in Central Africa clearing up to 8 feet 2½ inches, definitely however, from inclined take-offs. The greatest height cleared above an athlete's own head is 23¼ inches by Franklin Jacobs (U.S.), who cleared 7 feet 7¼ inches despite a physical height of only 5 feet 8 inches at New York on January 28, 1978.

The greatest height cleared by a woman above her own head is 10¼ inches by Tamami Yagi (Japan) (b. November 15, 1958), who

4x100 METERS RECORD HOLDERS: The victorious U.S. team of (left to right) Collins, Wiley, Williams and Riddick.

stands 5 feet $4\frac{1}{2}$ inches tall and jumped 6 feet $2\frac{3}{4}$ inches at Matsumoto, Japan, on October 19, 1978.

Longest Career. Duncan McLean (born Gourock, Scotland, December 3, 1884) won the South African 100-yard title in February, 1904, in 9.9 seconds, and at age 91 set a world age-group record for 100 meters in 21.7 seconds in August, 1977—more than 72 years later.

Dimitrion Yordanidis completed a marathon race in 7 hours 33 minutes at the age of 98 in Athens, Greece, on October 10, 1976.

Blind 100 Meters. The fastest time recorded for 100 meters by a blind man is 11.5 seconds by Kozuck, a Polish runner, in 1976.

One-Legged High Jump. Arnie Boldt (b. 1958), of Saskatchewan, Canada, cleared a height of 6 feet $6\frac{3}{4}$ inches indoors in 1977, in spite of the fact that he has only one leg.

Longest Race. The longest race ever staged was the 1929 Transcontinental Race (3,665 miles) from New York City to Los Angeles. The Finnish-born Johnny Salo (killed October 6, 1931) was the winner in 79 days, from March 31 to June 18. His elapsed time of 525 hours 57 minutes 20 seconds gave a running average of 6.97 m.p.h. His margin of victory was only 2 minutes 42 seconds.

Endurance. Mensen Ernst (1799–1846), of Norway, is reputed to have run from Istanbul, Turkey, to Calcutta, in West Bengal, India, and back in 59 days in 1836, so averaging an improbable 94.2 miles per day. The greatest non-stop run recorded is 186 miles in 31 hours 33 minutes 38 seconds by Max Telford (b. Hawick, Scotland, on February 2, 1935) of New Zealand at Wailuku, Hawaii, on March 19–20, 1977. Telford ran 5,110 miles from Anchorage, Alaska, to Halifax, Nova Scotia, in 106 days 18 hours 45 minutes from July 25 to November 9, 1977.

The 24-hour running record is 161 miles 545 yards by Ron Bentley, 43, at Walton-on-Thames, Surrey, England, November 3–4, 1973.

The fastest recorded time for 100 miles is 11 hours 30 minutes 51 seconds by Donald Ritchie (b. July 6, 1944) at Crystal Palace, London, on October 15, 1977.

The greatest distance covered by a man in six days (*i.e.* the 144 permissible hours between Sundays in Victorian times) was $623\frac{3}{4}$ miles by George Littlewood (England), who required only 141 hours $57\frac{1}{2}$ minutes for this feat on December 3–8, 1888, at the old Madison Square Garden, New York City.

The fastest time for the cross-America run is 53 days, 7 minutes for 3,046 miles by Tom McGrath (N. Ireland) from August 29 to October 21, 1977.

The greatest lifetime mileage recorded by any runner is 195,855 miles by Earle Littlewood Dilks (b. 1884) of New Castle, Pennsylvania, through 1977.

WOMEN'S RELAY RUNNERS: The British team which holds the 4 × 200 meters record consists of (left to right) Sonia Lannaman, Sharon Colyear, Donna Hartley and Verona Elder. (See record table, pages 174–175.)

Most Olympic Gold Medals. The most Olympic gold medals won is 10 (an absolute Olympic record) by Ray C. Ewry (U.S.) (b. October 14, 1873, d. September 29, 1937) with:

Standing High Jump	1900, 1904, 1906, 1908
Standing Long Jump	1900, 1904, 1906, 1908
Standing Triple Jump	1900, 1904

The most gold medals won by a woman is 4, a record shared by Francina E. Blankers-Koen (Netherlands) (b. April 26, 1918) with 100 m., 200 m., 80 m. hurdles and 4×100 m. relay (1948) and Betty Cuthbert (Australia) (b. April 20, 1938) with 100 m., 200 m., 4×100 m. relay (1956) and 400 m. (1964).

Most Olympic Medals. The most medals won is 12 (9 gold and 3 silver) by Paavo Johannes Nurmi (Finland) (1897–1973) with:

1920 Gold: 10,000 m.; Cross Country, Individual and Team; silver: 5,000 m.
1924 Gold: 1,500 m.; 5,000 m.; 3,000 m. Team; Cross Country, Individual and Team.
1928 Gold: 10,000 m.; silver: 5,000 m.; 3,000 m. steeplechase.

The most medals won by a woman athlete is 7 by Shirley de la Hunty (*née* Strickland) (Australia) (b. July 18, 1925) with 3 gold, 1 silver and 3 bronze in the 1948, 1952 and 1956 Games. A recently discovered photo-finish indicates that she finished third, not fourth, in the 1948 200 m. event, thus unofficially increasing her total to 8. Irena Szewinska (*née* Kirszenstein) of Poland has also won 7 medals (3 gold, 2 silver, 2 bronze) in 1964, 1968, 1972 and 1976. She is the only woman ever to win Olympic medals in track and field in four successive Games.

WORLD RECORDS—WOMEN

RUNNING

Event	min.sec.	Name and Nationality	Place	Date
100 meters	10.88*	Marlies Oelsner (East Germany)	Dresden, East Germany	July 1, 1977
200 meters (turn)	22.06*	Marita Koch (East Germany)	Erfurt, East Germany	May 28, 1978
400 meters	48.94*	Marita Koch (East Germany)	Prague, Czechoslovakia	Aug. 31, 1978
800 meters	1:54.9	Tatyana Kazankina (U.S.S.R.)	Montreal, Canada	July 26, 1976
1,500 meters	3:56.0	Tatyana Kazankina (U.S.S.R.)	Podolsk, U.S.S.R.	June 28, 1976
1 mile	4:23.8	Natalia Maracescu (née Andrei) (Rumania)	Bucharest, Rumania	May 22, 1977
3,000 meters	8:27.2*	Lyudmila Bragina (U.S.S.R.)	College Park, Maryland	Aug. 7, 1976

HURDLES

100 meters (2' 9")	12.48*	Grazayna Rabsztyn (Poland)	Fürth, West Germany	June 10, 1978
400 meters (2' 6")	54.89*	Tatyana Zelentsova	Prague, Czechoslovakia	Sept. 2, 1978

FIELD EVENTS

Event	ft.	in.	Name and Nationality	Place	Date
High Jump	6	7	Sara Simeoni (Italy)	Brescia, Italy	Aug. 4, 1978
Long Jump	23	3¼	Vilma Bardauskiene (U.S.S.R.)	Prague, Czechoslovakia	Aug. 29, 1978
Shot Put	73	2¾†	Helena Fibingerova (Czechoslovakia)	Nitra, Czechoslovakia	Aug. 20, 1977
Discus Throw	232	0	Evelyn Jahl (née Schlaak)	Dresden, East Germany	Aug. 12, 1978
Javelin Throw	227	5	Kathryn Joan Schmidt (U.S.)	Fürth, West Germany	Sept. 11, 1977

† Fibingerova set an indoor record of 73 feet 10 inches at Jablonec, Czechoslovakia, on February 19, 1977.

PENTATHLON

4,839 points (with 800 m.)	Nadezda Tkachenko (U.S.S.R.)	Lille, France	Sept. 19, 1977

(100 meter hurdles, 13.49 sec.; shot, 52 ft. 3¼ in.; high jump, 5 ft. 10½ in.; long jump, 21 ft. 3½ in.; 800 meters, 2 min. 10.62 sec.)

Event	min. sec.	Team	Place	Date
4×100 meters	42.27*	East Germany (Johanna Klier, Monika Hamann, Carla Bodendorf, Marlies Oelsner)	Potsdam, E. Germany	Aug. 19, 1978
4×200 meters	1:31.6	British Team (Verona Elder, Donna Hartley, Sharon Colyear, Sonia Lannaman)	Crystal Palace, England	Aug. 20, 1977
4×400 meters	3:19.2	East German National Team (Doris Maletzski, Brigitte Rohde, Ellen Streidt, Christina Brehmer)	Montreal, Canada	July 31, 1976
4×800 meters	7:52.3	U.S.S.R. National Team (Tatyana Providokhina, Valentina Gerasimova, Svetlana Styrkina, Tatyana Kazankina)	Podolsk, U.S.S.R.	Aug. 16, 1976

JAVELIN THROWER Kathy Schmidt hurled the javelin 227 feet 5 inches on September 11, 1977.

800 METER AND 1,500 METER CHAMPION: Tatyana Kazankina of the U.S.S.R. (leading here) set new marks for these distances in 1976.

Most Wins at One Games. The most gold medals at one celebration is 5 by Nurmi in 1924 (see above) and the most individual is 4 by Alvin C. Kraenzlein (U.S.) (1876–1928) in 1900 with 60 m., 110 m. hurdles, 200 m. hurdles and long jump.

Mass Relay Record. The record for 100 miles by 100 runners belonging to one club is 7 hours 56 minutes 55.6 seconds by Shore A.C. of New Jersey, on June 5, 1977.

The women's mark is 10 hours 47 minutes 9.3 seconds by a team from San Francisco Dolphins Southend Running Club, on April 3, 1977.

The best time for a 100 × 400 meter relay is 1 hour 34 minutes 00.6 seconds by the Tarnverein Länggasse, Bern, Switzerland, on April 19, 1975.

A 13-man relay team from the Los Angeles Police Revolver and Athletic Club ran from the steps of the Capitol, Washington, D.C., to Los Angeles City Hall (3,871.6 miles) in 20 days 5 hours 20 minutes in May, 1974.

The longest relay ever run, and the one with the most participants, was by 1,607 students and teachers who covered 6,014.65 miles at Trondheim, Norway, from October 21 to November 23, 1977.

Pancake Race Record. The annual Housewives Pancake Race at Olney, Buckinghamshire, England, was first mentioned in 1445. The record for the winding 415-yard course (three tosses mandatory) is 61.0 seconds, set by Sally Ann Faulkner, 16, on February 26, 1974. The record for the counterpart race at Liberal, Kansas, is 58.5 seconds by Sheila Turner in the 1975 competition.

Trampolining

Origin. The sport of trampolining (from the Spanish word *trampolin*, a springboard) dates from 1936, when the prototype "T" model trampoline was developed by George Nissen (U.S.). Trampolines were used in show business at least as early as "The Walloons" of the period, 1910–12.

Marathon Record. The longest recorded trampoline bouncing marathon is one of 1,248 hours (52 days) set by a team of 6 in Phoenix, Arizona, from June 24 to August 15, 1974. The solo record is 179 hours (with 5-minute breaks per hour permissible) by Geoffrey Morton of Broken Hill, N.S.W., Australia, March 7–14, 1977.

Most Titles. The only men to win a world title (instituted 1964) twice have been Dave Jacobs (U.S.) the 1967–68 champion, Wayne Miller (U.S.) the 1966 and 1970 champion, and Richard Tison (France) in 1974 and 1976. Judy Wills won 5 women's titles (1964–65–66–67–68).

Volleyball

Origin. The game was invented as Minnonette in 1895 by William G. Morgan at the Y.M.C.A. gymnasium at Holyoke,

Massachusetts. The International Volleyball Association was formed in Paris in April, 1947. The ball travels at a speed of up to 70 m.p.h. when smashed over the net, which measures 7 feet 11½ inches. In the women's game it is 7 feet 4¼ inches.

World Titles. World Championships were instituted in 1949. The U.S.S.R. has won five men's titles (1949, 1952, 1960, 1962 and 1978). The U.S.S.R. won the women's championship in 1952, 1956, 1960, 1970, and 1973. The record crowd is 60,000 for the 1952 world title matches in Moscow, U.S.S.R.

Most Olympic Medals. The sport was introduced to the Olympic Games for both men and women in 1964. The only volleyball player to win four medals is Inna Ryskal (U.S.S.R.) (b. June 15, 1944), who won a silver medal in 1964 and 1976 and golds in 1968 and 1972.

The record for medals for men is held by Yury Poyarkov (U.S.S.R.), who won gold medals in 1964 and 1968, and a bronze in 1972.

Marathon. The longest recorded volleyball marathon is one of 51 hours 5 minutes played by two teams of six (no substitutes) from the U.S. Army Field Station, West Berlin, W. Germany on July 7–9, 1978.

One-Man Team. Bob L. Schaffer of Suffern, New York, specializes in taking on 6-man teams single-handedly. His won-lost record since August 16, 1963 is 2,102 wins to only 3 losses.

Walking

Longest Annual Race. The Strasbourg-Paris event (instituted in 1926 in the reverse direction) over 313 to 344 miles is the world's longest annual walk event. Gilbert Roger (France) has won 6 times (1949–53–54–56–57–58). The fastest performance is by Robert Rinchard (Belgium) who walked 325 miles in the 1974 race in 63 hours 29 minutes, so (deducting 4 hours of compulsory stops) averaging 5.12 m.p.h.

Longest in 24 hours. The best performance is 142 miles 448 yards by Jesse Castaneda (U.S.) at the New Mexico State Fair in Albuquerque, September 18–19, 1976. The best by a woman is 109.8 miles by Anne Van De Meer (Netherlands) at Rouen, France, on May 20–21, 1978.

Most Olympic Medals. Walking races have been included in the Olympic schedule since 1906. The 20-kilometer event in Montreal in 1976 was the 25th Olympic race. The only walker to win three gold medals has been Ugo Frigerio (Italy) (1901–68) with the 3,000 m. and 10,000 m. in 1920 and the 10,000 m. in 1924. He also holds the record of most medals with four (having additionally won the bronze medal in the 50,000 m. in 1932), which total is shared with Vladimir Golubnitschiy (U.S.S.R.) (b. June 2, 1936), who won gold medals for the 10,000 m. in 1960 and 1968, the silver in 1972 and the bronze in 1964.

Most Titles. Four-time Olympian, Ronald Owen Laird (b. May 31, 1938) of the New York Athletic Club, won a total of 65 U.S. National titles from 1958 to 1976, plus 4 Canadian championships.

OFFICIAL WORLD RECORDS (Track Walking)
(As recognized by the International Amateur Athletic Federation)

Distance	hr.	min.	sec.	Name and Nationality	Date	Place
20,000 meters	1	23	12	Ronald Weiser (E. Ger.)	Aug. 30, 1978	Czech.
30,000 meters	2	11	53.4	Raul Gonzalez (Mexico)	May 19, 1978	Norway
50,000 meters	3	52	23.5	Raul Gonzalez (Mexico)	May 19, 1978	Norway
2 hours		16 miles		Raul Gonzalez (Mexico)	May 19, 1978	Norway
		1,638 yards				

Road Walking. The world's best road performances are: 20,000 meters, 1 hour 23 minutes 12 seconds by Roland Wieser (East Germany) at Prague, Czechoslovakia, on August 30, 1978; 50,000 meters, 3 hours 41 minutes 19.2 seconds by Raul Gonzalez (Mexico) at Prague, Czechoslovakia on June 11, 1978.

Greatest Mileage. Dimitru Dan (born July 13, 1890, *fl.* 1976) of Rumania was the only man of 200 entrants to succeed in walking 100,000 kilometers (62,137 miles), in a contest organized by the Touring Club de France on April 1, 1910. By March 24, 1916, he had covered 96,000 kilometers (59,651 miles), averaging 27.24 miles per day.

DIFFERENT WALKS OF LIFE: Dimitru Dan (left) of Rumania was the only finisher in a walking race of 100,000 kilometers (62,137 miles). Plennie Wingo (right) walked 8,000 miles backwards in 1931–32. He used special glasses to see where he was going.

WORLDWIDE WALKER:
George Schilling was the
first man reported to have
walked around the world,
in the 1890's.

Walking Backwards. The greatest exponent of reverse pedestrianism has been Plennie L. Wingo (b. 1895) then of Abilene, Texas, who started on his 8,000-mile transcontinental walk on April 15, 1931, from Santa Monica, California, to Istanbul, Turkey, and arrived on October 24, 1932. He celebrated the walk's 45th anniversary by covering the 452 miles from Santa Monica to San Francisco, California, backwards, in 85 days, aged 81 years.

The longest distance reported for walking backwards in 24 hours is 80 miles by Lindsay R. Dodd (England), April 9–10, 1976.

"Non-Stop" Walking. Thomas Patrick Benson (b. 1933) of Great Britain, walked 314.33 miles at Moor Park, Preston, England, in 123 hours 28 minutes December 19–25, 1975. He did not permit himself any stops for resting and was moving 99.41 per cent of the time.

Walking Around the World. The first person reported to have "walked around the world" is George M. Schilling (U.S.) in the late 1890's, but the first verified achievement was by David Kunst, who started with his brother John from Waseca, Minnesota, on June 10, 1970. John was killed by Afghani bandits in 1972. David arrived home after walking 14,500 miles on October 5, 1974.

Tomas Carlos Pereira (b. Argentina, November 16, 1942) spent 10 years, April 6, 1968, through April 8, 1978, walking 29,825 miles around all five continents.

The Trans-Asia record is 238 days for 6,800 miles from Riga, Latvia, to Vladivostok, U.S.S.R., by Georgyi Bushuyev, 50, in 1973–74.

Walking Across America. John Lees, 27, of Brighton, England, on April 11–June 3, 1972, walked 2,876 miles across the U.S. from City Hall, Los Angeles, to City Hall, New York City, in 53 days 12 hours 15 minutes (53.746 miles per day).

Walking Across Canada. The record trans-Canada (Halifax to Vancouver) walk of 3,764 miles is 96 days by Clyde McRae, 23, from May 1 to August 4, 1973.

Water Polo

Origins. Water polo was developed in England as "Water Soccer" in 1869 and was first included in the Olympic Games in Paris in 1900.

Olympic Victories. Hungary has won the Olympic tournament most often with six wins, in 1932, 1936, 1952, 1956, 1964 and 1976. Five players share the record of three gold medals: George Wilkinson (1879–1946) in 1900–08–12, Paulo (Paul) Radmilovic (1886–1968) and Charles Sidney Smith (1879–1951) in 1908–12–20—all G.B.; and the Hungarians Deszö Gyarmati (b. October 23, 1927) and György Kárpáti (b. June 23, 1935) in 1952–56–64.

Radmilovic also won a gold medal for the 4×200 m. free-style relay in 1908.

Most International Appearances. The greatest number of internationals is 244 by Ozren Bonacic for Yugoslavia between 1964 and September, 1975.

Marathon. The longest match on record is one of 63 hours 13 minutes between two teams of 15 from Camp Hill Edwardians Swimming Club, Birmingham, England, on March 24–27, 1978. Breaks and substitutions were in accordance with N.C.A.A. regulations.

Water Skiing

Origins. The origins of water skiing lie in plank gliding or aquaplaning. A 19th-century treatise on sorcerers refers to Eliseo of Tarentum who, in the 14th century, "walks and dances" on the water. The first report of aquaplaning was from the Pacific coast of the U.S. in the early 1900's.

A photograph exists of a "plank-riding" contest in a regatta won by a Mr. H. Storry at Scarborough, Yorkshire, England, on July 15, 1914. Competitors were towed on a *single* plank by a motor launch. The present-day sport of water skiing was pioneered by Ralph W. Samuelson on Lake Pepin, Minnesota, on two curved pine boards in the summer of 1922, though claims have been made for the birth of the sport on Lake Annecy (Haute Savoie), France, in 1920. The first World Water Ski Organization was formed in Geneva, Switzerland, on July 27, 1946.

Jumps. The first recorded jump on water skis was by Ralph W. Samuelson, off a greased ramp at Lake Pepin in 1925. The longest

WATER SKI TRICKSTER (left): Maria Carrasco scored 5,570 points in Milan, Italy in September, 1977. LONGEST SKI JUMP (right): Wayne Grimditch jumped 180 feet in Georgia in 1975.

jump recorded is one of 180 feet by Wayne Grimditch, 20 (U.S.), at Callaway Gardens, Pine Mountain, Georgia, July 13, 1975. A minimum margin of 8 inches is required for sole possession of the world record.

The women's record is 128 feet by Linda Giddens (U.S.) at Miami, Florida, in August 1976.

Slalom. The world record for slalom on a particular pass is 4 buoys (with a 37-foot rope) at 36 m.p.h. by Kris LaPoint (U.S.) at Horton Lake, near Barstow, California, on July 15, 1975, and also by his brother, Bob LaPoint in Miami in August, 1976.

The women's record is 3 buoys on a 39-foot line by Cindy Hutcherson Todd (U.S.) at Groveland, Florida, on July 16, 1977.

Tricks. The highest official point score for tricks is 7,080 points by Carlos Suarez (Venezuela) at Milan, Italy, on September 3, 1977.

The women's record of 5,570 points was set by Maria Victoria Carrasco (Venezuela) at Milan, Italy, on September 3, 1977.

Longest Run. The greatest distance traveled non-stop is 1,124 miles by Will Coughey (New Zealand) on Lake Karapiro, New Zealand, in 30 hours 34 minutes, February 26–27, 1977.

Highest Speed. The water skiing speed record is 125.69 m.p.h. recorded by Danny Churchill (U.S.) at the Oakland Marine Stadium, California, in 1971. A claim of 134.33 m.p.h. by Grant Torrens (Australia) in February, 1978, is awaiting ratification. Donna Patterson Brice (b. 1953) set a feminine record of 111.0 m.p.h. at Long Beach, California on August 21, 1977.

Most Titles. World overall championships (instituted 1949) have been twice won by Alfredo Mendoza (U.S.) in 1953–55, Mike Suyderhoud (U.S.) in 1967–69, and George Athans (Canada) in 1971 and 1973, and three times by Mrs. Willa McGuire (*née* Worthington) of the U.S., in 1949–50 and 1955 and Elizabeth Allan-Shetter (U.S.) in 1965, 1969, and 1975.

Allan-Shetter has also won a record eight individual championship events.

Barefoot. The first person to water ski barefoot reportedly was Dick Pope, Jr., at Lake Eloise, Florida, on March 6, 1947. The barefoot duration record is 2 hours 37 minutes by Paul McManus (Australia). The backwards barefoot record is 39 minutes by McManus. The best officially recorded barefoot jump is 52 feet by Keith Donnelly at Baronscourt, Northern Ireland, on July 9, 1978. The official barefoot speed record (two runs) is 110.02 m.p.h. by Lee Kirk (U.S.) at Firebird Lake, Phoenix, Arizona, on June 11, 1977. His fastest run was 113.67 m.p.h. The fastest by a woman is 61.39 by Haidee Jones (Australia).

Weightlifting

Origins. Amateur weightlifting is of comparatively modern origin, and the first "world" championship was staged at the Café Monico, Piccadilly, London, on March 28, 1891. Prior to that time, weightlifting consisted of professional exhibitions in which some of the advertised poundages were open to doubt. The first to raise 400 lbs. was Karl Swoboda (1882–1933) (Austria) in Vienna, with 401¼ lbs. in 1910, using the Continental clean and jerk style.

Greatest Lift. The greatest weight ever raised by a human being is 6,270 lbs. in a back lift (weight raised off trestles) by the 364-lb. Paul Anderson (U.S.) (b. 1932), the 1956 Olympic heavyweight champion, at Toccoa, Georgia, on June 12, 1957. (The heaviest Rolls-Royce, the Phantom VI, weighs 5,936 lbs.) The greatest by a woman is 3,564 lbs. with a hip and harness lift by Mrs. Josephine Blatt (*née* Schauer) (U.S.) (1869–1923) at the Bijou Theatre, Hoboken, New Jersey, on April 15, 1895.

The greatest overhead lifts made from the ground are the clean and jerks achieved by super-heavyweights which now exceed 560 lbs. (see table on page 185).

The greatest overhead lift ever made by a woman is 286 lbs. in a continental jerk by Katie Sandwina, *née* Brummbach (Germany) (born January 21, 1884, died as Mrs. Max Heymann in New York City, in 1952) in *c.* 1911. This is equivalent to seven 40-pound office typewriters. She stood 5 feet 11 inches tall, weighed 210 lbs., and is reputed to have unofficially lifted 312½ lbs. and to have once shouldered a 1,200-lb cannon taken from the tailboard of a Barnum & Bailey circus wagon.

STRONGEST WOMAN:
Jan Suffolk Todd has raised 458 lbs. in the two-handed dead lift in competition.

Power Lifts. Paul Anderson as a professional has bench-pressed 627 lbs., achieved 1,200 lbs. in a deep-knee bend, and dead-lifted 820 lbs. making a career aggregate of 2,647 lbs.

International Powerlifting Federation records in the Superheavyweight division have been set by Donald C. Reinhoudt (U.S.) with a squat of 931 lbs. (April 16, 1976), a dead lift of 881½ lbs. and total of 2,420 lbs. (May 3, 1975) and Doug Young (U.S.) with a bench press of 611½ lbs. (March 4, 1978).

Ronald Collins (G.B.) with a 1,655-lb. lift in Liverpool, England, on December 15, 1973, when his body weight was 165 lbs., became the first man to lift a total 10 times his own body weight. Since then 7 other lifters have achieved this, but only Collins has repeated.

The newly instituted two-man dead lift record was raised to 1,410 lbs. by Clay Patterson and Doug Young in San Marcos, Texas, on October 1, 1977.

Hermann Görner (Germany) performed a one-handed dead lift of 734½ lbs. in Dresden on July 20, 1920. He once raised 24 men weighing 4,123 lbs. on a plank with the soles of his feet and also carried on his back a 1,444-lb. piano for a distance of 52¼ feet on June 3, 1921. Görner is also reputed to have once lifted 14 bricks weighing 123½ lbs. horizontally, using only lateral pressure.

Peter B. Cortese (U.S.) achieved a one-arm dead lift of 370 lbs. —22 lbs. over triple his body weight—at York, Pennsylvania, on September 4, 1954.

The highest competitive two-handed dead lift by a woman is 458 lbs. by Jan Suffolk Todd (born May 22, 1952) (U.S.) at Stephen-

THE LIGHTWEIGHT RECORD in the Snatch competition went to Roberto Urrutia of Cuba with a 314-pound lift in September, 1977.

ville Crossing, Newfoundland, Canada, on June 24, 1978. She weighed 196¼ lbs. Her squat, a record 480 lbs., and bench press of 187 lbs., made a record three-lift total of 1,125 lbs.

It was reported that a hysterical 123-lb. woman, Mrs. Maxwell Rogers, lifted one end of a 3,600-lb. car which, after the collapse of a jack, had fallen on top of her son at Tampa, Florida, on April 24, 1960. She cracked some vertebrae.

A dead lift record of 2,100,000 lbs. in 24 hours was set by a 10-man team in relay at the Darwen Weightlifting Club, Darwen, England on August 19, 1978.

Most Olympic Gold Medals. Of the 90 Olympic titles at stake, the U.S.S.R. has won 26, the U.S. 15 and France 9. Ten lifters have succeeded in winning an Olympic gold medal in successive Games. Of these, three have also won a silver medal.

MOST SUCCESSFUL OLYMPIC WEIGHTLIFTERS

Louis Hostin (France)	Gold, light-heavyweight 1932 and 1936; Silver, 1928.
John Davis (U.S.)	Gold, heavyweight 1948 and 1952.
Tommy Kono (Hawaii/U.S.)	Gold, lightweight 1952; Gold, light-heavyweight 1956; Silver, middleweight 1960.
Charles Vinci (U.S.)	Gold, bantamweight 1956 and 1960.
Arkady Vorobyov (U.S.S.R.)	Gold, middle-heavyweight 1956 and 1960.
Yoshinobu Miyake (Japan)	Gold, featherweight 1964 and 1968; Silver, bantamweight 1960.
Waldemar Baszanowski (Poland)	Gold, lightweight 1964 and 1968.
Leonid Zhabotinsky (U.S.S.R.)	Gold, heavyweight 1964 and 1968.
Vasili Alexeev (U.S.S.R.)	Gold, super-heavyweight 1972 and 1976.
Norair Nourikian (Bulgaria)	Gold, featherweight 1972; Gold, bantamweight 1976.

Most Olympic Medals. Winner of most Olympic medals is Norbert Schemansky (U.S.) with four: gold, middle-heavyweight 1952; silver, heavyweight 1948; bronze, heavyweight 1960 and 1964.

Schemansky achieved a world record (heavyweight snatch of 361½ lbs. on April 28, 1962, at Detroit) at the record age of 37 years 10 months.

OFFICIAL WORLD WEIGHTLIFTING RECORDS

(As of December 1978)

Flyweight
(114½ lb.–52 kg.)

Snatch	241¼	Kon lon-Chi (N. Korea)	U.S.S.R.	Mar. 16, 1978
Jerk	311¾	Alexander Senchine (U.S.S.R.)	U.S.S.R.	Dec. 1978
Total	545½	Alexander Voronin (U.S.S.R.)	W. Germany	Sept. 18, 1977

Bantamweight
(123¼ lb.–56 kg.)

Snatch	265½	Koji Miki (Japan)	Japan	Oct. 25, 1976
Jerk	332¾	Mohamed Nassiri (Iran)	Iran	Aug. 2, 1973
Total	578½	Norair Nourikian (Bulgaria)	Canada	July 19, 1976

Featherweight
(132¼ lb.–60 kg.)

Snatch	286½	Gyorgyi Todorov (Bulgaria)	Bulgaria	May 25, 1976
Jerk	364¾	Nikolai Kolesnikov (U.S.S.R.)	Czech.	June 12, 1978
Total	640¼	Nikolai Kolesnikov (U.S.S.R.)	Czech.	June 12, 1978

Lightweight
(148¾ lb.–67.5 kg.)

Snatch	314	Roberto Urrutia (Cuba)	W. Germany	Sept. 20, 1977
Jerk	397¾	Vyacheslav Andreyev (U.S.S.R.)	U.S.S.R.	Nov. 17, 1978
Total	700	Yanko Rusev (Bulgaria)	Bulgaria	May 1, 1978

Middleweight
(165¼ lb.–75 kg.)

Snatch	347	Yordan Vardanyan (U.S.S.R.)	U.S.S.R.	May 7, 1977
Jerk	433	Alexander Logoutov (U.S.S.R.)	U.S.S.R.	Nov. 1978
Total	766	Yordan Vardanyan (U.S.S.R)	U.S.S.R.	May 7, 1977

Light-heavyweight
(181¾ lb.–82.5 kg.)

Snatch	378	Blagoi Blagoiev (Bulgaria)	W.Germany	Dec. 1978
Jerk	464	Yordan Vardanyan (U.S.S.R.)	U.S.	Oct. 6, 1978
Total	832	Yordan Vardanyan (U.S.S.R.)	U.S.	Oct. 6, 1978

Middle-heavyweight
(198¼ lb.–90 kg.)

Snatch	398	David Rigert (U.S.S.R.)	Czech.	June 16, 1978
Jerk	488½	David Rigert (U.S.S.R.)	Czech.	June 16, 1978
Total	881¾	David Rigert (U.S.S.R.)	U.S.S.R.	May 14, 1976

(220½ lb.–100 kg.)

Snatch	396¾	Nicolas Kolesnik (U.S.S.R.)	U.S.S.R.	Dec. 17, 1978
Jerk	496	Vladimir Kononov (U.S.S.R.)	U.S.S.R.	Sept. 1978
Total	876¼	Vladimir Kononov (U.S.S.R.)	U.S.S.R.	Sept. 1978

Heavyweight
(242½ lb.–110 kg.)

Snatch	407¾	Valentin Khristov (Bulgaria)	E. Germany	Apr. 10, 1976
Jerk	523½	Valentin Khristov (Bulgaria)	U.S.S.R.	Sept. 22, 1975
Total	920¼	Valentin Khristov (Bulgaria)	U.S.S.R.	Sept. 22, 1975

Super-heavyweight
(Over 242½ lb.–110 kg.)

Snatch	442	Sultan Rakhmanov (U.S.S.R.)	U.S.S.R.	Apr. 25, 1978
Jerk	564¼	Vasili Alexeev (U.S.S.R.)	U.S.S.R.	Nov. 1, 1977
Total	981	Vasili Alexeev (U.S.S.R.)	U.S.S.R.	Sept. 1, 1977

Wrestling

Earliest References. The earliest depiction of wrestling holds and falls are from the walls of the tomb of Ptahhotap (Egypt) indicating that organized wrestling dates from *c.* 2350 B.C. or earlier. It was introduced into the ancient Olympic Games in the 18th Olympiad in *c.* 708 B.C. The Graeco-Roman style is of French origin and arose about 1860. The International Amateur Wrestling Federation (F.I.L.A.) was founded in 1912.

Sumo Wrestling. The sport's origins in Japan certainly date from *c.* 23 B.C. The heaviest performers were probably Dewagatake, a wrestler of the 1920's who was 6 feet 7¾ inches tall and weighed up to 430 lbs., and Odachi, of the 1950's, who stood 6 feet 7½ inches and weighed about 441 lbs. Weight is amassed by over-eating a high protein stew called *chankonabe.* The tallest was probably Ozora, an early 19th century performer, who stood 7 feet 3 inches tall. The most successful wrestlers have been Koki Naya (born 1940), *alias* Taiho ("Great Bird"), who won 32 Emperor's Cups until his retirement in 1971, and Sadaji Akiyoshi (b. 1912), *alias* Futabayama, who won 69 consecutive bouts in the 1930's. Taiho was the *Yokozuna* (Grand Champion) in 1967. The highest *dan* is Makuuchi.

The youngest wrestler ever to attain the rank of *Yokozuna* was Toshimitsu Ōbata (*alias* Kitanoumi) in July, 1974, aged 21 years 2 months. Jesse Kuhaulva (b. Hawaii, June 16, 1944) *alias* Takamiyama was the first non-Japanese to win an official tournament, in July, 1972.

Best Records. In international competition, Osamu Watanabe (b. October 21, 1940) (Japan) the 1964 Olympic free-style featherweight champion, was unbeaten and unscored-upon in 187 consecutive matches.

Wade Schalles (U.S.) has won 615 bouts from 1964 to the end of 1977.

Most World Championships. The greatest number of world championships won by a wrestler is ten by the free-styler Aleksandr Medved (U.S.S.R.), with the light-heavyweight titles in 1964 (Olympic) and 1966, the heavyweight 1967 and 1968 (Olympic), and the super-heavyweight title 1969, 1970, 1971 and 1972 (Olympic). The only wrestler to win the same title in 6 successive years has been Abdollah Movahed (Iran) in the lightweight division in 1965–70. The record for successive Graeco-Roman titles is five by Roman Rurua (U.S.S.R.) with the featherweight 1966, 1967, 1968 (Olympic), 1969 and 1970.

Most Olympic Titles. Three wrestlers have won three Olympic titles. They are:

Carl Westergren (Sweden) (b. Oct. 13, 1895)		Ivar Johansson (Sweden) (b. Jan. 31, 1903)	
Graeco-Roman Middleweight A	1920	Free-style Middleweight	1932
Graeco-Roman Middleweight B	1924	Graeco-Roman Welterweight	1932
Graeco-Roman Heavyweight	1932	Graeco-Roman Middleweight	1936

Aleksandr Medved (U.S.S.R.)
(b. Sept. 16, 1937)

Free-style Light-heavyweight	1964
Free-style Heavyweight	1968
Free-style Super-heavyweight	1972

The only wrestler with more medals is Imre Polyák (Hungary) who won the silver medal for the Graeco-Roman featherweight class in 1952, 56–60 and the gold in 1964.

Heaviest Heavyweight. The heaviest wrestler in Olympic history is Chris Taylor (b. U.S., June 13, 1950), bronze medallist in the super-heavyweight class in 1972, who stood 6 feet 5 inches tall and weighed over 420 lbs.

Longest Bout. The longest recorded bout was one of 11 hours 40 minutes between Martin Klein (Estonia, representing Russia) and Alfred Asikainen (Finland) in the Graeco-Roman middleweight "A" event in the 1912 Olympic Games in Stockholm, Sweden. Klein won.

Yachting

Origin. Yachting dates from the £100 (now $200) stake race between King Charles II of England and his brother James, Duke of York, on the Thames River, on September 1, 1661, over 23 miles, from Greenwich to Gravesend. The earliest club is the Royal Cork Yacht Club (formerly the Cork Harbour Water Club), established in Ireland in 1720. The word "yacht" is from the Dutch, meaning to hunt or chase.

Most Successful. The most successful racing yacht in history was the British Royal Yacht *Britannia* (1893–1935), owned by King Edward VII while Prince of Wales, and subsequently by King George V, which won 231 races in 625 starts.

Highest Speed. The official world sailing speed record is 33.4 knots (38.46 m.p.h.) achieved by the 73½-foot *Crossbow II* over a 500-meter (547-yard) course off Portland Harbor, Dorset, England, on October 4, 1977. The vessel, with a sail area of 1,400 square feet, was designed by Rod McAlpine-Downie and owned and steered by Timothy Colman. The U.S. Navy experimental hydrofoil craft *Monitor* is reported to have attained speeds close to 40 knots (46 m.p.h.) in 1956.

Longest Race. The longest regularly contested yacht race is the biennial Los Angeles-Tahiti Trans Pacific event which is over 3,571 miles. The fastest time has been 8 days 13 hours 9 minutes by Eric Taberley's *Pen Duick IV* (France) in 1969.

Most Competitors. 1,261 sailing boats started the 233-mile Round Zealand (Denmark) race in June, 1976.

America's Cup. The America's Cup was originally won as an outright prize by the schooner *America* on August 22, 1851, at Cowes, England, but was later offered by the New York Yacht Club as a challenge trophy. On August 8, 1870, J. Ashbury's *Cambria* (G.B.)

failed to capture the trophy from the *Magic*, owned by F. Osgood (U.S.). Since then the Cup has been challenged by Great Britain in 15 contests, by Canada in two contests, and by Australia four times, but the United States holders have never been defeated. The closest race ever was the fourth race of the 1962 series, when the 12-meter sloop *Weatherly* beat her Australian challenger *Gretel* by about 3½ lengths (75 yards), a margin of only 26 seconds, on September 22, 1962. The fastest time ever recorded by a 12-meter boat for the triangular course of 24 miles is 2 hours 46 minutes 58 seconds by *Gretel* in 1962.

Little America's Cup. The catamaran counterpart to the America's Cup was instituted in 1961 for International C-class catamarans. Great Britain has won 8 times from 1961 to 1968.

Admiral's Cup. The ocean racing series to have attracted the largest number of participating nations (three boats allowed to each nation) is the Admiral's Cup held by the Royal Ocean Racing Club in the English Channel in alternate years. Up to 1977, Britain had won 7 times, U.S. twice and Australia and West Germany once each.

In 1975, a record number of 19 nations competed.

Olympic Victories. The first sportsman ever to win individual gold medals in four successive Olympic Games has been Paul B. Elvström (b. February 24, 1928) (Denmark) in the Firefly class in 1948 and the Finn class in 1952, 1956 and 1960. He has also won 8 other world titles in a total of 6 classes.

The lowest number of penalty points by the winner of any class in an Olympic regatta is 3 points [6 wins (1 disqualified) and 1 second in 7 starts] by *Superdocius* of the Flying Dutchman class sailed by Lt. Rodney Stuart Pattison (b. August 5, 1943), British Royal Navy and Ian Somerled Macdonald-Smith (b. July 3, 1945), in Acapulco Bay, Mexico, in October, 1968.

Largest Sail. The largest sail ever made was a parachute spinnaker with an area of 18,000 square feet (more than two-fifths of an acre) for Harold S. Vanderbilt's *Ranger* in 1937.

Most Numerous. The numerically largest class of sailing boats in the world is the "Sunfish" (U.S.), with a total in excess of 140,000. Made of plastic, it is a 14-foot sailing surfboard with a single sail.

The numerically largest class of centerboard sailing dinghy is the International Optimist, a 7-foot 7-inch wooden or plastic boat intended to be used by children. 105,000 are claimed worldwide. This boat is also the smallest in size and cheapest of any recognized international yachting class.

Highest Altitude. The greatest altitude at which sailing has been conducted is 16,109 feet on Laguna Huallatani, Bolivia, by Peter Williams, Brian Barrett, Gordon Siddeley and Keith Robinson in Mirror dinghy No. 55448 on November 19, 1977.

INDEX

PICTURE CREDITS